THE MIS

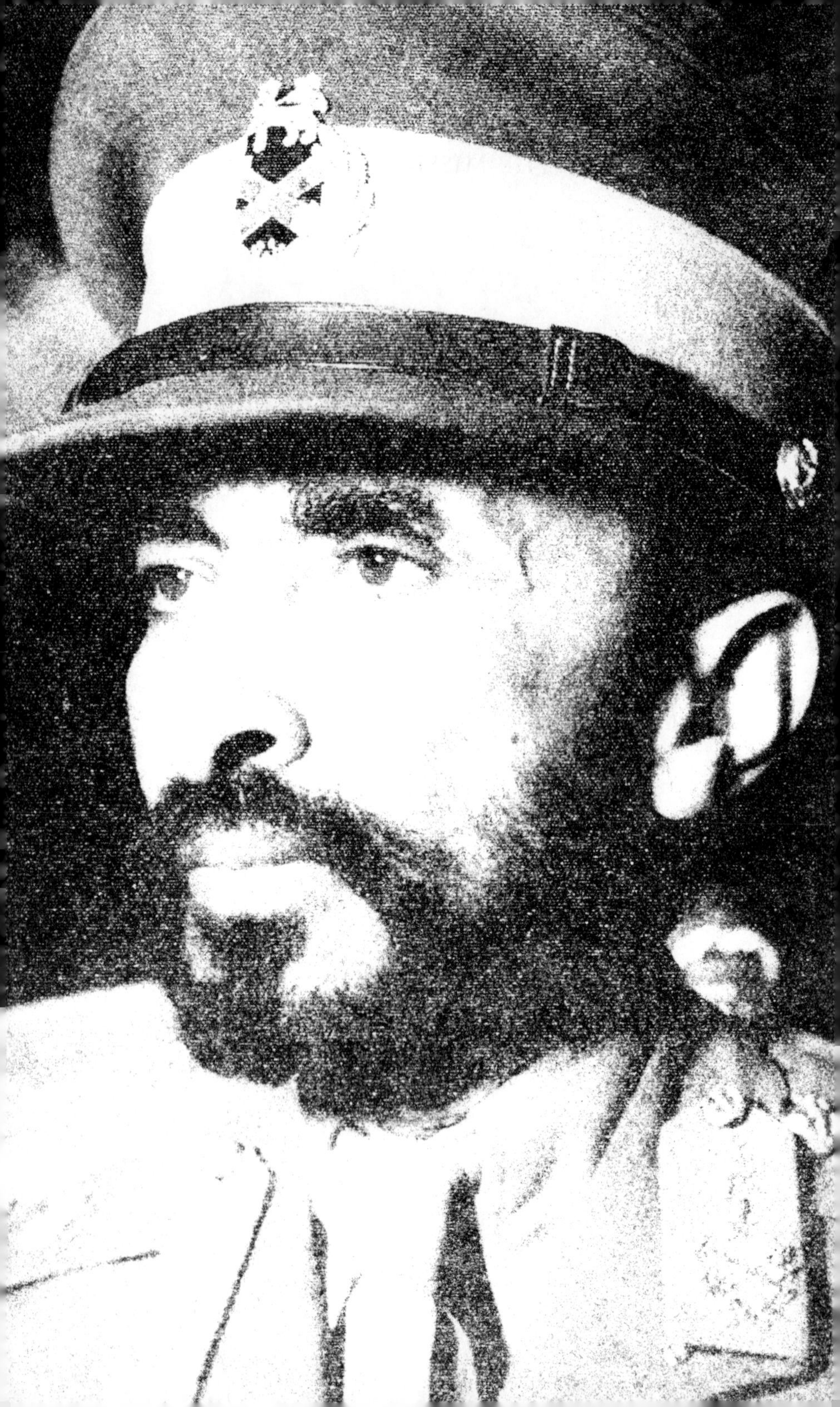

HANS WILHELM LOCKOT

The Mission

The Life, Reign and Character of Haile Sellassie I

INTRODUCTION BY MAXIM J. ANDERSON

Research Associates School Times Publications/
Frontline Distribution Int'l Inc.
and
Miguel Lorne Publishers, Jamaica
Tel: (773) 651-9888
Fax: (773) 651-9850
e-mail: frontlinebooks@prodigy.net

CHICAGO • JAMAICA • LONDON •
REPUBLIC OF TRINIDAD AND TOBAGO

First published in the UK by C. Hurst & Co. (Publishers Ltd.)
© Hans Wilhelm Lockot, 1989
Introduction © Maxim J. Anderson, 1993

ALL RIGHTS RESERVED
No part of this work or quotes used in connection with reviews written specifically for inclusion in a magazine or newspaper may be reproduced in any form or by any means without the prior written permission of Research Associates School Times Publications/Frontline Dist. Int'l, Inc. and Miguel Lorne Publications.

ISBN 0-94839-034-4
Library of Congress Catalog Card No. 96-069478
This impression is printed in paperback only, 2001
North America/US and Caribbean rights only.

CONTENTS

Author's foreword	*page* vii
Some traditional Ethiopian titles	viii
Introduction: The Rastafarian Movement and its Doctrine — A Current View by Maxim J. Anderson	ix
Map of Ethiopia	xxx
Genealogical Tables	46–7

Chapters

I.	Prelude	1
II.	Menelik's Heritage	5
III.	Yassu and Tafari	10
IV.	Ras Tafari	25
V.	The Emperor	44
VI.	Fighting the Desert	56
VII.	Animals and People	64
VIII.	Generation Gap	68
IX.	The Coup	73
X.	Aftermath of the Coup	85
XI.	Development and Assistance	88
XII.	The New Africa	98
XIII.	Revolution: The Young Generation	113
XIV.	Revolution: Crescendo	117
XV.	Revolution: Finale	121
XVI.	Epilogue	128

Appendix: Selections from the Speeches of Haile Sellassie I	133
Note on the Sources for the English Texts of the Emperor's Speeches	162
Index	163

FOREWORD

Haile Sellassie, the ruler, was a man obsessed by his task of leading Ethiopia into the modern world. He spared no effort, as far as his considerable abilities allowed, to do what he believed would be best to achieve that end. Faithful throughout his life to his self-imposed mission, he remained, up to the very end, 'every inch a king'.

In the eyes of many today, his image appears blurred, but the most striking characteristic of Western public opinion, where the person of Haile Sellassie is concerned, is ignorance – ignorance which only appears to deepen as the date of his fall and death recedes into the past. Stereotyped political slogans, unfounded accusations and simple slander are commonly accepted as fact.

So it is as an eye-witness who lived in Ethiopia from 1951 till 1975 during the most fruitful years of the Emperor's reign, and worked in the service of the Imperial government, that the author wishes to contribute to the long-overdue task of putting the Emperor's record straight – in an essay designed to fill gaps in factual knowledge for some readers, and to serve as a reminder for those readers who already possess that knowledge.

The author wishes to express his gratitude to the country of Ethiopia, which was a kind and indulgent host to him through all the years of his residence there; to its people who deserve the reputation of representing an ancient and independent culture of their own; to the numerous officials, scholars, experts, colleagues, staff members, collaborators and visitors to his place of work, the National Library of Ethiopia – which is a veritable treasury of information on all fields and periods of Ethiopian history and life; to all the men and women, friends and foes alike, who in countless meetings and discussions have in their various ways contributed to the substance of this book; and to the publisher, Mr Christopher Hurst, who has corrected slips of wording and in several instances tamed the author's unruly language and given it a more conventional and idiomatic form, thus quietly taking on himself the laborious work of editorship.

Fürstenfeldbruck, H.W.L
West Germany
June 1989

SOME TRADITIONAL ETHIOPIAN TITLES
(approximate translations)

Negus	King (abolished by Haile Sellassie, who was the last man to be crowned as a king, in 1928).
Ras	Duke (territorial ruler).
Dedjazmatch	Earl (territorial ruler).
Fitawrari	'Commander of the vanguard' – Commander-in-Chief of the army, marshal.
Kegnazmatch	'Commander of the right wing of the Army' – general.
Grazmatch	'Commander of the left wing of the Army' – general.
Balambaras	Commander of the fort.
Afe Negus	Lord Chief Justice. (Bearers of this title and of the three that follow were aides to the Emperor.)
Tsehafe Taezaz	Privy Seal.
Blatta	Counsellor – title implying learning and wisdom.
Blattengueta	Same as 'Blatta' – senior grade.
Kantiba	Mayor
Negadras	Trade commissioner.
Bejirond	Chief accountant.
Lidj	Literally 'child'. When used as a prefix to the name, it carries the meaning 'son of an important man who has not yet acquired a title of his own'. The 'important man' is in most cases a ruler – an emperor, king, ras or dedjazmatch; if he is of minor rank, he is likely to belong to the family clan of a ruler.
Woizero	Original meaning: woman of standing, a married lady. Present meaning: 'Mrs'.
Woizerit	Girl of standing, virgin. Present meaning: 'Miss'.
Ato	Original meaning: man of standing, esquire, gentleman. Present meaning: 'Mister'.

INTRODUCTION

THE RASTAFARIAN MOVEMENT AND ITS DOCTRINE: A CURRENT VIEW

by Maxim J. Anderson

In the light of recent reports[1] purporting to have solved the 'mystery' surrounding the 'disappearance' of H.I.M. Haile Sellassie I, Hans Wilhelm Lockot's book, *The Mission*, is timely. It reminds us, at the centenary of his birth, that the proverbial 'half' about the King of Kings has never been told. This is as true for the Emperor of Ethiopia as it is for the Rastafarians of the 'New World' who, over the last sixty-two years, have recognised his historical importance and exemplary works. Both Leader and followers are subject to misunderstanding, vilification and banishment to the margins of credibility by 'sophisticated' minds and their mocking audiences. Lockot, in his attempt at a 'just appraisal', goes far in dealing with some of the injustice perpetrated against the Emperor and, by extension, against Rastafarians as well.

Lockot's perceptive essay is that of an insider; in short, it is the account of an eye-witness, who evidently observed well the securing and nation-building task of 'an evolutionist living in times of revolution'. With his twenty-four years' experience of living in Ethiopia and working at the Imperial National Library, his observations carry their own qualification. That this is true is obvious from some of his revelations and analyses, but it also stems from the stated fact that he presented himself in early 1951 and, having put to the Emperor the proposition of 'building up' the National Library, gladly accepted his Majesty's 'command': 'You will do it.'

That said, it is perhaps as well to set the the tenor of this Introduction by acknowledging Lockot's concluding key remark: that, in spite of all the lies and media propaganda before and after the revolution in 1973, 'history will be the final judge.' Indeed. Six years after the failed palace coup, the Emperor, addressing Parliament on the duties and obligations involved in the overall process of 'development', said: 'We are content to let history judge the wisdom of our actions'. The world and Ethiopia did not have long to wait for that judgement, for already, in terms of national unity and 'development', not a few Ethiopians and others are contrasting the erratic post-revolution times with the dangerous era (i.e. post-partitioned Africa; colonial powers' territorial machinations; the First World War; fascist aggression leading to the Second World War) and the post-war years in which Ras Tafari/Haile Sellassie I manoeuvred and – detractors notwithstanding – brought Ethiopia through intact.

Many critics fail to recognise that the misconstrued 'autocratic rule' of the Emperor was, conversely, iconoclastic in its modernising objective and accommodation to youth; that, despite their impetuosity, the Emperor 'and the young people were pursuing the same goal – their views differed only about timing.' In 1935 Geoffrey Harmsworth noted that following his coronation the *Negusa Nagast* (King of Kings) 'turned his eyes towards Europe', for at an early stage he divined from where the 'danger would one day come'[2]. Undoubtedly this was a reference to Mussolini; but it also hinted at the onslaught of 'Western' ideas into Ethiopia. Thus, with the expansion of education and growth in numbers of young people sent abroad to study, and the marked increase of students in Addis Ababa from the former Italian colony of Eritrea, brimming with 'foreign ideas', the Emperor realised that their impatience revealed them to be a symptom of their heady times. Seeing this as a 'challenge' resulting from the disturbing process of modernisation, he 'was not prepared on any account to side-step this challenge with the progressive . . . youth'. In fact he encouraged them, as for instance in Workineh Gebeyehu's rise from humble beginnings to become, until his 'leadership' role in the attempted coup of December 1960, the 'most powerful man in Ethiopia after the Emperor'. In short, many of those who were then young owed their 'enlightenment' and subsequent rise in social status to the Emperor. Lockot is therefore in company with Harmsworth, who correctly opined: 'The name of Haile Sellassie . . . will, I believe, shine in history, no matter what the future holds in store . . .'[3]

The fresh approach evident in Lockot's essay is, in a secular sense, a tacit recognition[4] of the Rastafarian movement's insight on the epoch-making significance of the Emperor's endeavours. Moreover, its thrust focuses on two themes central to Rastafarians: namely, purposive change and history (i.e. with the former having an explicit relationship with the latter). Rastafarian 'Reasoning'* always takes as its point of departure the symbolic and practical relevance of 'ancient' history and its immanent bearing in the present. Thus the Emperor, whose heritage

---

*This word, with capital 'R', conveys a special religious-secular significance in the Rastafarian lexicon.

THE RASTAFARIAN MOVEMENT AND ITS DOCTRINE   xi

reaches back to the union between Solomon and the Queen of Sheba in the tenth century BC, was manifested terrestrially in 1892; opened the Book of which John spoke in Revelation 5:5 in November 1930; and, in Lockot's secular analysis, became the 'inventor of the new order'. This the Emperor achieved with a functional blend of the modern with the traditional. And to have more of the former in the mixture in order to effect purposive change, the Emperor as the twentieth-century moderniser *par excellence*, beginning in 1916, kept the state structures in a permanent state of flux by constant institutional reforms, introduction of new administrative methods and shifting of personnel.

Lockot takes admiring cognisance of the skill required in accomplishing those moves, and throughout his book highlights the qualities in the Emperor which struck the most disparate commentators. Thus the reader is struck by how 'consistent' the Emperor was in his works: That he was indefatigable; selfless; regal; dignified; disciplined; never lacking in decorum; beyond ridicule. To Harmsworth he was 'a wise man', suggesting more the 'prophet than the great military and political leader'.[5] For Mussolini he was the 'young, resolute and intelligent man who has *supreme power* in his hand in Ethiopia'.[6] 'Here then, as Lockot reveals, stands the historical figure whose temporal Reasoning (i.e. from a Rastafarian perspective) is a 'a weave of philosophy and history' – the precise mode Rastafarians ceaselessly endeavour to emulate. Here in history stands this essentially hard-working monarch who 'felt that he was serving as an exemplar to a nation' – and to struggling peoples everywhere. In fact, when the process that he had started gathered revolutionary momentum with the impatience of the youth, he kept his 'habitual composure' and eschewed bloodshed, preferring to settle things through negotiation. In Lockot's appraisal of events, the Emperor held on to power 'until he was sure that the reins of government would not be handed to civilians: the chatterers and speechmakers'. Those opportunists were incapable of sustaining the state. For more than fifty-seven years Haile Sellassie I had continued and furthered Menelik's unifying works primarily by securing Ethiopia's borders through the involvement of the country in ever-widening international relations, and by establishing 'a modern administration and legal codes', i.e. establishing a universalistic political order over archaic feudal particularism. Here, then, was the modern foundation upon which Ethiopia as an ancient polity would adapt and continue into the future.

As for 'understanding' more of the West than its technology, the Emperor – 'the artist of power'[7] – probed the writings of 'Frederick the Great of Prussia, Napoleon Bonaparte, Machiavelli . . ., Voltaire, Goethe' and others to prepare himself for his political mission of transforming Ethiopia.[8] It would have a voice in the world's halls of power, first by maintaining its ancient independence and sovereignty, and also by introducing current ideas and building new politico-social and economic structures. So, if the Ethiopian empire was to hold its own internationally, it is necessary to be knowledgeable about the philosophies sustaining the existing powers. Ethiopia's entry into the League of Nations in 1923 is therefore understandable from the perspective of *realpolitik*. That move, Rastafarians affirm, 'emphasised Ethiopia's distinct place in world history'; it also revealed Ras Tafari's statesmanship in manoeuvring into positions of power. However, it set the stage for Geneva in June 1936 when the world powers' collective conscience was stripped bare and their compounded hypocrisy left prostrated, only to be rolled over by the iron wheels of fascism (as the Emperor predicted) less than three years later.

The theme of power relations is highlighted in Lockot's book, and the fact that the Emperor spent much time in his library at Debre Zeit studying the subject exemplifies why Rastafarians should not shy away from what is considered by some to be 'dangerous babylonian' literature. Haile Sellassie I being the Perfect Exemplar in the Rastafarian world-view, we are shown that Frederick the Great, Napoleon and Goethe, in their respective actions and conceptions, are all part of the scheme of things. Both philosophy and strategy play their part in conducting the 'power game'. For instance, the Emperor obtained financial assistance and armaments from Hitler's Third Reich in order to fight its fellow-fascists; he deliberately went into exile in the very country that had opposed Ethiopia's entry to the League of Nations, in order to oppose the aggression of Italy, which had supported its entry – was this Machiavellianism or the 'fulfilment of prophecy'? Equally, the Emperor 'was not defeated by the revolution. While still in the possession of power he surrendered without a fight.' With hindsight, that decision can be seen to have been the correct one. It foretold the subsequent 'Red Terror' and all the suffering and internal disintegration it entailed. 'Should he', asked Lockot, 'have bled the peoples of the Horn to death to serve as pawns on the great-power chess board?' Of course not. The Emperor as the peacemaker and unifier 'did not see this as his mission'.

From the above brief review of Lockot's essay we have sought to show that the Rastafarian movement relates the historical figure of Haile Sellassie I to its spiritual and temporal endeavours. That the

THE RASTAFARIAN MOVEMENT AND ITS DOCTRINE xiii

Emperor's role as Exemplar is a *sine qua non* is by now a commonplace. This being so, little mention is made here of the religious aspect of the movement, which is well covered in the literature. Even so frequent mention is made of the Doctrine in order to explain the movement's current position. However, to grasp the movement and its current doctrinal developments, it is essential to have at least a tentative understanding of antecedents (away from the stale clichés) which are central to the Rastafarian manifestation within the 'New World'. In short, the movement emerged via an ancient Ethiopian-Egyptian-Hebraic-West African religio-cultural line of descent. This 'line', from a Rastafarian analysis, led to Haile Sellassie I being seen as the physical and spiritual incarnation of that historical process at first by only a few.

In making this affirmation, however, the present writer must also say that perhaps few Rastafarians would take this approach. For them the Bible is the only source, the only literary tradition to adhere to. Others[9] see things differently, and constantly search ancient and 'obscure' cross-cultural material for evidence of their version of the Truth. Thus it is principally the concept of the divinity of H.I.M. Haile Sellassie I that unites us. Some Rastafarians will therefore find much in Lockot's analysis and language with which they disagree; likewise a few will perhaps be critical of this somewhat 'overtly secular' treatment of the movement.

The Rastafarian movement has grown, and in so doing has become more complex in its body of doctrine.[10] The reasons for this development are varied, and therefore a full picture is not possible here. Suffice it to say that they are historical and, at the same time, adaptive to the current force of events. The movement has undergone crucial socio-political changes in its sixty-two years' history,[11] the most significant,[12] as Lockot hinted in another connection, being the 'disappearance' in 1974–5 of the only remaining Christian empire. Then the new challenge to the central tenet and the Central Personality of the movement (i.e. the Emperor) came not directly from 'Rome' – viewed in Rastafarian Doctrine as 'the Beast' of Revelation – but, tellingly, from within Ethiopia and from ideologues in Moscow, Havana and elsewhere.

At this juncture we should outline and summarise selected antecedents directly related to the 'culture-line' birth of the movement in Jamaica.[13] This is necessary because of the widespread conceptual errors that have been made and tediously repeated by numerous writers on the movement and Doctrine.

It has been stated that 'since at least the beginning of the twentieth century, Jamaican blacks have identified with Ethiopia on account of its biblical symbolism.' This assertion is historically wrong.[14] So too is that made by Ken Post in his thesis on the advent of 'Ethiopianism' in Jamaica. Post ingenuously attempts to articulate Rastafarian Doctrine with South African and American meanings and versions of African peoples' self-realisation. True, the history and culture of the ancient kingdom of Ethiopia became the pivot on which this consciousness turned, and the Bible was indeed central as source material. Psalm 68:31 was given fresh vigour in the general combat with outright denigration of Black peoples and all things African. Drawing on a text[15] which explained away 'Ethiopianism' as the main clause in a 'mythical charter', Post opportunely narrows the Jamaican-Ethiopian identification to 1935, the year of Mussolini's aggression against Ethiopia. With an eye on the Rastafarians, he says that 'Jamaican Ethiopianism' became more specific, more 'limited'. As already suggested, he too was in error.[16]

'Ethiopianism', shorn of its overtones in colonialist and polemical 'Left' thinking, also operated at a deeper level. The Coronation of the Emperor in 1930 brought to the fore, within the Jamaican context, antecedents which reach far into 'New World' African peoples' historical experience. The surfacing of Ethiopia in Jamaica in the 1930s has much to do with specific aspects of the latter's history.

In a convincing study on examples of 'Hebrewism' in West Africa, Joseph Williams supported his African findings by examining Ashanti survivals in Jamaica, where he resided for five years. The evidence that Ashanti retentions existed in adapted form in this ex-slave colony was overwhelming, and he noted by way of comparison certain 'characteristic traits' as observed by Bryan Edwards in the eighteenth century. To Edwards the designated 'Koromantyn' slave displayed 'courage and stubbornness, or what an ancient Roman would have deemed an elevation of soul'.[17] But those 'traits' were merely externals within a broader pattern of protest and resistance to enslavement. Care should therefore be taken not to read into them such stereotyped 'finality of type' as some writers[18] have done. Being mindful of historical stereotypes, it is nonetheless true that the Akan-speaking peoples' cultural influence in Jamaica's early and subsequent development of an autochthonous culture[19] is central to an understanding of current Jamaican social forces of which the Rastafarian movement represents the most recent. Williams speaks of the 'Ashanti dominance among the descendants of the slaves'. To him the strongest cultural index of that 'dominance' is religion viewed through the prism of a belief in a Supreme Being and Myalism, or its antithesis Obeah* – possibly the survival of yet 'another Hebraic influence'[20] – manifesting itself as a positive force in herbal and psychosomatic medicine where the ritual dance is pivotal.

Related to the Reasoning outlined here, T. Edward Bowdich also studied the distant past in an attempt to prove connections between the 'Ashantee' of West Africa on the one hand and dynastic Egypt and Ethiopia on the other. Briefly, he 'considered' these West African people 'to be part of the civilized Ethiopians of Herodotus and Diodorus, pressed westward [by] Egyptian emigrants . . ., and afterwards driven . . . still further westward by the sweeping expedition of Ptolemy Evergetes'.[21] Be that as it may, Bowdich also noted the significance of the ritual dance among other historic African peoples such as the 'Phoenician priests' who, he says, 'worked themselves to the height of frenzy . . . then raved or prophesied, as if possessed by some invisible power . . .' He then affirms that he had 'frequently seen the fetish women or priestesses' do a similar dance in 'Ashantee'.[22] Leaving aside his misunderstanding of what he called stupefaction – what Leonard Barrett referred to as 'altered states of consciousness'[23] – Bowdich mentions that the 'Ashantees' believe the actions and revelations of the 'priestesses'[24] to have been 'consigned' to them by the 'Supreme Deity', 'Yancoompon'.[25] He endeavours to demonstrate diffusion of Ptolemaic Egyptian religious ideas to the 'Ashantees': 'notwithstanding the polytheism' of the former, they too 'acknowledge but one Supreme God',[26] and within their cosmology the Almighty God 'does not degrade himself' with temporal matters, but leaves them for 'fetish' superintendents. Drawing on Strabo, he compared the 'Accras' theology with that of the ancient Ethiopians. According to Bowdich, the latter 'had their penates; so have the modern'.[27]

Thus whereas Williams posits a diffusion of ancient Hebrew religio-cultural practices from Jerusalem via Upper Egypt, Meroe, then west to Gao among the Songhais and finally south to the Ashanti,[28] Bowdich conjectures an Egyptian-Ethiopian migration of ideas into West Africa, principally among the Akan-speaking peoples. Again, one should be wary of such diffusionist theory, which more often than not attempts to disprove African autochthonous cultural innovation and development.[29]

*Myalism = a magico-religious system originating from Akan-speaking regions of West Africa including spirit possession, ancestor worship, herbal medicine etc.
Obeah = a religious system co-existing with Myalism, but regarded by most Jamaicans as a negative force.

There is, however, an historical connection with ancient Israel which Rastafarians in general do not deny and of which they are forever mindful. The historically significant union of Queen Makeda (the Queen of Sheba) and King Solomon in the tenth century BC is justified in the Solomonic Line of which Haile Sellassie I is *Eyesos Kristos* (Jesus Christ) in His Kingly character and therefore represents the mystical manifestation of the Creator traversing the terrestrial plane, as he has done in different epochs and in the guise of various personages. The *Kebra Nagast* account of the 'diffusion' of Judaism into Ethiopia is, from the perspective of Doctrine, accepted by the Rastafarian movement as interpreted through the main source, namely the Bible. According to James Bruce, the net importance of that union was 'the foundation of an Ethiopian monarchy, and the continuation of the sceptre in the tribe of Judah, down to this day'.[30] To Rastafarians it foretold things 'new' – though, through insensitivity to Rastafarian Doctrine, it is seen by some as 'final' portending the 'apocalypse'. But this is not the point, which is change. For as Jesus Christ said: 'The Queen of the South [i.e. Ethiopia] shall rise up in the judgement with this generation, and shall condemn it; for she came from the uttermost parts of the earth to hear the wisdom of Solomon; and behold [one] greater than Solomon is here.'[31] The simplest explanation possible of an aspect of Rastafarian Doctrine is that the foregoing signified, symbolically, that the sun shall remove from Jerusalem and shine henceforth over Axum.[32]

Without attempting a more detailed account of the doctrinal significance of the *Kebra Nagast*, it is perhaps enough to say that Solomon, on receiving the son born of his union with the Queen of the South (Menelik/David), blessed[33] him and enjoined the first-born son of his high priest Zadok and the sons of the priestly class to accompany Menelik I on his return to his mother's country. However, in fulfilment of the removal of the sun from Jerusalem and the 'continuation of the sceptre in the tribe of Judah . . .', according to the Ethiopians, Menelik and his companions removed the Ark of the Covenant, and took it to Ethiopia.[34]

These selected antecedents are considered useful for an understanding of the philosophy of the current Rastafarian movement and Doctrine, and they go beyond mere 'mythical constructs' or historical conjecture based on 'apocryphal legends'. For Rastafarians the objective truth rests firmly on their knowledge of the heritage of H.I.M. Haile Sellassie I, and that goodly heritage has its objective roots in the antecedents outlined above , and also within the Bible interpreted through Rastafarian religious and secular doctrines. Not infrequently, implicit recognition of the ancient origins and spirituality of that heritage emanates from other learned sources too. For instance, the 'Gold Sceptre(s)' presented by King George V of Great Britain to 'His Majesty Haila Selassie, King of the Kings of Ethiopia [sic]' takes on a whole new and explicit meaning to Rastafarians. E.A. Wallis Budge wrote that these sceptre(s) (a gold and ivory one was presented to Empress Menen) 'have been designed with the view of making them to possess a historical, religious and symbolic character in accordance with the traditional history of "unconquered Abyssinia".' Furthermore, because the Sceptre(s) are replete with representations of the 'Pentacle', which 'tradition asserts' was set in King Solomon's (magical) ring, 'it is right that both the name [Yahweh] and the Pentacle should appear on the Sceptre of a King of Abyssinia of the Solomonic Line.'[35] There are numerous other 'historical and religious' symbols on H.I.M. Haile Sellassie I's significant Coronation 'gift'. Suffice it to say that what is known and recognised implicitly the Rastafarians boldly make explicit and simple for all who care to listen.

But what has all this to say about the current position of the Rastafarian movement? The sceptic may still object that there appears to be no logical and realistic connection between the movement and the historical figure of Emperor Haile Sellassie I; that the emphasis on antecedents is at best atavistic with no bearing on present reality or, at its worst, seems to be telling 'only a Jamaican story'. According to the Reasoning, both objections are groundless. Rastafarians are connected to the Emperor in the ways already outlined and expanded below. Rastafarian Doctrine and the movement that flows from it are universal and know no geographical boundaries. This is now an important factor requiring further research. However, one cannot grasp the essence, the 'logic' of the movement without an understanding of the soil, the environment, the nutrients which nurtured the seed that has now come into full bloom. The inner motive force of the Rastafarian Doctrine and movement has hitherto been much misunderstood. The majority of writers on the subject are no more than superficial investigators, and in his own 'appraisal' and particular view of the Emperor Lockot intimates that other writers on him are so too.[36] Most have made only tentative excursions into the works, life and times of the Emperor and, equally, into Rastafarian Livity,* with objectionable ulterior motives.[37]

*'Livity': a Rastafarian/Jamaicanism; there is no English word that precisely conveys its real meaning. Simply, it approximates to 'that which is sentient'; the spirituality and totality of life's experience.

Leaving aside such considerations for the moment, philosophical and historical Reasoning shows that from the perspective of the Bible and the (largely oral) teachings of the *Kebra Negast* and the Rastafarian intuitive mind, adherents of the Rastafarian world-view know full well that certain influential and intellectual power-wielders recognise the historical verity of Rastafarian Doctrine and its conceptual connection with Judaism and Christianity; that, moreover, both from the religious[38] and cultural perspectives, Rastafarians are not 'fantasisers' who consciously re-interpret their (sub-conscious) West African culturo-religious antecedents within an Ethiopian religio-cultural reality, and finally that the committed Rastafarians' affirmation of Emperor Haile Sellassie I as *Kristos* (Christ) in His Kingly character[39] is the logical capstone on their monumental spiritual and physical edifice.

Again, Lockot tends to confirm the Rastafarian historical claim, though from a critical and secular angle. A somewhat similar, though perhaps unintentional confirmation can be deduced from Budge's explanation of the 'Gold Sceptre'. The significant symbols engraved on it link the Rastafarian movement and Doctrine symbolically and historically with Old Testament Israel by way of ancient and modern Ethiopia. Equally, the historical links evident from the conjectures and data cited above on West Africa's link with dynastic Egypt, Ethiopia and ancient Israel place the Rastafarian spiritual and secular views within this ancient cultural-religious complex. In an analytical sense, Ethiopia exemplifies the Old Testament being religiously superseded by the New as already suggested in the *Kebra Nagast*, and then the Conversion from Judaism to Christianity in the fourth century AD; and presently by the Rastafarian lineal conception, by means of the 'Line', of the Emperor as *Kristos*. Conceptually Ashanti and the rest of West Africa represent, in the Western Hemisphere, 'archaic' but functional religio-cultural patterns deriving from the Old Testament. In the latter, for example, is to be found the practice of *obi*,[40] which is traceable to Egyptian ophiolatary (snake-worship) and 'necromancy' in Israel. In this respect Rastafarian Doctrine does not sectarianly reject West African Myalism, Kumina, (syncretic) Pukumina and the 'Christian' revivalism deriving from them, or even their antithesis Obeah with its healing propensity; rather, it supersedes the Old, especially by rejecting blood-sacrifice and the 'witchcraft' practices in Obeah. In a secular sense, this 'revolutionary' movement is an 'extension of the traditional African religion but with even more intensive religious commitment, in that [some of the movement's adherents] offer up their lives in the cause of the revolution. *Their techniques have less of an aura of "Magic" than those of their ancestors, because the enemy's tactics have changed and this indicates a refinement of the old ways.*'[41]

The Rastafarian movement, in short, came into being via an Ethiopian/African-Jamaican Line. Specifically, the Maroons* were, historically, the first within the re-emergence of the Line in the Americas. In terms of open resistance, they held that primary position until Cudjoe met Colonel Guthrie under the Cotton Tree in 1739.

Henceforth they became Treaty-bound. From that time onwards the enslaved generality symbolically took away the Maroons' *Abeng*.† The Akan ('Koromantyn') spirit and martial behaviour no longer 'belonged' to a distinct African social group, but became more dispersed among the African (and 'Creole') population. This 'spirit' then became sublimated within the African-Jamaican culture as heightened resistance to slavery, which largely had religious inspiration and was led by spiritual leaders such as Sam Sharpe in 1832. And with the later teachings of Marcus Garvey and others, the coronation of Negus Tafari as H.I.M. Haile Sellassie I (the Power and Instrument of the Trinity) on 2 November 1930, representing a 'Timely Move', the Rastafarian movement surfaced from the antecedent culture-complex here posited.

The topical issue of the increasingly visible Rastafarian movement since 1974–5 has taken on a wider interest now that Rastafarians – representing a 'social category' of Africans in the diaspora – are 'settled' within the 'immigrant' communities beyond the Caribbean region in the cities of North America and Europe.[42] Having travelled and broadened their experience, individuals and groups within this 'foreign wing' of the movement are further along the road of doctrinal development, along with visible manifestations of secularisation,[43] due not only to their geographical setting, but also to material and sociological factors and the currently popular 'Dread' concept and its concomitant sub-culture which has little or nothing to do with true Rastafarianism.[44] It therefore follows from this maligned concept that the development of a suggested 'social theory'[45] to explain the movement should not be confined exclusively to giving a descriptive account of Rastafarian doctrine in a secular sense; rather, it must, by taking cognisance of this 'foreign wing', aim to con-

---

*Free Africans living in their own communities with their own leaders who took to the hills and fought the slave-owning regime.
†*Abeng*: a horn used by the Maroons for communication in battle during their martial phase, and later in ceremonial. Currently it has a symbolic and philosophical significance for radicalised elements.

tribute actively to the current welfare and social development of the communities of which Rastafarians are constituent parts.[46]

This is necessary because Ras Tafari is an evolving religio-cultural and incipient political movement.[47] It is presently the most modern and culturally radical, yet the most vilified and patient social group to emerge out of African-Caribbean (Creole) culture.[48] It is viewed as 'a natural and logical development from the social, economic and psychological circumstances of the Jamaican society'.[49] According to Carole Yawney, the movement should be seen as a 'popular front, in a cultural and symbolic sense'.[50] In reviewing George Simpson's pioneering works on the movement, Joseph Owens concluded, in agreement with Simpson, that Rastafarians are 'utopians for having dared to propose an ideal [futuristic] poise for Jamaican culture'.[51] Such a slanted view, it is clear, stems from the inability of most commentators on the movement and its so-called 'apocalyptic' doctrine fully to appreciate its inherent boldness. Equally, such boldness frightens most other dominant social groups in the various societies and urban communities where Rastafarians have become vocal and active interest groups. Generally these dominant groups, especially in Jamaica but also in the Caribbean generally, abhor and fear the words and actions of this 'New World' phenomenon – this culturally 'revitalising force'.[52] Further, many from such hostile groups see Rastafarians, more so at home but also in the black communities abroad, as challengers of 'the entire society on the grounds of conscience, moral commitment and cultural identity'.[53]

In like manner, sectarian theologians and hedonistic members of society look on Rastafarians as latter-day Jeremiahs, unwelcome 'preachers' of 'messianic' doom and, more threateningly, of the supersession of the rich, belonging to their 'great tradition', by the majority-poor fixed to their 'little tradition'.[54] Ironically, a majority of the class from which Rastafarians come generally align themselves with the dominant classes in a unanimous consensus against the uncoventionality of the movement.[55]

On a more objective and secular level, the movement is seen, undoubtedly by not a few of those in positions of power, as (potentially) 'revolutionary'. In Sheila Kitzinger's functional analysis, Rastafarian Doctrine is not to be slighted. For 'the Ras Tafari faith is by its nature quasi-political, and the movement itself can only be understood as a politico-religious cult.'[56] Joseph Owens went further and warned society of the so-called cult's 'hidden agenda': 'The movement is disfunctional in the sense that its adherents seek the destruction of the society within which the cult operates.'[57] Speaking of the involvement of

Rastafarians in Jamaican society, Rex Nettleford revealed that such involvement is indispensable from a 'desire for fundamental change'. According to Owens, Nettleford 'sees in Rasta the most salutary kind of revolutionary, in fact, the only real revolutionary',[58] i.e. revolutionary in a culturally developmental and philosophical sense. Earlier, Owens had written: 'The Rastafarian inspiration is not something handed down (*"traditum"*) but is re-lived and re-created in each generation . . .'[59]

Reflecting on social change, W.E. Bowen analysed the potential for development offered by these contemporary challengers of the values and hegemony of the 'upper classes', and predicted a future of socio-political conflict with eventual victory for the 'inferior group'; he saw Rastafarian builders of the future becoming the 'dynamic standard-bearers of a new Jamaican society'.[60] Beckford and Witter, in their critique of Jamaica's political economy, hint at this potential but nevertheless passed it over in their work.[61]

Thus, as a continuation of Cudjoe, Nanny, Tacky, Sam Sharpe, Paul Bogle, Alexander Bedward[62] and Marcus Garvey's earlier efforts, Rastafarians like Howell, Hibbert, Dunkley and Hindes became noticeable as so-called 'ideological extremists'[63] from 1930 onwards. The movement, in a temporal sense, began as 'a counteraction to the imperialistic outcome' of colonial politics and cultural Eurocentricism, and has developed into an 'all-encompassing quest by Africans in the disapora [seeking to chart an independent path to development and, ultimately, their own] destiny'.[64] In this wider sense of the movement's objectives, Rastafarians could be termed 'neo-Garveyites' or exponents of 'liberation theology'. For as an elder Rastafarian wrote, 'they are those who pass through great tribulations in Jamaica by the name Rastafari, and in other lands by different names. They are those that shall not take the beast by force of armament [if you bow before force, God and History shall record your Judgement] but [via the Rastafarian triadic formula] Word, Sound and Power.' The Rastafarian is one 'who draws his reservoir of strength through faith and humility'[65] – based on the redeeming Knowledge of H.I.M. Haile Sellassie I as the Perfect Exemplar. He does so, philosphically and assuredly, from the perspective of Time: Far-I (i.e. looking into the distant future).

In conjunction with the foregoing claim, the Rastafarian world-view is time-bound and is non-discriminatory in its condemnation of social injustice. It is universal in its perceived redemptive application: I an I*

---

*Approximating to 'we', but even this approximation is too simple. It is an expression meaning the whole gamut of humanity ranging from the individual to God.

'have weighed [the imperialist powers]'. I an I 'have weighed [the dependent and underdeveloped governments]'. I an I 'have weighed all in the balance of justice. They have been found wanting.' And what of this belligerent, ecologically-threatened, nationalistic world ridden with race-hatred? This: 'Either collective extinction or collective survival [humanity], which one?'[66] Ras Sam Brown also had a universal message: 'We are those who are destined to free not only scattered [Black peoples] but all people, animals, herbs and all life forms.'[67] For 'we are avowed to create a world order of one brotherhood,' and 'our duty is to extend the hand of charity to any brother in distress . . .'[68] Thus, notwithstanding the perceived 'vagaries', subtleties and idealism seen by some, deep reflection and objective analysis will, as hinted at by Owens, reveal 'a definite ascendancy of universalism over particularism'[69] in the Rastafarian Doctrine and movement. When one considers Haile Sellassie's endeavours to unite a disparate polity into one nation; his Pan-Africanist stance; his consistency in the pursuit of collective security, especially for the small and less powerful states; and his ideals with regard to the League of Nations and then the United Nations, interpreted by Rastafarians as tentative movements towards the Brotherhood of Man; – the universalistic and humanistic characteristics of the current Rastafarian movement should not come as a surprise.

To a large extent, therefore, the burgeoning of the movement within the metropolises is due to its universalistic appeal against socio-economic injustices rather than to faddish sub-cultural externals.[70] Giving a socio-political summing-up of the movement in 1982, Carl Stone stated: 'In our [Jamaican] society the most powerful ideological force is Rastafarianism not Marxism and (contrary to most studies on the movement) Rasta appeal has nothing to do with full or empty bellies.'[71] This observation takes us beyond the derogatory sociological analysis (of a kind still current) of Orlando Patterson, who prefaced his findings as follows: 'Bizarre on the surface, the millennarian cult of Rastafari . . . is understandable in terms of social-psychological withdrawal.'[72]

In response to such criticism one can say that the movement's appeal has more to do with the process of cultural counteraction already mentioned. In an overtly secular sense, a commentator on the movement[73] has suggested that 'Rastafarianism arose primarily because of the suppression of the culture of non-European peoples. And this suppression began long before the development of what is today regarded as advanced capitalism.' Even so, the secular 'ideological [motive] force' discerned by Stone among Jamaican Rastafarians is naturally not to be found with a fully identical motive-form in the Northern metropolises. The movement's motive-form outside the Caribbean has, on the positive side, taken the assertive forms of cultural identity within multicultural, multi-racial politics. On the negative, reactive side is a fashionable 'ethnic' 'Dread' trend, predominantly among sections of the 'rebellious' young. A tentative but obvious conclusion would be that the difference in motive-forms has much to do with the social, economic, political and historical characteristics specific to those metropolises. These variables affect the 'ideological' thrust of both Doctrine and movement, and tend to take more of an organisational form in such cities as London, New York and Toronto. The initiative for this, of course, stems from the nature of these societies, but the impetus originated in Shashamane (in Ethiopia), Kingston (Jamaica), Port of Spain (Trinidad), and St. George's (Grenada).

Thus in the metropolises numerous organisations such as the Ethiopian World Federation, the Twelve Tribes of Israel, the Rasta Union of Zion and the Rastafarian Advisory Service (RAS) have their aims and objectives, inspiration and meaning rooted in Ethiopia/Africa, the Caribbean and Britain. A similar plethora of Rastafarian organisations will be found in the United States and Canada, equally inspired by Haile Sellassie I, and connected with the Caribbean[74] and Africa. These organisations are all important for an understanding of the development, historical and potential, of the movement, for central to these organs is acceptance of the practical emphasis given by the Emperor to the necessity to organise and centralise. Here it should be mentioned that it was he who first established the principle and example of organisation which practically internationalised and involved Rastafarians. This took shape in the Ethiopian World Federation (EWF) in 1937. The first chartered Local 17 was established in Kingston in August 1938. From the EWF headquarters in New York there came seventeen years later an historic announcement that 'five hundred acres of . . . fertile land'[75] had been granted to the people of the West by the Emperor. Henceforth the hope of repatriation[76] took on realistic meaning for many Rastafarians.

Organise and centralise: this is the twin goal of Rastafarians everywhere. Their chief problem, however, is their marked tendency for fissiparous behaviour and to produce egocentric personalities. Nevertheless they refer constantly to the ideal inherent in the League of Nations and the United Nations and the Emperor's practical and symbolic involvement with those organs. Equally, Rastafarians will cite the quartering of the Organisation for African Unity in Addis Ababa when it was founded in May 1963. Historically they refer to the entire reorganisation of Ethiopia by the Emperor – more fully after the death of Menelik II in 1916, when Lidj Yassu reigned briefly and there was an interregnum with Empress Zauditu culminating in Ras Tafari's elevation to power in 1928–30 as H.I.M. Haile Sellassie I, the Conquering Lion of the Tribe of Judah. Rastafarians will further cite the first written Ethiopian Constitution of 1931. As the Emperor said at the time, it was 'a Constitution for our reign, . . . that is based on law and bring our people into partnership in the work of government . . .' Its revision in 1955 furthered the original aim of moving towards a constitutional monarchy. Rastafarians are conscious of the several schools and the University which, through the Emperor, were organised and put into the service of the modernisation programme. The establishment of a standing army, replacing the outmoded *ad hoc* feudal army that existed before and after Adowa and, most important, the modernisation of the Ethiopian state which was now to be run by a relatively efficient public administration, was complemented by non-arbitrary Legal Codes whereby former 'slaves' and vassals became citizens equal before the law with nobles. For the Rastafarians these are practical examples of the organisational endeavours and ability of Emperor Haile Sellassie I – accompanied, as Lockot recounts, by hard physical work.[77] Yet the Rastafarians continue to indulge in 'personalitism' and 'groupism', which results in greater factionalism. Thus the relation between the historical person of the Emperor and the Rastafarian movement tends at present to suffer contradictions owing to these disruptive tendencies.

This essay on the Emperor *vis-à-vis* the Rastafarian movement has sought to depart, like Lockot's book, from the usual stale repetitions. Nevertheless, we must finally say here that in relating their doctrinal views in accordance with history, Rastafarians are time and again charged with fantasising[78] or extrapolating a world-view from known facts or 'legends'. There are some who dismiss 'Rastafarianism' as oversimplistic or reductionist in tenor; they shun the 'scientific' approach – completely missing the point that Rastafarians hold as a principle: 'Man Know Thyself.'[79] But with a broader outlook and understanding, these accusers would realise that Rastafarians are – in opposition to extrapolation – intuitive thinkers; that in their approach to life they are *not* akin to Pilate's stamp and temper, i.e. asking a question and then walking away without waiting for an answer. . .

So, by historically relating the Emperor with Rastafarians in the light of Lockot's attempt at an objective 'just appraisal', we conclude by remarking on the significance to the Rastafarian movement as a whole of the year in which this essay is being written: 1992. RAS, as the co-ordinating body, has with the wide approval of other Rastafarian organisations, named 1992 'the Year of the Creator' – the centenary of H.I.M. Haile Sellassie I's manifestation on the Terrestrial Plane in July 1892. Thus, in the Rastafarian symbolic interpretation, it is not coincidental that a number of historical events converge in 1992: from the half-millennium of Columbus' 'mistaken discovery' to even the tricentenary of the 'wicked' pirate-infested Port Royal (the old commercial capital of Jamaica) slipping beneath the waves at noon on a fine day in June 1692. Even so, although all things are intertwined, the centenary of the Emperor – notwithstanding any purported 'discovery'[80] – remains the primary event in the calendar for Rastafarians. And because we who belong to our time are too close to it, we have to conclude that in regard to the Emperor's works, life and times – 'history will be the final judge.' The future will, indeed, correct the inaccuracies that win approval today and confirm the Rastafarians' currently slighted truth.

July 1992

NOTES

1 That the 'remains' of the Emperor have been 'discovered' *in situ* beneath a 'latrine'. It is said that an official 'interment' is scheduled for July 1992. See *Focus on Africa*, vol. 3, no. 3, April–June 1992: 16–20. Rastafarians view this as being more than a coincidence, and under the auspices of the RAS an international contingent of Rastafarians is set to mark His Imperial Majesty's centenary in Addis Ababa in the same month.
2 Geoffrey Harmsworth,*Abyssinian Adventure* (London, 1935), p. 189. This writer's comments are contrasted with those of Lockot's for the simple reason that he was a journalist on the *Daily Mail*, which supported Italy against Ethiopia in 1935. As can be seen in a number of articles in the 1970s and 1980s, this newspaper does not consider the Rastafarians' viewpoint objectively.
3 Harmsworth, p. 186.
4 Lockot, p. 40.
5 Harmsworth, pp. 191–2.
6 D.A. Talbot, *Haile Selassie I: Silver Jubilee*, The Hague, 1955, p. 23. Emphasis added.
7 This is a recurring theme in Lockot's essay. The Emperor says in his autobiography: 'From the age of thirteen onwards, although my physical strength may not have been great, my spiritual and intellectual powers began to increase gradually and thus had the entrance gate of this world open.' Edward Ullendorff, *The Autobiography of Emperor Haile Sellassie I: My Life and Ethiopian Progress, 1892–1937*, transl. from Amharic and annotated (London, 1976).

8. See Talbot, p. 20.
9. See E.S.P. McPherson, *The Black Churches: A Historiographic Taxonomy of Religions in Jamaica*, bk. I (R.A.S., London, 1988), for 'other' approaches to Rastafarian Doctrine. Currently, a growing number of Rastafarians are focusing on both Ethiopia and West Africa, notably Ghana, as a source and for current inspiration.
10. The *Encyclopedia of Religion*, vol. 3, 1987, p. 96. Hereafter I shall compound 'doctrines' and refer only to Doctrine.
11. For a brief 'mid-way' account of the movement's history, see the seminal work of M.G. Smith, Roy Augier and Rex Nettleford, *Report on the Rastafari Movement in Kingston, Jamaica* (ISER, UCWI, 1960, repr. 1972), *passim*.
12. Although Rastafarian Doctrine has no equivalent to the '*Fatwa*', some Binghi Rastafarians will nonetheless disdain this view of a change.
13. The principal reason for the focus on Jamaica is straightforward. First, the movement originated on this tiny island. Secondly, it is from there that the movement has made an impact on the world. Although there are as yet no 'pilgrimages' to the parish of St Thomas, or to the capital, Kingston, historically we should bear in mind Mecca/formerly Becca, centuries after. See James Bruce, *Travels of James Bruce Esquire into Abyssinia to Discover the Source of the Nile* (London, 1790).
14. The *Encyclopedia of Religion*, vol. 3 (1987), pp. 95–6. In truth African-Jamaicans identified their religious outlook with Ethiopia more consciously with the advent of George Leile's Ethiopian Baptist Church, *ca*. 1783.
15. Bengt Sundkler, *Bantu Prophets in South Africa* (London, 1948).
16. Ken Post, *Arise Ye Starvelings: The Jamaican Labour Rebellion of 1938 and its Aftermath* (The Hague, 1978), pp. 160–3.
17. Quoted in J.J. Williams, *Hebrewism of West Africa: From Nile to Niger with the Jews* (1930, repr. New York, 1967), p. 2 (Bryan Edwards on the 'Koromantyn' and their leadership role in the 'Rebellion' in 1760. To him those intractable 'Koromantyns' were responsible for every major uprising in Plantation Jamaica.) 'Although various tribes entered Jamaica, the most dominant were the Ashanti-Fanti peoples who were closely interrelated in origin and language. Despite a strong Yaruba-Ibo complex in some places, the Ashanti-Fanti culture-complex dominated Jamaica as a whole.' Leonard Barrett, *The Sun and the Drum: African Roots in Jamaican Folk Tradition* (London, 1976), p. 16.
18. By this is meant that one should be cautious about their motives. What interest do they serve? See Robert I. Hill, *Cuba and Porto Rico with the other Islands of the W.I.* (New York, 1888): 'The Jamaican negroes are sui generis; nothing like them, even in their own race, can elsewhere be found – not even elsewhere in the W.I. They are omnipresent . . .' (quoted in Williams p. 1).
19. Rex Nettleford, in *Caribbean Cultural Identity*, refers to the difficult and painful process of 'indigenisation'.
20. Williams, pp. 50–1.
21. T. Edward Bowdich, *An Essay on the Superstitions, Customs and Acts common to the Ancient Egyptians, Abyssinians and Ashantees* (Paris, 1821), pp. 10–11.
22. Ibid., p. 15.
23. Barrett, *The Sun and the Drum, op. cit.,* pp. 105–6.
24. Cf. I Samuel 28: 7–25.
25. i.e. Williams' Nyame/Nyanacompong of the Ashanti.

THE RASTAFARIAN MOVEMENT AND ITS DOCTRINE xxvii

26 Bowdich, p. 41. See also Dennis Forsythe: 'Akhenaten has been dubbed "the first individual in history" as it was he who established monotheism by recanting on his devotion to some 2,000 gods and elevating Aten, the Sun God, as Supreme God . . . etc.' *Rastafari: For the Healing of the Nation*, Kingston, 1983: 26.
27 Bowdich, p. 42.
28 It should be borne in mind that the Ashantis claim a northern (ancient Ghana) origin.
29 Although it is not possible to pursue this hypothesis further here, some historians have claimed Ethiopia as the mother of Egyptian civilisation, and Egypt as the father of the Israelite civilisation.
30 Bruce, p. 106.
31 Matthew, 12: 42; Luke 11:31.
32 I Kings, 11: 11–12 and chap. 14, *passim*; Isaiah 1, *passim*.
33 Bruce, pp. 107–8.
34 *Kebra Nagast* (The Glory of the Kings). Of this book Sylvia Pankhurst wrote that its principal aim was to establish 'a standard of ethics for the guidance of the people and the Kings'. *Ethiopia: A Cultural History*, p. 100.
35 Sir E.A. Wallis Budge, *Notes on the Gold Sceptre . . . presented by H.M. King George V to H.M. Haile Selassie . . .* (London, 1930). Psalm 68:31 was 'engraved in Amharic' on the 'right hand side' of the 27-inch sceptre. Crucially, the head of the sceptre contains 'a magical cross found drawn in an Ethiopian manuscript' which indicates 'the exalted position in the world which Abyssinia has gained under the protection of the Cross of Christ, before which the enemies of [Ethiopia], both invisible and visible, fled.' See *passim*.
36 Lockot, preface and p. 127.
37 See Ken Post, op. cit.; Ernest Cashmore, *The Rastafarians* (Minority Rights Group report no. 64, 1984); Horace Campbell, *The Rastafari Intervention: . . .* (Univ. of Sussex, Society of Caribbean Studies, 1979), etc.
38 See *Encyclopedia of Religion*: 'religion, the problem of definition', p. 646. See also *Encyclopaedia Judaica*, vol. 15, section on Solomon.
39 There are many who question Rastafarians about the events of 1974/5 and the reality of 'death'. Some Rastafarians would not even consider the question; others simply dismiss both the questioner and the question. Still others would refer the questioner to Mark 16: *passim*; Luke 23:44–8; – 24: *passim*; Acts 10:34–43.
40 N.J. Gardner *History of Jamaica* (London, 1873), p. 187. See also I Sam. 28:7 – 'Necromancy was practised in Israel' though forbidden by law, see Lev. 19:31; 20:6, 27 etc., 2 Kings 21: 6; Isaiah 8: 19.
41 Barrett, p. 153. Emphasis added.
42 Somewhat paradoxically from the perspective of repatriation to Africa within the Doctrine. However, emigration northwards is understandable from the socio-economic perspective of poor people(s) fleeing 'underdeveloped capitalism'.
43 i.e. within Semaj's 'Phase Three' in the history of the movement. L.T. Semaj 'Inside Rasta: The Future of a Religious Movement', *Caribbean Review*, vol. XIV, no. 1 (1985).
44 The appellation 'Dread' has now been emptied of its former content ('Dreadlocks'/Latter-day 'Nazarites'–Numbers 6:1–8, Judges 13: 5–7; 16:15–22), which conveyed a more specific Rastafarian identity. Originating in Jamaica, the term is now universally used for anyone who resembles a Rastafarian. See Velma Pollard,

'Dread Talk . . .', *Caribbean Quarterly*, vol. 26, no. 4 (Dec. 1980); J.V. Owens, *The Rastafarians of Jamaica*, Kingston, 1976; George Beckford and Michael Witter, *Small Garden . . . Bitter weed*, London, 1980, chap. 8; and Rex Nettleford, who speaks of the cultivation of 'a ferocious theatricality' by Rastafarians.

45 Semaj said of this 'theory': 'Religion or mythology cannot be the primary' means for discovering 'concrete solutions in social problems. At best religion . . . can facilitate the development and formulation of solutions to social problems.' In sum, a 'Social Theory is an organised set of values which explain what you are for, what you are going to do and how you [are] going to do it.' 1989: 25–26 and 1985: 38, respectively.

46 'There is no conflict between serving one's country *materially* and serving God *spiritually*'. H.I.M. Haile Sellassie I, quoted in Talbot, p. 403, emphasis added.

47 Nettleford in Owens, 1976, vii.

48 See Rex Nettleford, *Caribbean Cultural Identity: The Case of Jamaica*, Institute of Jamaica, 1978: 187–8. '[Being one] of Plantation America's most authentic expressions of organic revolt . . .' – 'It is as though the Rasta-man is prophet, priest, and advocate – in short the society's cultural conscience.'

49 Rex Nettleford, *Mirro, Mirror: Identity, Race and Protest in Jamaica*, London Kingston, 1970, 100.

50 Carole Yawney, *Volunteer Ethiopians: African Consciousness among the Rastafarians of Jamaica*, Canadian Assoc. for African Studies, 1975: 2.

51 Owens, 1975.

52 Nettleford, 1970.

53 Nettleford, in Owens, 1976: viii.

54 Edward Braithwaite, *Contradictory Omens: Cultural Diversity and Integration in the Caribbean*, Mona, 1974.

55 This irony highlights Lockot's view on recognition of Haile Sellassie *vis-à-vis* Ethiopians in general. Mengistu Haile Mariam noted: 'The recognition of Ethiopia in the Caribbean is unique in its claims – in particular the black people of Jamaica opt to say that they are Ethiopians . . . This sentiment . . . stronger than in any Ethiopian, gives a very great feeling which is difficult to express.' Summary of World Broadcasts/BBC Monitoring, 3rd series, ME/1053 B/2, 23 April 1991. Although this writer of this Introduction generally agrees with Lockot's assertion about 'speechmakers and chatterers', this does not mean that he endorses Mengistu's defunct regime. However, it is reasonable to assert that at that particular juncture in Ethiopia's history the armed forces were the only organised group with the means at hand to halt the state's disintegration through excess of revolutionary fervour. However, Mengistu's oppressive seventeen-year dictatorship witnessed what amounted to genocide. See *Focus on Africa*, op. cit.

56 Sheila Kitzinger, 'Protest and Mysticism: the Rastafari Cult of Jamaica', *J. for the Scientific Study of Religion*, vol. VIII, 1969: 257.

57 Owens, 1976: 94–5.

58 Ibid., 96.

59 J.V. Owens, 1973: 166.

60 W.E. Bowen, 'Rastafarianism and the New Society', *Savacou*, 5 (June 1971): 49–50.

61 Beckford and Witter, 1980, chapters 7, 10.

62 McPherson, 1985.

THE RASTAFARIAN MOVEMENT AND ITS DOCTRINE xxix

63 Post, 1978: 188.
64 Semaj, 1985: 8.
65 Ras Sam Brown, 'Treatise on the Rastafarian Movement', *Caribbean Studies*, vol. 6, no. 4 (April 1966): 40.
66 Owens, 1976: 217–18, 147, respectively.
67 Brown, 1966: 39.
68 Ibid., p. 40.
69 Ownes, 1976: 28.
70 By this is meant 'dreadlocks'; 'ganja' abuse; 'trendy' I-speech; showy display of red, gold and green badges and attire; reggae music emptied of its message content, and so on.
71 See Semaj, 1985: 37.
72 Orlando Patterson, 'Ras Tafari: The Cult of the Outcasts', *New Society*, 12 Nov. 1964: 15. See Owens, 1975: 88, for categorisation of the movement as 'escapist-adjustive', 'pseudo-religious', 'birth-pangs out of economic deprivation', etc. Lord Scarman's Report (*The Brixton Disorders, 10–12 April 1981*, HMSO, London, 1981) alleges Rastafarian 'sadness'.
73 Carl Stone, in Louis Lindsay, *Methodology, and Change: Problems of Applied Social Science Research in the Commonwealth Caribbean*, Mona, 1978: 271.
74 See letter from Brother Moody in regard to the closing of the Jamaican embassy in Ethiopia. *Weekly Gleaner*, 3 March 1992: 20.
75 Report, 1960, *passim*.
76 According to Ras Michael A. Lorne at the 1983 Rastafarian Conference in Jamaica: 'Repatriation . . . this is a goal that I an I will never sacrifice. We cannot give up a massive continent for a little two-by-two square which they throw us into. To accept [the islands] as your homeland is to acquiesce to slavery . . .' *Focus on Rastafari: selected presentations from Rastafari Focus '88*, Commonwealth Institute, London. Published by RAS, 1988.
77 As long ago as 1935, a visiting journalist noted: 'People . . . are amazed at the progress of modern Ethiopia. That it has come about through the efforts and wisdom of one man who is only a few years over forty is all the more astonishing.' Harmsworth, p. 131.
78 See Post, 1978, p. 167. E.g. Rastafarian Doctrine is polemicised and reduced to an 'ideology' *a la* Engels – a form of ' "false" cognition of reality, in the sense that between that reality and action it interposes imaginary motive forces, like the will of God'. Such a conceptual framework is inadequate for analysing the movement, for it denies its credibility before the 'analysis' even begins!
79 R.G. Collingwood, *The Idea of History*, Oxford, 1986.
80 See note 39 above.

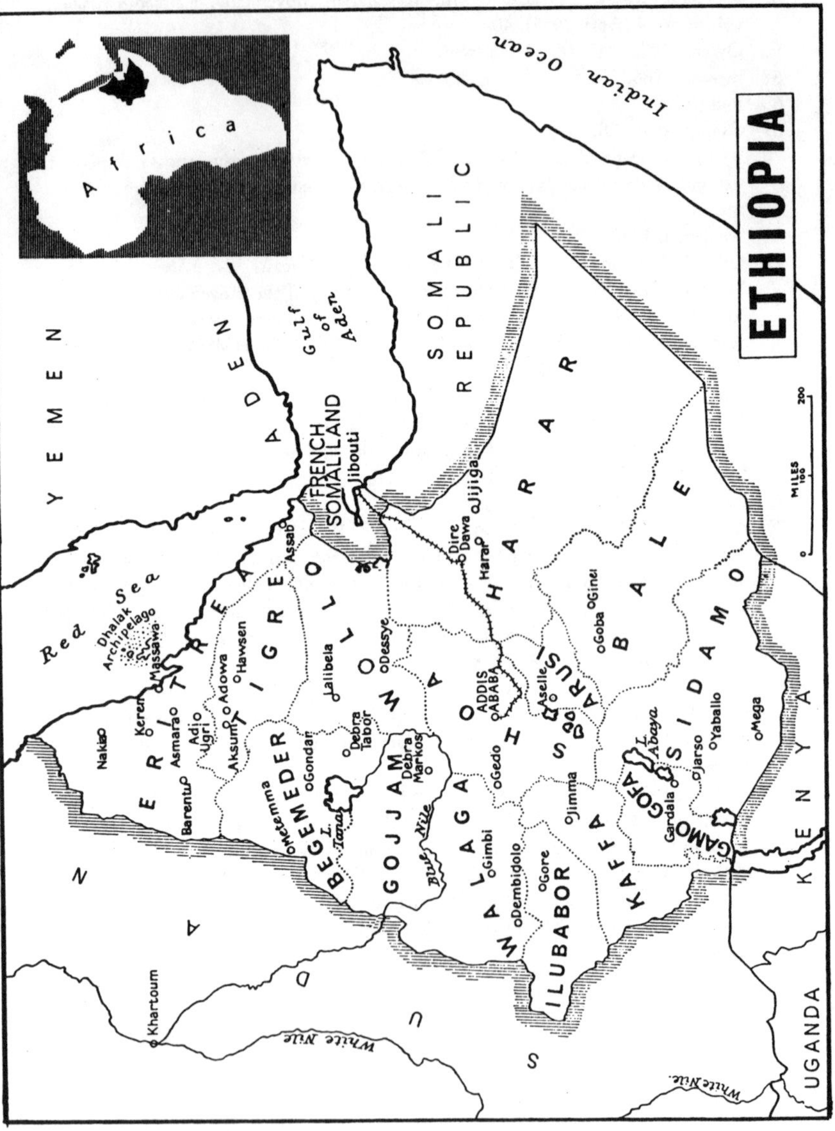
ETHIOPIA
Africa
YEMEN
ADEN
Red Sea
Dhalak Archipelago
Massawa
Gulf of Aden
FRENCH SOMALILAND
Jibouti
SOMALI REPUBLIC
Indian Ocean
ERITREA
Nakfa
Keren
Asmara
Barentu
Adi Ugri
Aksum
Adowa
Hawsen
TIGRE
Assab
BEGEMEDER
Gondar
Metemma
L. Tana
Debra Tabor
Lalibela
WOLLO
Dessye
GOJJAM
Debra Markos
Blue Nile
SHOA
ADDIS ABABA
Dire Dawa
Harar
Jijiga
HARAR
WALLAGA
Gimbi
Gedo
Dembidolo
ILUBABOR
Gore
KAFFA
Jimma
ARUSI
Aselle
BALE
Goba
Ginel
SIDAMO
L. Abaya
Jarso
Yaballo
Mega
GAMO GOFA
Gardala
SUDAN
Khartoum
White Nile
KENYA
UGANDA
MILES
0
100
200

I. PRELUDE

The Roman empire after its conversion to Christianity, the Byzantine empire, the Habsburg, Romanov and Hohenzollern empires – all of them have vanished, but none covered so long a span of time as the Ethiopian empire, and no other survived up till so recent a date. With the fall of Haile Sellassie, Christian empires ceased to exist. Who was Haile Sellassie, the man who occupied this extraordinary place in world history?

Haile Sellassie has been derided as a ridiculous, archaic figure driven by greed and vanity; denounced as having committed acts of unbelievable cruelty and wickedness, praised as broadminded, kind and generous, admired for his strength of character and self- discipline, acknowledged as a clever pragmatist or merely as a sly businessman who exploited or fooled those with whom he had to deal, extolled as a far-sighted politician, stigmatised as unpredictable and prone to erratic whims in his seemingly pathological distrust of all and sundry: these and other representations of the Emperor are to be found in the contemporary literature. The only message to the bewildered reader seems to be 'Truth is what you believe, find your own version of it.' But the truth is surely there to be found if it is sought in a spirit of openness. So, who was Haile Sellassie? As the date of his fall recedes into the past, it is surely time for a just appraisal to be attempted.

He was a man of exceptionally consistent character, with an unwavering sense of destiny. If there is anything immediately striking about his personal development, it is the absence of any distinct phases, crises or drastic changes of view. Lidj Tafari emerged on the political stage very young, already with many accomplishments and with strong consistent features. He left it in his eighties, still the same. But to see his personality whole, it is not enough to examine all that is known of his origins, his talents and his education. Some hints of what was to follow – his style and the way he ruled, as well as the way he fell – are to be found at the time when he was beginning his ascent to power during the first two years of the First World War, 1914-16. It was then that the career of Tafari arrived at the crossroads. There was indeed a crisis at that time, and it was one of historic proportions. The choice he made then determined the whole subsequent course of his life, and left a permanent imprint on all his actions and prospects as Emperor.

Historical records of those years are blurred. Many of the facts of the drama that unfolded in Ethiopia at that time remain hidden behind a veil of incidental data and indeed may never be revealed. Too many of those who were repositories of the vital secrets have died. Perhaps a few classified reports may still exist, far away from public view in the Foreign Ministry archives of the great powers, and if they emerge one day some new light may be shed on the events. Today it is impossible to give a full account, and all that can be done is to point to the stage and introduce the actors.

Before we introduce the human actors, it is necessary to mention the three great giants behind the scenes that pulled the strings and made the puppets dance. The first was the Christian religion, represented in its longest-surviving form by the ancient Ethiopian Orthodox Church; the second was the rising giant of Islam; and the third, lower in rank and dignity but more effective in action, was Western philosophy. This last had many embodiments: in the policy of the great powers, represented by their accredited diplomatic missions in Addis Ababa; in the shape of the First World War, which brought one epoch to a close and laid down new rules that the world would have to obey thereafter; and, finally, in its men of genius. Of these, Frederick the Great of Prussia, Napoleon Bonaparte, Machiavelli, Augustine of Hippo, Thomas à Kempis, Voltaire and Goethe were the stars that occupied the firmament of Lidj Tafari in his early youth, influenced as he then was by his father Ras Makonnen and by his teachers. After becoming Emperor, he had little time for private reading, but he would return repeatedly, even in old age, to the study of books written either by, or about, these seven great men. He apparently did not care for the literature of his own time, but during the enforced leisure of his exile in England, he sought to remedy this lack of knowledge, at least to a sufficient extent. Among the seven, Voltaire and Goethe were in the second rank having joined the constellation later due to their having been admired respectively by Frederick the Great and Napoleon. Machiavelli's work had a strong impact on Tafari as a young prince and later as Regent; this waned gradually under the influence of Frederick's polemical writings against the Florentine. He was in the habit of reading the two medieval authors, Augustine and Thomas, in translation while staying in Addis Ababa.

The list of preferred authors is not complete because he read other medieval works, preferring to do so in the original Latin. His small personal library of Latin books and other classics was hidden away in the palace of Debre Zeit, about 40 kilometres from the capital. Here he would occasionally read for some hours in complete privacy. Nothing more is known of this strange small library, except that most of the books showed clear signs, by markings, of his having studied them. Apart from the Emperor himself, only servants were allowed to enter this place.

The most admired of the seven figures, the ones who exercised the greatest influence on the young Lidj Tafari as well as on the mature Emperor, were the two rulers. Frederick the Great was his model of the enlightened ruler, the liberal philosopher who happened to occupy a throne. Frederick's maxims – 'The King is the first servant of the state', and 'Under my rule, anybody may try to obtain salvation according to his own fashion' – were of fundamental importance to him; he even thought that those principles provided a sufficient foundation for all religions to coexist and be reconciled in his country. Furthermore, he had adopted the 'Prussian' values: independent judges, incorruptible civil servants, a disciplined army. He also happened to resemble Frederick in his love of animals and abhorrence of hunting.

In Napoleon, the son of the French Revolution who rose to power on its ruins, he saw the lucky combination of modern man with plebiscitary Emperor, loved and admired by the whole population. For him, Napoleon was the great legislator – the *Code Napoléon* was part of the inspiration for the voluminous instrument of modern Ethiopia's legal codes – and he was also the Emperor with the bee, the symbol of industry, in his coat-of-arms.

After the liberation from Italian rule, the old-fashioned ideals of the Emperor were still shared by some members of his old guard, but no longer by the foreigners working in Ethiopia or by the younger generation of teachers. In later years, the German Cultural Institute (Goethe-Institut) in Addis Ababa presented the creations of modern art and the essence of modern thought to young Ethiopians in a skillful and imaginative way. Goethe, strangely, was never featured in any presentation given by the Institute.

We need to look closely at the critical years 1914–16, as well as the few years before the war, to get a clear impression of the future Emperor. According to accounts given by historians, there entered on the stage a young Crown Prince who was handsome and gifted but at the same time hot-blooded and unrestrained, and with many weaknesses of character. This was Menelik's grandson Lidj Yassu who, instead of staying in the capital minding his proper business, was drifting about the provinces, indulging in amorous and other excesses. More seriously, his lack of a sense of historic responsibility was displayed when he began to incline towards Islam and practise Muslim rites. He was even on the verge of converting to Islam, something that would have brought Ethiopia under Muslim rule. He did this under the influence of his numerous Muslim friends and possibly also of his father, who had been a Muslim ruler before converting to Christianity for reasons of state. The prospect of such treason on the part of an Ethiopian Christian prince led to an uprising of the feudal lords. The Orthodox Church was also enraged, and the Crown Prince was accordingly deposed, excommunicated and banished. The leader of the revolt against the apostate Crown Prince was Dedjasmatch Tafari Makonnen, governor of Kaffa and formerly of Harar; as a great-grandson of King Sahle Selassie of Shoa, he was of Solomonic descent. The fact that he was also a true believer made him a natural successor to the throne.

We now turn to some established facts. Taking advantage of the serious illness of the Emperor Menelik, the tangled internal situation and intrigues among those competing for national leadership, and the policy of détente pursued by the German Chancellor von Bülow, the missions of the Entente powers, Great Britain and France, had managed in the years before 1914 to reduce considerably the hitherto strong German influence at the imperial court in Addis Ababa. This was exerted by Menelik's personal political adviser Zintgraff, his physician Dr Steinkühler and the philologist Pinnow (employed as tutor to his grandson Yassu). After the outbreak of war, by contributing to the overthrow of the Emperor Yassu, they prevented Ethiopia from being brought into the war on the side of Germany and its allies.

Dejasmatch Tafari Makonnen would not have been considered by anyone to be a pretender at that time, since he had neither the legitimate right, the personal standing, the power or a sufficient body of followers to reach out for the crown. However, he saw his chance to use the extraordinary situation that had now arisen as a step in his own ascent to power. The true context of these events has so far not been made clear in historiography.

II. MENELIK'S HERITAGE

Menelik had not, up to this time, achieved his political aim of a Greater Ethiopia encompassing the whole Horn of Africa, from the Nile to the Red Sea coasts and the Indian Ocean. This would have been to restore the territory of the ancient Ethiopian empire of Aksum. Imperial Germany appeared as one of the great powers which was *not* pursuing expansionistic aims in this part of Africa, and Menelik thus saw it as a natural ally against those three colonial powers – Britain, France and Italy – which had confined Ethiopia to the role of a land-locked country, denying it access to the sea. The three had also refused him the frontier of the Nile which he had demanded in his official letters to foreign governments, and moreover, in the Tripartite Treaty of 1906, they had divided his country into so-called spheres of interest, thus distributing the skin of the lion among themselves before the beast had even been killed. A special mission sent by the German Emperor to Menelik in 1905 (and led by the diplomat von Rosen, a man with experience of dealing with 'oriental' countries,) led to a treaty of friendship being concluded between them. Accordingly, the diplomatic mission which Menelik sent to Europe in 1907 moved along the route Berlin-Vienna-Budapest-Rome-Constantinople, without ever touching Paris or London. As strongly as he could, Menelik was trying to impress his own views, plans and political goals on his grandson and chosen successor, Lidj Yassu. Menelik requested Wilhelm II to send a German philologist as tutor to educate the young prince – Yassu had previously been instructed by a German governess – as well as a political adviser and a personal physician to take care of Menelik himself. All these requests were granted, and the three German aides (mentioned above) arrived at the Ethiopian court in 1909.

After 1907, Menelik's health, both physical and mental, steadily worsened. In the last few years of his reign, he lost control of his own actions and words, and thus of events – except for some short intervals when, by sheer willpower, his strength returned and he appeared to have regained possession of his mental faculties. These intervals became rarer, and ceased altogether in the last two years of his life. He was the first Emperor of the Shoan, southern Solomonic line – and, if the royal code of Ethiopia, the Fetah Nagast or 'Law of Kings', were to be strictly interpreted, he was also the last, since he had no son. According to the

'Law of Kings', as written in a sacred book in medieval times,* only the male line of Solomonic descent counted where the right of succession to the throne was concerned. This ruled out the southern Solomonic princes who were still alive, since they were all descendants by the female line – these were the Crown Prince Lidj Yassu, his uncle and guardian Ras Tesamma, and his cousins Dedjasmatch Tafari Makonnen and Kegnasmatch Imru. Although it was doubtful whether the 'Law of Kings' was actually still valid, since neither of Menelik's two immediate predecessors, the famous Emperors Theodoros II and Yohannes IV, had reigned in accordance with its rules.

There was now a strong movement in Ethiopian society towards the restoration and maintenance of old values. This was in reaction to Menelik's dangerous modernistic plans. This conservative movement was led by the strongest social force in Ethiopia, the Orthodox Church, and by the powerful Rases of the northern provinces. The latter, by restoring the validity of the 'Law of Kings', became pretenders themselves. Among the feudal lords in the north and north-west, there were now several living descendants through the male line of the Solomonic dynasty. Most important, the traditionalist course was shared by the Empress Taitu, who was opposed to her husband's plans.

Indeed, it has been alleged that Menelik's decline in his last years was due to the slow administration of poison by Taitu. This story was especially favoured in Germany, where a reputable magazine even carried it in an editorial during Menelik's lifetime (*Die Zukunft*, vol. 70, 29 Jan. 1910, pp. 137–52). Here 20 May 1909 is given as the date when Menelik's physician-in-ordinary Dr Steinkühler identified potassium cyanide in the urine of the ailing Emperor, sending a confidential report on his discovery to the German minister in Addis Ababa. The minister ordered him to send the same report to 'all Chiefs of Mission' – i.e. those of Britain, France and Italy, as the result of which Menelik's three German aides were obliged to resign their posts.

The Empress, who bore her title as Menelik's spouse and not in her own right, was nevertheless, with a short interruption, the strongest political influence in Ethiopia up till Menelik's death. Clever and unscrupulous, she saw the chance to bestow the dynasty on her own family – as soon as it was clear that there would be no undisputed successor to the throne when Menelik died. This she would effect by transferring the crown to her nephew Ras Gugsa, feudal ruler of Beghemder and hus-

---

* See also below, page 10.

band of Menelik's daughter (and her step-daughter) Zauditu, who became Empress after the fall of Yassu. The couple had separated because Zauditu also had no son, and Ras Gugsa therefore had to take another wife in order to become eligible to found a new dynastic line. In spite of this, he retained the full support of his former spouse, the Empress Zauditu.

It was obvious that Crown Prince Lidj Yassu, Menelik's chosen successor, stood in the way of such scheming, and so it was essential, if it was to be successful, that Menelik should die before Lidj Yassu reached maturity and could be installed as the new Emperor. The coronation of the Emperor Yassu V of Ethiopia by the Orthodox Church would have made things final. In the event, Taitu failed in her plan. In one of his last lucid moments, in 1911, Menelik abdicated the throne in favour of the Crown Prince, and declared Lidj Yassu the new Emperor of Ethiopia. However, the solemn coronation by the Ethiopian Orthodox Church was delayed by the Crown Council, which continued to act as guardian to the seventeen-year-old monarch.

Yassu, however, was now able to exercise his newly-acquired power. He elevated his father, the Ras Mikael Wolde Giorgis, to the rank of Negus and submitted the rulers of Beghemder, Godjam and Tigre to the King of Wollo, thus making these northern Rases his father's vassals. Ras Gugsa meanwhile staged a revolt in the north in order to seize the crown, but this move failed and he was deposed and arrested by the Crown Council. None the less, the young Emperor reinstated him to his rightful dignity as the governor of Beghemder; he also restored the rich and politically important governorship of Harar to the heir-apparent, his team-mate and cousin Tafari Makonnen. Empress Taitu had succeeded in posting there one of her followers, Dedjasmatch Balcha, and having Tafari transferred from his father's governorship to the backward province of Sidamo in the south – which had deprived him of much of his domestic power and his contacts with the foreign outposts in Harar. It is difficult to establish the exact date at which young Tafari returned to his father's province and became governor of Harar, since nearly all sources give different dates. Possibly Lidj Yassu had succeeded some months earlier, when still Crown Prince, in restoring Harar to Tafari, using his influence with the dying Menelik and thus counteracting Taitu's intrigue aimed at depriving the southern Solomonide line of their power-base.

For centuries Harar had been independent and had become a political and commercial centre on the Horn before Menelik conquered it.

Menelik had entrusted the administration of his new province to his cousin, friend and closest adviser Ras Makonnen (father of Lidj Tafari), who later achieved fame when the Ethiopian forces won their great victory at Adua over the Italians in 1896. He was not commander-in-chief, but because he was the only Ethiopian with expert knowledge of foreign methods of warfare and modern military science at that time, all the other military leaders, whose reputations were based on traditional warfare, including the commander-in-chief, had consented to follow his guidance when Ethiopia was confronted by the army of a European power.

Harar had a British consulate, it was the centre of Catholic missionary activity on the Horn, and a number of foreign experts and businessmen were active there. The orphaned Dedjasmatch Tafari was powerless. Lidj Yassu – himself still a boy – and Ras Tesamma were his only protectors, the latter not counting for much except for the short span of a few months – during which he gained the upper hand in his struggle against the Empress Taitu – before his sudden death. Nobody else in the empire had an interest in restoring Harar to young Tafari, even though, in his southern province of Sidamo, he had tried from scratch to introduce reforms. These included expelling slave-traders and establishing new contacts with British outposts in the south – in contrast to the then governor of Harar, Dedjasmatch Balcha, who was only concerned with raising revenue and had no intention of introducing reforms for the benefit of the people.

Menelik took the utmost care to ensure the succession of Lidj Yassu. Already in 1908, he had the twelve-year-old prince anointed as Crown Prince of Ethiopia in a solemn church ceremony, and the Rases of the empire were sworn to their allegiance. Ras Tesamma was then appointed Regent and guardian of the Crown Prince, to rule until Yassu came of age and could be crowned as Emperor. There followed a feud between the nominal Regent and Empress Taitu, who actually ruled through the Crown Council. In this Taitu appeared to be the loser, since Ras Tesamma succeeded in exposing her intrigues and had her ousted from the Crown Council and banished to a convent. This was in 1910, but already by 1911 Ras Tesamma was dead – the suddenness of his demise led some sources to maintain that it was due to poisoning, but this has never been verified. No other regent was appointed, the Crown Council took over Yassu's guardianship, and Taitu's influence increased again inconspicuously; although no longer a member of the Crown Council, she slipped back to the palace as Menelik's spouse and to care for him. When Yassu became Emperor in 1911, he urged the Crown Council to bring forward the date of his coronation, but it was not then disposed to do so. Later, when Menelik's death was announced on 12 December 1913, it became urgent for him to be crowned as the rightful Emperor of Ethiopia, but his rivals managed again to have the coronation postponed. In order to rally support for his cause, Yassu left the capital, where he was surrounded by rivals. Also, his life was in constant danger because of the frequent feasts and banquets he was required to attend. In the provinces he had a vast following, partly due to the great authority which his father, the Negus Mikael of Wollo, enjoyed throughout the Galla country, but also because of his own popularity. From his father's court he pursued what he saw as the mission that Menelik had bequeathed to him: of reconciling the country's two great religions, Christianity and Islam, and pursuing a policy directed against the colonial powers which were now in occupation of the Red Sea coast.

III. YASSU AND TAFARI

Menelik had summoned the young prince Tafari to Addis Ababa, to be educated for a time at court along with the Crown Prince. There are photographs that show the two young great-grandsons of the Shoan King Sahle Sellassie together. Rarely can two youthful companions have been more different. The small, delicately-built, studious and disciplined introvert Tafari with strikingly large and radiant black eyes, is dwarfed by the younger Crown Prince – tall, strong, handsome and seemingly a pugnacious extrovert. Menelik observed this contrast with pleasure; each of the two princes represented qualities that were lacking in the other, and he therefore believed that the genius and talents of the highly gifted pair would be complementary and blend into one remarkable combination of strength. Just as Lidj Tafari's father, Ras Makonnen, had been a trusted adviser and indispensable support to him, Menelik was sure that Tafari in his turn would be a perfect lieutenant to Yassu. 'There goes the future of Ethiopia', Menelik is reported to have said to his German political adviser as he watched the two boys leaving his presence. The two would make an excellent team.

Then, suddenly the world was at war, and the team split up. The ways of the two princes diverged; each was still the faithful servant of Menelik's mission, but saw the fulfilment of that mission as going in a different direction. Whether or not the two actually quarrelled, they were natural opposites, and Tafari knew his cousin too well to be under any illusion that he could influence him once he had decided on the way he was going to pursue.

According to the Law of Kings, Tafari's claim to the throne, though much less well-founded than the claims of other pretenders from the north of the country, was better than that of Yassu. But because his claim had been overruled by Menelik, this point did not count with Tafari: being aware of the risks of Yassu's policy and its possible danger for the country, he determined to topple his cousin. Once Yassu was overthrown, Dedjasmatch Tafari would be the last and only representative of Menelik's political concept; all the other Rases and princes being traditionalists.

When the Great War broke out, Emperor Yassu saw the time as ripe for action. He thought that if he entered the war on the side of the Central Powers it would be possible for him, by building an alliance with Islamic forces in Africa, to tip the scales of the war decisively and chase the colonial powers from the Horn. Turkey, the largest Islamic empire, had already entered the war, and in the Sudan the embers of the Mahdi's revolt, which still smouldered in spite of his defeat in 1898, could easily be rekindled. With both shores of the Red Sea ablaze, the sparks would fly over Egypt and make the British position there untenable: the Suez Canal would fall to Germany's African allies, and from there the blaze would spread across North Africa and even beyond the Straits of Gibraltar to western Morocco. There would be Jihad against the foreign colonialists! In the other direction, hands could be joined with the German colonial army fighting in East Africa. Germany was still a colonial power, but having long since (in 1890) rid itself of the Sultanate of Zanzibar, the most powerful and influential maritime Islamic principality in East Africa, Yassu's plan now appeared considerably easier to realise than before. How should Yassu start his campaign? An obvious way was to try and spur the peoples living around the coasts of the Horn to revolt against their oppressors, at the same time mustering his own armies for an invasion of those areas.

For a decade Mohammed ibn Abdallah, assuming the title of Hajj and even Khalifa as representative of an Islamic religious order, and known to the British as the 'Mad Mullah', had waged a bitter colonial war in Somaliland, which the British had only won after a major military effort. The British action had been supported by Christian Ethiopia on no less than four occasions. Between 1899 and 1903 Ras Makonnen had sent military units totalling 24,500 men against the Mullah, on Menelik's orders. They fought bravely and achieved some successes, but failed to capture the Mullah who, after his defeat, managed to slip away as if by a miracle either to Italian Somaliland or perhaps even to hiding places in Ethiopia where he had friends and sympathisers. From his hide-outs he made several small raids into British-ruled territory.

After the beginning of the First World War, the Mad Mullah resumed his fight. As the Mahdi had done in the Sudan, he now operated as a figure symbolising the struggle of Islam against alien rule. This now appeared to Yassu as the right approach – and he took advantage of the opportunity it afforded him to take his first steps on the international stage. He got in touch with the Mad Mullah and sent him arms and ammunition; he even went so far as to propose marriage to the Mullah's daughter, an action which it was thought would serve as a bright beacon visible to the whole world, showing that the two great religions had entered into a mutual bond and were further unified by brotherhood in arms.

The Mullah, fervent Muslim as he was, did not want to be taken by surprise. He had accepted the arms, but he vividly remembered the defeats his troops had suffered after the intervention of Ras Makonnen's Ethiopian army. He possibly considered Yassu's offer as somewhat rash and precipitous, and remained cool towards a marriage project. At the very least, time was needed for more explicit negotiations. It is not known what conditions he would have agreed to, since no written statement has ever been traced, but any proposal that looked like an unconditional submission to Islam by Ethiopia would have been seen by Yassu to be out of the question and unacceptable.

It was not only the great foreign powers, with their changing patterns and policies, that had stood in the way of Menelik's plans: a greater problem was presented by the religions, which blocked his path, like immoveable rocks. If his territorial ambitions were fulfilled, Ethiopia would become a country with a Muslim majority – already they constituted about two-fifths of the population. Menelik tried to bring about conversions to Christianity. Processions of priests, splendid in their ornate festive robes, swarmed about the new provinces: liturgies were celebrated, holy water was sprinkled, and prayers were said – the people were converted and baptised. But this was to no avail: when the priests left, the people returned to their former ways and things remained as they had been before. Islam was too strong. Nor was there any point in converting the leaders either. The principle that whoever ruled a country could impose his own religion (*Cuius regio eius religio*) did not apply in Africa, as had been amply demonstrated by Yassu's father, Ras Mikael of Wollo. After converting to Christianity himself, he had tried by every possible means, including persecution, to convert his subjects too – and failed. He therefore soon abandoned any further efforts in this direction, and left matters as they stood. By so doing he retained the extraordinary popularity which he also enjoyed with all the other Galla tribes, in the north as well as in the south.

The Orthodox Church saw the predicament it faced and was alarmed. There was the danger that the Christian foundations of the Ethiopian empire could be flooded over by the growing numbers of Muslims, who from time immemorial had been their arch-enemies. The Church did not see that the two religions shared any common ground: in its view, the people had to be true believers, and the other side would be no more than tolerated, if they were not actually persecuted. The Church had embraced the political concept of Empress Taitu, shared by the Rases in the north (except for Ras Mikael of Wollo) and, with few exceptions, by the other nobles. First and foremost, according to this concept, the newly-won territories had to enjoy a semi-colonial status, in the manner of the ancient Ethiopian empire of Aksum: peoples were left independent within existing units, but they were obliged to pay heavy and regular tribute to the central government. Thus the empire had to be divided into two distinct parts, each with a different status. This was in contrast to Menelik's concept, which was the integration of the whole population within one legal order. Taitu had dismissed her husband's plans as megalomaniac dreams, endangering the very existence of the Ethiopian state.

By tripling Ethiopia's size, Menelik had put a new state on the map. In so doing he had made the southernmost province of Shoa the centrepiece of the empire, and founded a new capital, Addis Ababa, which was now also the geographical centre, since it was approximately equidistant from the nearest borders in all directions. But how would this centre look if there were political turmoil or war in the state? Taitu's plan to remove the centre back to Gondar and situate the core of the empire once again inside the easily-defended mountain fortress had the wholehearted support of the Church, whose ancient holy sites were all in the north. The semi-colonial regions of the south could either be incorporated as semi-dependencies – or, if need be, abandoned again without harming the central government. The aims of foreign policy did not go beyond the recovery of Eritrea, which would be added to the core since it still had a Christian majority persisting from ancient times: under the tutelage of the colonial power, the different religions had become accustomed to living together peacefully. Eritrea was perhaps the only matter on which all parties in Ethiopia agreed, including Menelik's progressive heirs and their followers.

The imaginative young Emperor was determined to remove the obstacles in his way by solving religious questions on the same broad scale as he proposed to solve problems concerning the map of Africa. If it was to be his destiny to rule over a country divided between two religions, there had to be a way of adhering to both of them without betraying either. As he saw it, they had some common ground, since both recognised Jesus Christ, and both had prophets and saints. How could he be an Emperor of Ethiopia without humiliating and discriminating against a major part of his subjects? The Crescent had to be incorporated into the imperial crown as well as the Cross, and new heraldic figures had to be added to the national flag. It was the only way that he could carry out his grandfather's last wish.

Could the numerous peoples and tribes of the empire be integrated within a uniform legal order? As Yassu saw it, there was no possibility of achieving this unless the two great religions first became integrated into the new state on an equal footing under the imperial crown. The numerous smaller African traditional religions that existed in Ethiopia could not stand their ground indefinitely against the two giants, and before long would fall to one or the other. If this was not possible, Menelik's vision would have been void – thus his heir, Emperor Yassu, had to make great efforts to bring it to reality. He would not neglect Christian customs or forget the signs of Christian dignity, but at the same time he was unhesitatingly prepared to adopt Muslim practice. As a prince of Solomonic descent, he saw himself as having an unchallengeable right to the Christian Ethiopian crown. His father the Negus Mikael of Wollo, who had converted to Christianity long ago during the reign of Menelik's predecessor Yohannes IV, and who as a Galla ruler had borne the name Mohammed Ali, was descended from the great Imam Ahmed ibn Ibrahim al Ghazi, known as Ahmed Gragne, the conqueror who had devastated Ethiopia in the sixteenth century. Through this line, Yassu thought that it would be possible to establish himself as a descendant of the Prophet Mohamed, the founder of Islam. Scholars and scribes had been ordered to conduct research into Yassu's genealogy, and were now busily engaged in that task. In a unique personal union, by his double descent from the biblical King Solomon and from the founder of Islam, Yassu hoped to reconcile the two religions under the crown, legalise his position as protector of religion with their respective leaders, and gain momentum for his planned alliance with the forces of Islam in the war.

In the eyes of Lidj Tafari, the plans of his younger cousin were not only unrealistic, but highly dangerous. The Ethiopian Orthodox Church, the strongest single force in the country, would never accept a solution to the religious problem as fantastic as that envisaged by the gifted but immature young Emperor: moreover, Tafari knew of no historical precedent in any country for a religious merger of this kind. For the landlocked and backward state of Ethiopia to go to war against the three great colonial powers that surrounded it, without any need to do so, seemed sheer madness. After the defeat that would inevitably follow, independent Ethiopia would disappear from the map and her territory would be divided up among the colonial powers along the lines that they had already agreed in the Tripartite Treaty of 1906. There were definite advantages in staying neutral. How much better it would be just to wait and see! If the Allied powers lost the war, it would become easier, by political means, to manoeuvre them off the Horn of Africa; if they won, Ethiopia could raise her claims in the context of a new world order, which the victors were expected to establish, and in the context of the friendly neutrality she had maintained during the critical years of the war. On the latter point, Tafari was wrong only in his timing. In the aftermath of the war, it became clear that the time had not yet arrived for consequences of that kind. There had to be another world war for the restoration of Eritrea to the Ethiopian empire to become feasible: Ethiopian claims to Italian Somaliland, raised by Haile Sellassie in pursuance of Menelik's vision, were rejected in 1948 by the peace conference of foreign ministers in Paris.

Lidj Tafari tried to influence his cousin, who was clearly heading for oblivion, but Emperor Yassu could not be stopped. Was it possible that he, Tafari, should join him in such an enterprise even if he was bound by his oath of allegiance to do so, and then probably meet an early death as he led the country into inevitable catastrophe? It would mean the end of Menelik's mission, to which both the two young men were the only surviving heirs, since all the rest of the Ethiopian leadership were traditionalists.

The province of Harar was the natural base for the planned military invasion of British Somaliland. Starting his preparations there, Yassu – to his consternation and disbelief – met with passive resistance from his appointed governor, Tafari. The irate Emperor transferred his cousin to the south, reappointing him as governor of far-away Kaffa, where he would have no occasion to interfere with events in the north and centre of the country. Tafari had not plotted against Yassu before, but now – and only now – he revolted. In a crucial step, he did not leave for Kaffa but went instead to Addis Ababa and joined the traditionalists opposed to Yassu.

In his memoirs, Haile Selassie tried to present Yassu's imperial grant of Harar to Dedjasmatch Tafari – fixed in writing so that third parties, especially the Crown Council or Ras Gugsa and other pretenders, should not be tempted to snatch the province from him again and thus diminish the internal power-base of the Shoan Solomonides – as a 'treaty' concluded between them which Yassu broke, thus incurring the blame for having split up the team. However, such an interpretation is absurd: no nobleman in the country, let alone the Emperor, would ever have concluded a treaty with one of his subjects or with any other party not on equal terms with him: the only exceptions would have been marriage contracts, in which two families agreed to share their power even if one of the two was less powerful previously than the other. The orphaned Tafari had no allies and no power, except what he received by way of support from his cousin the Emperor. However, not a word of the Amharic text of the so-called 'treaty' would need to be altered for it to convey the meaning, in translation, later claimed for it by Haile Sellassie. (The niceties of the Amharic language, which is extraordinarily rich in forms conveying hidden meanings and permitting a variety of interpretations and afterthoughts, makes it all but impossible, in a rational translation, to exhaust the meaning of a given text.)

Yassu was not aware that his war preparations and his negotiations with the Ottoman Empire, the Mahdi in the Sudan, the Mad Mullah and many other Muslim chiefs in the Horn, as well as his heraldic experiments with the imperial insignia, could not be kept secret and were soon being subjected to public discussion in the capital. Britain and France, through their secret agents, had made extraordinary efforts to collect authentic evidence which, by being published, would expose the Emperor as an apostate who was forsaking Ethiopian tradition. The Orthodox Church had to be convinced that Yassu was on the way to becoming a convert to Islam: but this was done by means of deception, because he had never intended anything of the kind.

The Ethiopian Rases, conscious of the situation and suspicious of foreign intentions, were rather amused by the reports, with details of his numerous love affairs, that were being used to discredit the young Emperor. But they were highly apprehensive of his religious experiments, and at the same time they had to be on the alert because if Yassu was riding for a fall all on his own, their chances of obtaining the throne were rising once again. Internal rivalries for the succession regained momentum. However, Dedjasmatch Tafari seemed not to be involved in any of this. When he came to Addis Ababa, nobody in the country saw him as a contender. Among the royal princes – sons of kings with the rank of Ras – a Dedjasmatch (son of a Ras) who had only recently been transferred to a minor post had no pretensions to equal standing, let alone to a leading role. Compared with those seasoned and impressive warriors, products of the Ethiopian highlands, the gentle and scholarly prince who happened to be the son of a Ras was someone who could comfortably be overlooked, although his knowledge of foreign affairs and his good contacts with the foreign missions in Addis Ababa caused him to be considered a useful ally.

With his mutinous refusal to go to Kaffa, Tafari's journey to the throne had begun. And he was determined – above all – to go it alone in his bid for the imperial crown. Yassu had to be deposed from the imperial throne, and the feudal rivals who were struggling for it kept at bay, so that Menelik's concept, of which he saw himself now as the only remaining standard-bearer, could be kept intact. Yassu's plans would be disastrous for the country; specifically they would lead to the end of independent statehood, in which Ethiopia had taken pride for more than two millennia. Having been his confidant, Tafari was familiar with the Emperor's designs, and this knowledge would prove to be a deadly weapon against Yassu, provided he could also rally the traditional forces in the country, especially the Church. Through his mutiny, he had taken the side of the Entente powers in the 1914–18 war; thus Britain and France immediately became his tacit allies, and from this time forward they did whatever was in their power and was also in their own best interests, to promote Tafari's ambition. This perfect conformity of interests continued after the end of the war, because by then the Western powers were interested in stabilising the political situation in the Horn. This meant defusing the timebomb that Emperor Yassu had planted there. They continued with their support of Tafari at least till his coronation as Emperor in 1930, and even after that. There could be no doubt that he was the most desirable candidate for the throne. He was well-educated and disciplined, he had a clear-cut programme, and he showed those consistent lines of thought and behaviour from which he never wavered throughout his life. There was nobody equally trustworthy in the offing: any of the other royal contenders, once on the throne, could have resumed Yassu's pernicious policies. Great caution had to be employed if the foreign help granted to Tafari was to be effective. It had to be given in secret and effectively without strings: there was no way the recipient's hands could be bound. The exact details of the political investment made by the two Western powers have never been disclosed, nor are they ever likely to be.

Whenever, on his road to power, Tafari's material assets were compared to those of his adversaries – whether in money, weapons (ranging from machine-guns to aircraft), or assistance from officers of foreign armies as instructors for his troops and even as fighters in his battles – his side always had the advantage. Although he possessed wealth and knew how to husband it, being somewhat parsimonious and avoiding any extravagances, Tafari gave the impression of being even wealthier than he actually was. The other royal contenders for the imperial throne were neutralised by the balance of arms in their internal struggle; each blocked the others' way to the throne while remaining unaware of Tafari's ambition until it was too late to stop him.

Foreign powers could not directly influence the actions of Ethiopian princes or the country's internal affairs, but occasionally by supporting an Ethiopian endeavour they could at the same time serve their own interests, and make political investment. This, as we have seen, was the case in the World War when the interests of the powers and of Tafari coincided. Had Tafari succeeded by serving foreign interests, or had he exploited foreign interests to achieve his goals? Neither of these interpretations is correct, because neither possibility would ever have been enough in itself to secure success, which was primarily the result of Tafari's own personality, and his combination of capabilities and qualities.

Tafari's father Ras Makonnen – Menelik's cousin and friend, governor of Harar and commander of the Ethiopian forces in the victorious battle of Adua – had also served as Menelik's emissary to Europe. He attended the coronation of King Edward VII in 1902 and conducted diplomatic missions to Rome, Paris and London on the Emperor's behalf. During his stay in Italy in the 1890s before the battle of Adua, he negotiated the fine detail of the Treaty of Uccialli – which in outline had been concluded in Ethiopia – and secured an Italian loan, with the province of Harar as collateral. The loan was immediately spent on the purchase of urgently-needed arms and ammunition – later used to defeat the Italians at Adua. In Italy he also attended as many military parades and manoeuvres as possible to obtain a first-hand impression of the strength and tactics of his adversary. On his return, he brought with him to Harar a quantity of professional military literature, and after studying several of Napoleon's famous battles, became a great admirer of the Corsican. The feats of other military leaders, including some of the spectacular battles fought by Frederick the Great, were included in his curriculum. To prepare for his diplomatic missions, he tried to master Europe's history and current political situation in rough outline – knowledge of which was extremely rare among the Ethiopian nobility of his time. Foreign travellers and diplomats in Ethiopia reported their surprise at the extent of Ras Makonnen's knowledge and the shrewdness of his judgement.

His son Tafari, accustomed from early childhood to rigid discipline, was given a prince's education in the European style: in other words he was required to absorb a vast amount of learning. His principal guide was a learned priest of the Ethiopian Church, Abba Samuel, who had supplemented his own traditional learning by studying with the French missionaries. Foreign instructors and tutors, such as Dr Vitalien, physician-in-charge at the hospital in Harar, and the fathers at the French Catholic mission there, also played a part. This connection with the Catholics, for obvious reasons, was not publicly admitted, but it became well known, none the less, and Tafari's enemies later nicknamed him 'the Catholic'. Supervising his son's education and acting occasionally as instructor himself, Ras Makonnen naturally tried to indoctrinate the boy with his own ideas and predilections. But it was soon apparent that Tafari did not share his father's military bent. Instead he learned languages – quickly and with remarkable ease – and took a special interest in foreign history and literature. He was able to share his father's admiration for Napoleon and Frederick the Great, but the focus of his interest shifted to the political and cultural aspects of those monarchs' careers. As to his solid knowledge of Latin – and, connected with it, his studies of medieval authors – this can only be attributed to his French Catholic tutors; no other source is traceable. The importance he attributed to the works of Machiavelli seemed inconsistent with the views of either his father, Abba Samuel or the French missionaries. The decisive influence here was probably Dr Vitalien, who was of French colonial extraction, having come from the Caribbean and been educated by Jesuits: this remained a strong influence with Tafari throughout an important period of his life, and only gradually waned after he became Emperor. It was a characteristic of the young Tafari, as of the old Haile Sellassie, that despite his great interest in history and literature he could be satisfied with short outlines provided by his tutors or advisers and was disinclined to read more widely in such vast fields. He chose only a small number of topics, but worked over those thoroughly and repeatedly. Late in his reign, he was reading new works from abroad on his historical and literary idols.

When Tafari was twelve years old, his father made him governor of a district and conferred on him the princely title of 'Dedjasmatch' – something Ras Makonnen was not empowered to do on his own authority, but which Menelik at once confirmed. Titles of nobility were not hereditary in Ethiopia; they could be given by the Emperor only after the recipient had assumed a high function in the army or administration. As long as he remained in private life, even the son of a king would bear only the title of 'Lidj' – literally 'child', and meaning the son of an important man. It could be borne by any nobleman's son, but some preferred in their later years to use the title 'Ato' ('mister'), which could be used indiscriminately by any free-born Ethiopian. It was not unusual in Ethiopia for a man of royal descent, even a Solomonide, to hide behind this common prefix. In a society where, right up till the revolution, descent counted for more than wealth or the actual position that one held, everybody knew who was who – foreigners, on the other hand, could never understand the intricacies of family connections. In his later years, Haile Sellassie stopped the old practice of conferring ranks of nobility, seeking to replace them entirely by grades of civil servants in the administration and by military ranks for the armed forces. It was possibly in anticipation of his early death – and because of Menelik's severe illness – that Ras Makonnen made sure in good time that his son acquired the title of Dedjasmatch. If Yassu did not become Emperor, there would be nobody in a position to raise him to that rank (which later became a precondition for his further ascent) as his first step on the ladder. Although the new Dedjasmatch did not yet have the power of jurisdiction and decision – this remained in the hands of a guardian appointed to him – he was now obliged to attend court proceedings and hearings, and in time the reponsibility for some minor decisions was placed in his hands. Like a pupil learning his alphabet, Tafari learned the administrative practices of his country, and became familiar with the taxation system and with such matters as the fight against slave-trading in the province of Harar, already begun by his father.

The success of Ras Makonnen's educational endeavours with his son are documented. A special diplomatic mission sent to Menelik by Emperor Wilhelm II of Germany visited Harar in January 1905. Its members – diplomats, eminent scientists and businessmen – were highly impressed by the maturity and composure of the twelve-year-old Lidj Tafari, who received them because his father was absent on an official journey, and showed no shyness when talking with them. Only when they asked the prince for permission to take his photograph did he politely refuse, saying that he could not grant such a request without an instruction from his father. A description of this first encounter between the boy who became Haile Sellassie and a foreign delegation was published in Germany with the report of the mission in 1907.

In the course of the audience, the leader of the delegation presented Tafari with a fine gold watch. The gift greatly surprised the young prince, who none the less enjoyed the experience. After graciously accepting the watch, he put it aside and thanked the donor politely and without any sign of emotion. It seems that a curtain fell early in Tafari's life, concealing his thoughts and feelings from the world. Later, as

Emperor, he always made his decisions alone, and never divulged his views or plans even to his closest confidants, or engaged in any discussion. After patiently listening to the arguments put forward by ministers in his Private Cabinet, or to the reports of foreign experts and advisers, he often stunned his followers with a decision that no one had foreseen. 'Nobody knows what Jan Hoy* thinks!' was a stock saying among the population. The many journalistic reports published on interviews granted by Haile Sellassie are informative about the background and opinions of the journalists concerned, but contain nothing more than guesswork on the Emperor's views and his personality. Still, all decisions made by the young Tafari as much as by the old Haile Sellassie served a single goal, namely his concept of the modern Ethiopian state. This concept was not one he had copied from anywhere, but was his original and very individual achievement. The needle of his compass had always pointed in the one direction, but was the direction in fact mistaken, because it did not finally save him from ruin? It is significant that even in his fall Haile Sellassie stuck to his self-imposed rules.

The natural tendency to keep people at a distance, and so always to command respect – whether compounded of admiration or fear – could already be seen in the young Tafari. However, this made impossible the kind of emotional following enjoyed by Yassu, who was the darling of the Shoa highland people as well as of the Galla (especially in his father's realm, Wollo). The famous Ethiopian emperors of the past – including Menelik, the best-loved of them all – had been extraordinarily tall, with powerful constitutions, and had thus embodied the popular image of a warrior-king. The handsome and gifted Yassu, with his easy, straightforward behaviour and physical appearance that evidently took after his grandfather Menelik, had immediately won the hearts of the people. He appeared to have all the qualities people wanted to see in their emperor, and in both parts of the empire he was the popular choice.

While Lidj Yassu's strength was his popularity, his weakness was the insufficiency of his birthright. If the 'Law of Kings' was strictly applied, he was ineligible for the throne. Menelik had done everything in his power to make good that deficiency, throwing his great authority into the scales and using the force of his will and vision to the full. On the occasion when the Crown Prince was solemnly anointed by the Abuna*

---

* Jan Hoy: Amharic for 'His Majesty' or 'Your Majesty'.
* Abuna. The head of the Ethiopian Church, then under the nominal control of the Coptic patriarchate in Alexandria, but independent from the 1950s.

of the Ethiopian Orthodox Church, and the Rases were sworn to their allegiance, Menelik uttered his famous curse, which has frequently been alluded to by historians, although it has been quoted in a number of different versions. The accepted wording of the report of this event is as follows: 'On this day the Emperor's mind was clear, and he had summoned all the princes, and the Abuna and Lidj Yassu were there. Menelik blessed Lidj Yassu, and raised his voice to explain: "By the will of God, he shall be your Emperor. You shall be obedient to him! Cursed be the man who opposes him! Whoever raises his hand against him shall be struck by my curse! What that man does shall end in failure, the sons he begets shall be black dogs, he shall be condemned to die a miserable death, and nobody shall know his grave!"' The people of Ethiopia became familiar with this curse, and Haile Sellassie's admirers and critics alike felt the spell. They were not surprised at the final outcome.

Literary versions of the curse, according to which the Crown Prince himself would be cursed if he proved unworthy and did not measure up to what was expected by an emperor, are a free invention, a favour granted to Haile Sellassie by contemporary historians.

Yassu was twenty years old when he was deposed as Emperor and banished. The Entente powers only succeeded at the last moment in their endeavours to bring him down. If his intention to be identified confessionally with both his Christian and Muslim subjects was unrealistic, his warmongering plans were not and he was well on the way to bringing about an uprising of the Islamic peoples of the Horn against their colonial masters. Already the three colonial powers – Italy, France and Britain – had been compelled to reinforce their garrisons at Massawa, Djibouti, Zeila and Berbera, moving units from other war theatres to resist the dangers that were daily becoming more real in the Horn.

The situation was recognised by the German legation in Addis Ababa, but only when it was too late for an intervention from that quarter to be organised. Since the beginning of the war, the legation had had no communication with Berlin, and the supply of funds was cut off. The dragoman of the legation, shuttling between Addis Ababa and Yassu's camp, could only provide verbal support; there was nothing Germany could do to speed up the supply of arms and ammunition to the Mad Mullah, or create a link between the Emperor's army and the German colonial forces fighting in East Africa. The powerlessness of the German Legation was in contrast to the Allied legations in Addis Ababa, which had unrestricted finances at their disposal.

The Emperor was excommunicated by the Church, and his troops in

Harar were thereupon ordered by the army commander-in-chief (who was answerable directly to the Empress) to arrest him. There was great confusion among the troops, most of whom were loyal to Yassu. Instead of arresting him, they let him slip out of Harar – which he did openly, passing through the army lines with his few followers. Nobody dared to arrest him. Yassu turned now to other Galla regions where he knew he could still muster forces loyal to him to reinforce the army of his father, King Mikael of Wollo. In a fury, Ras Mikael, in support of Yassu, immediately turned his forces against Addis Ababa, which caused a panic there, because the Shoans could not field an army to equal them. The units in Harar could not be relied on if they were now to fight against the King of Wollo instead of being led against the British in Somaliland.

A large consignment of machine-guns was granted by the Entente powers, but they were yet to arrive from the French Territory of Djibouti. During the critical phase of about three weeks till the arrival of the weapons, the Shoans used against King Mikael the stratagem of feigning negotiations, ostensibly aimed at the reinstatement of Yassu. King Mikael was deceived, and refrained from attacking. There was an additional piece of bad luck when a messenger, sent by Yassu to ask his father to hold back his attack for a few days longer until he could arrive himself with reinforcements, failed to get through. After the simulated negotiations broke down, King Mikael's horsemen rode – on a rather misty day – wave after wave into deadly bursts of machine-gun fire, which made the battle of Segelie not only decisive but also a bloody massacre. King Mikael was taken prisoner and died later in jail. The machine-guns, which had saved the day for the Shoans, had their political price, for suddenly Dedjasmatch Tafari was their leader. It was, of course, he who had bought the weapons, or procured them at a nominal price which the Ethiopian commander-in-chief, Menelik's old general Habte Giorgis, was able to pay.

It was in vain that Lidj Yassu tried later to gather together a sufficiently strong force to regain the crown. He was captured in 1921 and imprisoned successively in two fortresses. For a time, he was treated like an animal by being kept in an open cage – the object of this was to display his moral deterioration. Notwithstanding this, his image still loomed large among numerous tribes in the provinces. Finally, on the outbreak of the Abyssinian war in 1935, Haile Sellassie had him killed for the sake of unity of the home front. This did not prevent some of the tribes that had remained loyal to Yassu from fighting on the Italian side in the Abyssinian war.

Haile Sellassie always regarded himself as having been the saviour of Ethiopia's independence. With his intervention, he had spared the country from becoming a colony, and prevented the huge loss of life which would have resulted from war. He had this view confirmed later by numerous writers and diplomats, who praised his political vision. Other comments on the part he played include highly improbable positions – such as the notion that he had merely served as a tool of foreign powers, or that the outcome of the African campaigns in the First World War was determined by him. The truth of the latter proposition cannot be known, but in Africa a single spark can set the savannahs alight. Because of the strong popular impact made by Yassu, he was a force to be reckoned with wherever he went, and even his numerous escapades with the daughters of local chiefs carried some political weight, because an aggressive daredevil was assumed to be a natural military leader. Backward Ethiopia was no match for the great powers, but if Yassu had been correct in his vision that he could count on the support of the Muslim populations of Africa, might not some of the results of the world war have been rather different?

The way chosen by the immature but imaginative Yassu to solve his empire's religious problem appeared ill-conceived and unrealisable, but was it really so? Even this question cannot be answered for certain. How well have historians come to terms with the part played by religion? Seen in the light of later ecumenical endeavours, which have vainly sought to reconcile churches and even great religions by reducing them all to political philosophy, Yassu's direct approach, trying to reconcile religion with religion, had an almost modern touch. What was a matter of life and death for the son of a Christian ruler of a Muslim population, who was also the ruler of an empire divided between two great religions, is no more to the sociologist of today than an intellectual puzzle of religion, philosophy and knowledge, in which any one of the three landscapes of the human mind can be confused with the others. Moreover, Lidj Yassu would have had on his side the momentum created by the war, that great furnace in which the destiny of mankind was being forged. He could try to weld elements together in its fires in a way that would not have been possible in normal times. Even when failing in this, his handling of the religious problem with sincerity and energy might have served his practical goal of raising the Muslim peoples in revolt against the colonialists, first in the Horn and then in the Sudan and adjoining countries.

IV. RAS TAFARI

After the fall of Yassu, Menelik's daughter Zauditu was crowned Empress, and Tafari, now elevated to the rank of Ras, was designated as Regent to rule in her name and as her successor to the throne. As Regent of the empire as well as Crown Prince, Ras Tafari appeared to be the most powerful man in the country, but appearances were deceptive: his greatest trials were still to come. For the next fourteen years, the bitter struggle for power went on behind the scenes, and Ras Tafari had to exercise all his skills and qualities to gain the upper hand and keep things that way. What seemed to be a matter of course, something that would evolve with time, was in fact a unique performance by an outsider: the pretenders in the north had not yet abandoned their own ambitions, and the Empress was still nurturing her plan to bring Ras Gugsa to power.

All of them – the Empress, the Rases in the north and the most powerful man at court, the army commander Habte Giorgis – were traditionalists who opposed modernistic innovation and still favoured the old plan of Empress Taitu to remove the capital of the empire to Gondar and keep the territories won by Menelik in a semi-colonial condition. Two different concepts of state were pitched against each other. Ras Tafari, the only remaining prince of the southern Solomonic line, was now fighting alone for the modern Ethiopian state. The Rases of the traditional party had sufficient knowledge of Europe and European affairs to understand, as they thought, the dangerous lure of the outside world: they wanted to limit foreign influence to imported goods and technology, whereas Ras Tafari wanted to adopt much more from Europe.

Having reached his new position single-handed, with few followers and only kinsmen of junior rank from Harar as companions, Ras Tafari was now isolated and surrounded by enemies – partly rival claimants who were superior to him in rank and power, and partly feudal nobles opposed to his views and plans. In the countryside those who still favoured Yassu – tribal people and some of the Ethiopian nobility – made up a large number. A never-ending succession of minor revolts now followed, flaring up in all parts of the country, in support of Yassu's bid for freedom and power. This did not even cease with Haile Sellassie's coronation as Emperor; the last such revolt was that of Ras Hailu, governor of Gojjam, in 1932, which had to be crushed in a military action, followed by the governor's dismissal. The strength Ras Tafari gained from his foreign support became a weakness in the context of internal politics, he was viewed with suspicion. Nor could he hope to become popular in Addis Ababa or in any province except his own. People distanced themselves from him, and populism was not his style. As Regent he was reputed to be in control of the whole empire, but in fact his power ended at the borders of the province of Harar, where the authority of his dead father extended to him. In no other province would anybody have heeded an order from the Regent.

Tafari's new title of Crown Prince implied the promise that he would one day be crowned as Emperor – as 'Negus Negest', or King of Kings. To achieve this, he first had to be crowned as a king. With the tacit consent of his enemies, this dignity was denied him, for two reasons. The first was that being only twenty-five years old, he was still considered too young for such a rank, and moreover a Dedjasmatch could not be made a King without first attaining the rank of Ras, for which he first had to qualify. A youth not yet capable of shouldering the tasks of his title needed a guardian: hence Wolde Giorgis was appointed as guardian to the Crown Prince and crowned as Negus instead of Tafari, whose title was thus kept 'in reserve'; if the Empress died, Wolde Giorgis would be crowned as Emperor, and Ras Tafari would continue as Crown Prince and heir-apparent to the throne. Whereas in his capacity as Regent Ras Tafari was independent, as Crown Prince he was subordinate to the King. Within this odd legal construction of course lay the possibility of conflict: the traditionalist party could try to keep a rein on the policies pursued by the Regent through the orders he would receive from the King. Ras Tafari was careful not to challenge his guardian and so give him an opportunity to interfere until Wolde Giorgis died three years later. Although they did not venture this time to appoint a new guardian for Ras Tafari, he was still denied the title of King. He would never be crowned as a King unless he could succeed in enforcing it by military force with a *coup d'état* – he now had to wait for a chance to do this. Ras Tafari was now at least equal in rank with his rivals in the struggle for the throne – also rivals with each other. As we have seen, Ras Gugsa, who like Tafari was the son of a Ras, enjoyed the favour of the Empress. She desired his succession, but could not raise him to the rank of King, since the Rases in the north, as sons of Kings, would have revolted if they had not been considered first.

The foreign powers believed they had obtained what they wanted, and that Tafari was the future Emperor. In fact, his chances were still the slimmest – next to nothing, in fact – and there were not many people in the empire who seriously believed that they could ever materialise.

There was little the foreign powers could do to help their favoured candidate, except by providing occasional material help in secret, and sending instructors to train his personal army, the basis of his domestic power, in Harar. To begin with, the Regent had no allies at all inside the country, and his further success would depend entirely on correct tactics and wise actions.

There was one considerable asset on Tafari's side, namely the country's strongest political force, the Ethiopian Orthodox Church. The fact that it had crushed Emperor Yassu and confirmed the new order was enough to keep the balance against the many weaknesses of Tafari's new position. To maintain this stronghold, he had to be careful to improve his relations with the Church and direct his future actions in a way that would not present a challenge to it, but there were factions within the Church that had to be reckoned with. The Itchegue, head of all the country's monasteries and the second-most powerful man in the Ethiopian Church hierarchy, saw modernisation as a pernicious influence on the Christian faith and, with the intention of turning the clock back, joined hands with Tafari's enemies. The feud between the Itchegue and Tafari continued for ten years until 1926, when the Regent succeeded in having him deposed.

Ras Tafari showed infinite patience. He needed time to remedy his weak points, and he knew what use to make of it. He had to create an image for himself in the minds of the population in order to earn their respect. It was also necessary for him to enlist the support of nobles from other provinces than his own. This would be done partly by traditional means, by fostering marriages between his family and the families of other rulers. He would also have to convince them of the superiority of his conception of the future Ethiopian state; of the advantages which the peoples of Ethiopia would obtain by following him; and of the need to adapt life in Ethiopia to the standards of the world outside its borders. By such adaptation, he could safeguard the country's independence and deter the colonial powers from grabbing Ethiopian soil with the pretext that they could develop such a backward country better than it would ever develop by itself. He would also be able to justify Ethiopia's claim to Eritrea and the other coastal lands of the Horn.

Tafari's chance came in 1926 when his most powerful adversary, the army commander Habte Giorgis died. In a rapid surprise action, Tafari moved his own troops from Harar into Addis Ababa; they stormed the imperial palace and forced the Empress to give up the supreme command of the armed forces and transfer it to him. By this move he forestalled his rivals and stripped the Empress of her power. Up till then she had used all possible means to get rid of her 'Regent and Crown Prince', but Tafari, knowing full well that he continually needed to be on the defensive, had always managed to avoid mistakes in the hidden feud which could be used against him. This was a smiling enmity typical of the country: the Empress pretended to have the warmest feelings towards her young kinsman; and indeed it seemed from the outside that relations between the two were excellent. Tafari took every care not to disturb that impression, because in the person of Habte Giorgis the Empress held the instrument of power, the Ethiopian army, in her hands. His sudden strike temporarily stunned the army, and he therefore had to act with the utmost speed to consolidate his advantage and reorganise the army leadership.

This time, the princes in the north, who were always prepared for military action, were clearly taken by surprise. They were not sure what should be their next move since Ras Tafari had meanwhile succeeded in winning over one of their number – his cousin, Ras Kassa of Tigre. Still, Tafari saw the danger that the Empress might now call in all her vassals from the provinces with their armies to reverse her forced surrender of her powers. The uneasy situation continued for nearly two years, with mounting danger of conflict. Then in 1928, before the hostile Rases could combine against him, Tafari tried to isolate the Empress's most powerful ally in the south, the Governor of Sidamo, Dedjasmatch Balcha. In his capacity of Regent, he summoned Balcha to Addis Ababa, but the Governor, not being used to taking orders from the Regent, at first flatly refused to obey. But then, in response to a secret message from the Empress, he changed his mind and came – bringing his army of 10,000 men. It was clear that on his arrival the Empress would take the supreme command from Ras Tafari and confer it on Balcha, thus decisively tilting the balance of power. The Regent thus sent a message to Balcha offering to negotiate with him and inviting him to a banquet: this offer was accepted. Negotiations accordingly took place during the banquet which Balcha attended accompanied by 500 of his followers and bodyguards: Ras Tafari was accompanied by only 200 men of his own bodyguard. Sumptuous hospitality and entertainment were dispensed. In particular, the foreign liquors – expensive but seemingly in unlimited quantities – that Tafari provided were received with acclaim. The effects of the drink were not uniform, because similar bottles were filled with different drinks: the followers of Tafari had to stay sober, even while they enjoyed the enormous meal. Ethiopian feasts of that kind used to continue for at least six hours, so in this instance the leaders had ample opportunity for their negotiations – which were not successful, because the Regent coldly rejected the demands of the Governor.

Meanwhile, Ras Tafari's emissaries had entered the camps occupied by Dedjasmatch Balcha's troops, carrying bags of money. Every soldier of Balcha's army was offered ten Maria Theresia silver dollars if he would leave immediately and return home. Thus, when Balcha returned he found the camps deserted, and even the five hundred men of his bodyguard were of no help to him when he was arrested. He was put in jail and only released well after the coronation of Haile Sellassie as Emperor.

Having gained the upper hand once again, Tafari could lose no time: in the same year, 1928, he occupied the imperial palace a second time with his troops from Harar and forced the Empress to consent to his being crowned as a King. Thus on 7 October 1928 the Negus Tafari was crowned, and finally the way to the imperial throne was open. It had taken twelve years for him to acquire the substance of a Regent's power and a Crown Prince's right, which up till then had consisted of the titles only. Like his great-grandfather, he was now Negus of Shoa, crowned by the Empress, with the full backing of the Orthodox Church. This fact was to have some significance in the final showdown still to come.

For Tafari the road to the throne was now open – but he was not walking that road alone. It was still in the balance which of the rivals would reach the goal. For Ras Gugsa who had been the late Empress Taitu's choice for the succession and was still the choice of the reigning Empress Zauditu, the outlook had been altered by the sudden and unexpected loss of his principal ally, Dedjasmatch Balcha. He could not intervene right away; time was needed to revise his plans, and to make good what he had lost by purchasing modern weapons and having the military trained in their use. He had also tried to enlist the support of the other Rases of the north, but they were not interested in helping a rival to the throne and preferred to 'wait and see', hoping that they might be able to seize a chance if the contest between Gugsa and Tafari ended in a stalemate. At the beginning of 1930, Ras Gugsa felt ready and started to proceed with his forces towards Addis Ababa. He was met at Zebit by the Shoan army led by King Tafari's military commander Dedjasmatch Mullugeta.

The superiority of the Shoan army in the quality of their equipment and the quantity of their machine-guns and cannons was not yet a decisive factor in the mountainous environment. For the first time in Ethiopia's history, two aeroplanes took part, flown by French pilots in a battle, making reconnaissance flights, dropping bombs, and showering the enemy with leaflets containing a proclamation of the Abuna of the Ethiopian Orthodox Church, which caused some disturbance among the Christian soldiers. Both sides fought hard and the battle was fierce, the balance tilting first one way and then the other until Ras Gugsa fell mortally wounded. With the death of their leader, Gugsa's army immediately collapsed, and it became plain that the future Emperor of Ethiopia would be King Tafari. This was on 31 March 1930, and two days later Empress Zauditu died. Tafari was crowned as Emperor on 2 November 1930, taking the 'throne-name' of Haile Sellassie I.

With his coronation, an interregnum that had started with the illness of Menelik and lasted twenty-two years, ended. The period had seen incessant struggles for the imperial throne between a number of rivals. To the outside world, the issue appeared a simple matter: always what Menelik had created was seen as represented by the central imperial government – but this in reality was no more than an expedient, provisional and without either stability or definite form. The power of the central government – significantly represented by women – was limited, because the Rases in the north ruled their regions like independent kingdoms, except for the obligation to pay yearly tributes and join with the empire's military forces in the event of war. The same applied to the newly-appointed governors in the south. They ruled entirely according to their own will, and often refused to pay any tribute money at all; they had become too powerful to be deposed. The strongest man in the country was Habte Giorgis, the army commander or Fitawrari; he saw his only task as being to protect the existing order, whether provisional or not. This meant preventing a *coup* from being launched at the centre, and provincial rulers from breaking away from the Empire. If they tried to do so he would immediately lead a punitive campaign against them. As long as the old Fitawrari was alive, nobody would dare to mount an attack on the imperial palace; what remained of Menelik's power – and it was considerable – would destroy them. When Tafari appropriated the supreme command for himself after his *coup*, he did not hesitate to re-distribute – immediately – the vast tracts of land owned by Habte Giorgis among his own followers. This gave them a more elevated rank, and so reinforced his own standing in the country.

Lidj Tafari had been compelled to stand on his own very early in life. He was thirteen years old when his father died in 1906, and his mother had already died before that. Only his great-uncles Ras Tesamma – later guardian to Yassu – and Menelik were left to care for him and give him further guidance, but that was to be for a short time only. Ras Tesamma died five years later, and there would soon be no value in protection by Menelik, whose authority was taken over by the Crown Council and Empress Taitu. The Empress did not deny Tafari the respect due to him on account of his famous and well-loved father, Ras Makonnen, and his present title, but she had no interest in advancing his interests, and moreover was eager to have all the Shoan Solomonides out of the way. His surviving great-great-uncle, Ras Kassa of Tigre, could not yet be counted for support because he too was a pretender to the imperial throne, claiming an even better birth-right than Tafari's: to validate his claim, Ras Kassa had to side with the traditionalists who were seeking to restore the rules of the Law of Kings. Tafari still had a long way to go before he could enlist the support of the Kassa clan. He had to increase his personal power in order to convince them that they would have better prospects by belonging to the family of a reigning Emperor than by risking total failure in a confrontation with the power of the two Empresses. In the alliance against him of the Fitawrari Habte Giorgis and Ras Gugsa, Ras Kassa would have had a weak hand. By the traditional means of conducting policy through marriage alliances, Tafari later advanced the process of winning over the clan of the Kassas.

Tafari had natural talent and a brilliant memory; he possessed the spark of eagerness and interest which give the essential impetus to learning; like many other outstanding men, he was driven by a desire to equal and later outshine an admired father; and he had had to bear the burden of power early in his life. Thus, he was mature well beyond his years. When his father died, he already had a knowledge of several languages and a basic comprehension of the European world and its history as well as his own country. Most important of all, he had already prepared a blueprint for his life, the outline of a world view, into which his thoughts and plans fitted, and which would never subsequently change. All he did subsequently was to build according to that blueprint, filling in the gaps as these became apparent. His consciousness of having a mission to fulfill became his main source of strength. His actions would be more effective if they all served the same goal; they would create a stronger impression on the country over which he was ruling and on the outside world. Also, this consistency gave him the incentive to use all his skills and talents to the full, and released the energy needed to fight physical exhaustion and operate to the greatest advantage within the limited possibilities that were open to him in the early stages.

Tafari transformed the inspiration he had received from his father and his teachers into something new that was uniquely his. An essential part of his blueprint was provided by the example of Japan: that other empire had proved that a non-European nation could embrace modern civilisation and stand culturally and technically level on a par with the European countries. Haile Sellassie always believed that Ethiopia could achieve the same success as the Japanese if it followed the same path, despite the considerably higher technical level Japan had reached before coming out of its isolation. There is no record of this part of Tafari's plan earlier than the time of his regency, but it is likely to have been inspired already by his father. Ras Makonnen had followed military events abroad, and studied military literature and analyses of battles. Therefore, the news of the Russian defeat at the hands of the Japanese navy at Tsushima in 1905 must have had an electrifying effect on him. This was the second victory of a non-European country over a great European power – a case of David slaying Goliath. Here was a major parallel between Ethiopia and Japan – and Lidj Tafari added to the equation other cultural, historical and political aspects in line with his special interest.

Part of Tafari's success can be put down to the cautious and inconspicuous way in which he acted against his enemies. It was also vital for him to acquire popularity with the common people – at this time he was popular in his own province of Harar only – and he achieved a fairly rapid success in this endeavour in the capital. Menelik's budding 'New Flower' (as 'Addis Ababa' would be translated) was bursting into bloom, to become the heart of urban life in Ethiopia. Urban people, all huddled together, are aware of the obvious benefits of technical innovation, and depend much more on an efficient civil administration and judicial system than their brethren out in the countryside. Ras Tafari's determination to remedy the defects in those two systems within the limits of his slowly increasing power soon bore fruit, and was acclaimed not only by the common people but by a growing number of the administrators and judges as well. An increasing number of young Ethiopians were being sent abroad – mostly financed by the feudal lords – and on their return they formed a new intellectual élite and gravitated towards Ras Tafari.

At the same time they showed signs of becoming a new kind of opposition. They saw their own country in the lights of what they had seen abroad, and were critical of its structure, blaming its backwardness on those mainstays of the existing order, the Church and the Crown. In so doing they tried to find a rational explanation for the irrational ways of history, and claimed the benefits of power without accepting its responsibilities – an eternal dilemma.

Technical innovations such as electric light, the telephone, piped water and roads adapted to wheeled traffic had been introduced by Menelik, but had so far been installed only inside the grounds of the imperial palace and on a few trial sites outside. There was little Ras Tafari could do about this unless he paid for it himself. An efficient administrative system needed to be set up first for such things to be done, and its creation – covering the whole country and structured on modern lines – was one of Ras Tafari's incontestable achievements, and a heritage from which any subsequent government could benefit. Another achievement was bringing the country within the scope of modern law and reforming legal practice and judicial proceedings accordingly.

However Ras Tafari could not make his changes as revolutionary as he wanted. The hands of the 'Regent and Crown Prince' were still bound by the Empress and her Crown Council, and by his guardian King Wolde Giorgis. At the same time, he needed to prepare himself by studying administrative regulations and legal codes as practised abroad, and this could not be done overnight. After about five years, he was ready, his royal guardian had died, and then, with one strategic move after the other, he could advance.

He reorganised the ministries by defining their areas of competence and building offices for them, and by having scribes and functionaries appointed by the state. Formerly, the Emperor treated ministers as his executives, and used them in whatever capacity was needed and for which they seemed suited at a particular time. They conducted business in their homes, and if helpers were needed, these were employed as their servants. In 1924, Ras Tafari made the slave trade illegal throughout the country; any offenders brought to justice would face the death penalty. He issued regulations for the legal procedures of the courts, and established a special court of consular jurisdiction in Addis Ababa, to initiate legal proceedings and adjudicate on matters involving foreigners and Ethiopians jointly. He abolished the levies taken by landlords and governors over and above state taxes, and started systematically cutting down the privileges of the feudal nobles – who would henceforward be transformed into administrators.

He introduced a new regime regarding punishment, abolishing the barbarous practice of cutting off an offender's hand or leg. Prisoners were no longer to be chained to the wall; instead they were to be simply placed under guard. To press this point, Ras Tafari used his private resources to have a prison built with facilities for the prisoners to be trained and to work, and adequate sanitary arrangements. He decreed an end to the practice of usury, limiting the rate of interest to be paid, and fining offenders. Insolvent debtors had formerly been handed over to the creditor, who had been able to keep them in jail until all the money was paid; this practice too was now forbidden. These are a few of the individual measures which preceded the comprehensive legal codes and administrative regulations he was to institute. His success in getting particular plans carried out varied during his reign largely according to the exact degree of power he wielded, which increased as time went on. In every field – administrative, economic, industrial. social, educational, cultural – Ras Tafari, with his vivid imagination, first saw the outline, and then filled in the details later: he would proceed to action only when the means came immediately to hand, such as when he had an opportunity to bring in help from abroad. Already in 1931 he made Ethiopia a constitutional monarchy, and he improved it 1955 with a revised constitution, which reflected progress made over the intervening years. True democratisation is unattainable in the absence of an economically secure middle class, and to bring such a class into being was his primary goal. It needed time to grow, but remarkable progress was made during Haile Sellassie's reign.

No sector of public life was overlooked. He started reforms within the Ethiopian Orthodox Church – which led, significantly, to the appointment of Ethiopian bishops. The bishops had previously been foreigners, consecrated by the Coptic Patriarch in Alexandria, but once independence from Alexandria was achieved, the Patriarch of the Ethiopian Church was the local archbishop. He reformed the military, adopting European-style ranks and uniforms. The Ethiopian military ranks which these superseded had in ancient times been identical with the steps on the ladder of ascent in civil society, thus exceptionally permitting the rise of a commoner to princely rank. He founded military schools, to which foreign instructors were appointed. Weapons were imported in large quantity, including warplanes flown by foreign pilots.

Menelik had founded a school in his capital, which taught foreign languages and subjects never before studied in the country, and a large foreign-staffed hospital. Ras Tafari also founded schools, and through each phase of his reign steadily expanded the network of educational facilities. He could not raise the funds to build a second hospital, but was not prepared to take no for an answer, and built and staffed it – in Addis

Ababa – from his own privy purse. Thereafter, and later during his reign as Emperor, the number of hospitals in the capital and later in other parts of the country gradually increased. Seeing the slow pace at which educational and health facilities could expand with internal financing, he gave his encouragement and protection to any endeavour by foreign governments, churches, missionary societies and other institutions that could lead to schools, training establishments, hospitals and welfare and rehabilitation centres being set up. He would show his personal interest by visiting them, and wherever in his vast country a new school or hospital was being built with funds from abroad – and this could be in the context of cultural policy, missionary activity or technical assistance – the Emperor would appear in person at least once, trying by his personal involvement to speed matters up and encourage further efforts in the same direction. He lavished the same personal attention on the cultural institutions that served the goals of adult education in the capital, visiting the British Council, the US Information Service, the West German Goethe Institute, the French, Italian, Soviet and other cultural centres, attending concerts, art exhibitions, theatrical events – not only the ones arranged by foreigners, but also those of the Ethiopian cultural organisations fostering the development of national literature and visual arts. He attended performances of the Bolshoi Ballet from Moscow, the Moscow Circus and a Chinese circus and presented decorations to the acrobats at the end of the show. This Emperor was not narrow-minded – he wanted his people to experience the rich variety of the foreign world, to bring them to maturity and make them capable of meeting the challenges of modern world. But because he saw himself as the leader of social development in Ethiopia, and as the one who determined its course, he also wanted to be informed on the actual content of foreign cultural influence. Not one of these activities of the Emperor can be seen as a private distraction – each one was his duty, the more so because of his awareness that on such occasions he was the focus of public attention and so was always obliged to be perfectly composed in his behaviour and to represent the dignity of the state.

For Ras Tafari it was an urgent necessity to introduce printing into Ethiopia on a much larger scale, so that not only could the government's laws and decrees be published, but also books and periodicals could be printed within the country. He wanted to foster the development of modern Amharic literature and at the same time open his people's eyes to events taking place in the outside world. There had already been a small printing facility, run by an Armenian, in Menelik's time, but with negligible capacity and output. Ras Tafari could not obtain access to government funds for this end, and so with his own money he obtained two presses and built a printing office. From the latter he published in the late 1920s two periodicals – a weekly, in both Amharic and French, called *Berhanena Selam* (Light and Peace), which also served as the official gazette, and a monthly, *Kesate Berhan* (Revealer of Light). The office also produced government documents and religious books in Amharic. On his initiative, some ancient Ethiopian ecclesiastical works written in Ge'ez were translated into Amharic; this was a liturgical language understood only by scholars, priests and students of the church schools – and certainly not by the common people; it thus had a role in Ethiopia equivalent to that of Latin in medieval Europe. He edited and wrote introductions to the works himself.

Soon the government took up the challenge, and he succeeded in raising the funds to import another press to service the needs of ministries: the first weekly paper in Amharic, an official publication called *Aymero* (Knowledge), was printed on it. Later, as Emperor, he acted as patron of Amharic literary development, quietly defraying the costs of printing the writings of many a talented Ethiopian author out of the imperial treasury, and attending performances of their plays. By this time, in the early 1950s, a dozen printing presses were working in Addis Ababa, and several libraries and bookstores had sprung up. Before this, the very first monthly periodical in Ethiopia had appeared in Harar, in French only, printed and published by the French missionaries under their leader Mgr Jarosseau. Its ambiguous title, *Le Semeur d'Ethiopie* (The Sower of Ethiopia), suggested a connection with missionary activity, but in fact it treated the activities of the Regent, Ras Tafari, and published his early decrees, which were then still made known to the populace in Addis Ababa by means of hand-written posters and even by vocal proclamation.

Well qualified by his skill in languages, his knowledge of the international scene and his excellent contacts with the foreign missions in Addis Ababa, Ras Tafari was able immediately to take charge of the country's foreign affairs: in this capacity no one else could present a credible challenge to him. His rivals had not appreciated this, failing to see how his successes in foreign policy would also strengthen his hand at home. Expanding his power-base within the country was a slow process, calling for exceptional patience. However, seen from abroad, the situation looked different. As Ethiopia's representative, as Regent and future Emperor, he quickly gained a solid reputation, increased by his travels to

Europe and West Asia. On his journeys he would communicate his plans for the country and his views generally to the personages who met him, and this won him sympathy wherever he went. Of course he deepened the knowledge he already possessed, and made a multiplicity of new contacts. In 1923 he visited the British-ruled port of Aden, and in 1924 Djibouti, Egypt, Palestine, France, Belgium, the Netherlands, Luxembourg, Sweden, England, Switzerland, Italy and Greece. His visits encouraged both businessmen and workers in these countries to look for investment and work opportunities in Ethiopia before the Italian invasion.

Ras Tafari achieved a remarkable political success in 1923 with the admission of Ethiopia as a member-state of the League of Nations. The condition on which membership was granted – that the country should accept the obligation to abolish slavery – conformed with his own plans. In Harar Ras Makonnen had made moves in this direction, and Ras Tafari continued the measures taken by his father. Since the abolition of slavery was part of his blueprint anyway, the obligation he accepted on behalf of the whole empire could only strengthen his hand at home; he could now act against the practice in the provinces where it still prevailed with a new legal and moral justification. However, there were more implications to this task than at first appeared. If slavery had been immediately abolished by law, this could have made matters considerably worse for the majority of slaves, depriving them of their subsistence and protection and flooding Addis Ababa with jobless refugees. Other measures had to be taken first: notably, provision for the liberated slaves to be educated and integrated into the economic process. As with some of the Emperor's other aims, such as land reform, this required a gradual approach and careful timing, to avoid the chaos that would follow if the existing order were to collapse before it could be replaced. Haile Sellassie worked consistently towards that end, first as Regent and later as Emperor, and took it up again after the liberation. The goal was reached in about 1955.

Although Haile Sellassie had done what he could to meet his country's obligations as a member of the League of Nations, the League itself was not in a position to live up to its covenant. It could not protect Ethiopia against invasion, or avoid its temporary loss of independence; already it was half-paralysed by the shock-waves sent ahead by the inexorably approaching Second World War. The close involvement of Ethiopia's own history with the pre-history of that colossal war only further emphasised Ethiopia's distinct place in world history. Haile Sellassie's famous address to the General Assembly of the League of Nations on 30 June 1936 stands out both as a historic landmark and as a moral victory for the Emperor himself. It highlighted painfully the downfall of the League.*

. . . The issue which is today before the League of Nations' General Assembly is not merely to settle what Italy has done by way of aggression. I would assert that it is something that touches upon all governments of the world. This is a problem of the duty of governments to assist each other to establish world security; it is a question of the very life of the League of Nations; of the trust which the nations of the world can properly repose in treaties they have concluded; of the value attached to promises which the small nations have received as regards the inviolability of their territorial integrity and independence, so that these values be respected and properly esteemed; it is to assess whether the principles of equality of nations is to be confirmed or whether the small states will have to accept subjection to the powerful ones. In brief, it is not only Ethiopia that is at stake but the decent way of life of the peoples of the world who have thus been affected and wronged. The signatures appended to a treaty, is it that they attain their value only in so far as they are of use to the signatories in the pursuit of their personal, direct and immediate interests? . . . .

In the name of the Ethiopian people which is a member of the League of Nations, I request the Assembly that everything necessary be carried out to have the covenant respected. I now renew once more the protest which I have previously submitted on the grounds of the transgression of treaties to the detriment of the Ethiopian people and on account of the violence perpetrated against it. I declare before the world that the Emperor of Ethiopia, the Ethiopian government, and the people will not accept anything done to them by force. I further declare that they will do everything in their power to see international order triumph, to have the League covenant respected, and to have the authority and the territory which is theirs restored to them.

I ask the fifty-two nations who have given a promise to the Ethiopian people that they would come to their aid at the time of the aggression against them, in order to prevent the aggressor from defeating them – I ask these fifty-two nations for their support by upholding their promise. What are you willing to do for Ethiopia? You, great powers, who have promised to give guarantees of collective security, lest small nations be extinguished and the fate which has overtaken Ethiopia should befall them as well, have you considered what kind

---

* The excerpts from the Emperor's speech at Geneva are taken from his autobiography, *Haile Sellassie I: My Life and Ethiopia's Progress*, translated and annotated by Edward Ullendorff (Oxford University Press, 1976).

of assistance to provide, so that Ethiopia's liberty shall not be destroyed and her territorial integrity respected?

You representatives of the world assembled here! I have come to you to Geneva to carry out the saddest duty that has befallen an Emperor. What answer am I to take back to my people?

These unforgettable words were still echoing long afterwards. They motivated many people who flocked to help Ethiopia with its postwar development, eager to do their share in building a new world, but also with a feeling that there was a debt to be paid.

When Haile Sellassie made this speech, he was already a refugee. His defeat at the last decisive battle of Maichen, where he personally led the Ethiopian forces and took part in the action, settled Ethiopia's fate. He decided to go into exile rather than be captured – a disappointment to many of his followers, who expected him to stay in the country and lead the patriotic resistance, which was to continue the fight in the highlands and the south-west, and to harrass the occupying forces throughout the time of the 'Italian East African Empire'. No precedent existed for what he had done: to Ethiopians it was inconceivable that the Emperor, the Elect of God, should flee his country, whatever the circumstances. Some of his adversaries later accused him of cowardice, as if he had left the country alone and solely in order to save his life. But of course such an accusation was baseless: never in his life did he hesitate to risk his life whenever the pursuit of his goals and the defence of his imperial dignity demanded it. He saw that the Italian conquest would not be history's final judgement on his country, and that he himself could play an essential part in restoring it to its former standing. Now he had to play the political trump cards he held against the League of Nations to secure the assistance of the great powers in case there was any chance left for an independent Ethiopian state. If he had stayed with the resisting groups in Ethiopia, who had withdrawn into the unconquered mountainous area, the Italians would have spared no effort to capture him; he could support the Ethiopian patriots more effectively by representing their case abroad and pricking the conscience of the fast-forgetting world. He could also keep himself ready, and prepare himself for the future tasks that awaited him.

Subsequent events indicated further Haile Sellassie's vision of those events. His decision to leave the country was not taken in haste: it followed ample deliberations with his government, and the cabinet of ministers voted 21 to 3 in favour of his leaving provided that Ethiopian forces remained in control of the railway to the Red Sea port of Djibouti in French Somaliland. But time was running out, and it was only three days after his departure, on 5 May 1936, that the Italian army entered Addis Ababa. He had no easy way out. The private funds that he was able to take could not last long, since he had to support his family and the few trusted members of his staff whom he took with him into exile. For an Emperor of Ethiopia to live in a state of dependence on others, receiving allowances granted by foreign governments or hand-outs from private sources, was a dreadful prospect. However, Haile Sellassie overcame this predicament and maintained an appropriate dignity during every moment of his exile. He took the support that the British government offered as a rightful reparation, due to him and to the Ethiopian national cause for the injustice done to his country and for the breaking of promises. He tried to avoid publicity for another source of funds for his support during the last years of his exile, namely from American citizens of African descent, from the Caribbean, and from Southern Africa. As he had foreseen, his presence in England served to focus the world's attention on the fact that the 'Abyssinian problem' was far from being resolved: but something he had not foreseen was that he would also become a legendary figure to millions of Africans and people of African descent throughout the Americas. Groups sprang up spontaneously in various places identifying their political interests with his. This was to become a cultural movement as well: these people embraced the figure of the Emperor as a symbol of their own frustrations and hopes, often with religious fervour. The uncritical admiration of the Rastafarians offended people of sophisticated views, but they none the less did greater justice to Haile Sellassie for what he was and what he stood for than did most of his contemporaries.

During his exile, the Emperor had time at his disposal to give to his studies of contemporary thought, to read, observe current political events and form his views. Those views were always independent of current trends and the opinions of others, in contrast to his actions which had to depend on dominant trends and were adapted to Western public opinion. His guiding motivation for all political action had to be the immediate advantages that Ethiopia could gain after its liberation from the Italians due to the political and economic strength of friendly countries. Before the Abyssinian war, he had always still taken care to ensure that no country with colonial ambitions should ever be overrepresented on the Horn. Therefore he had preferred to look to neutral countries, such as Sweden, when chosing advisers or technical personnel. This policy was discarded after the liberation, by which time the colonial era was approaching its end anyway. Swedish advisers and assistants had been among the first to come and, after the liberation, the last to leave. Due to their long experience, their projects were among the most useful, especially in the fields of agriculture, building technology and public health. They also made a considerable contribution in the military sector, setting up the Ethiopian Air Force centre at Debre Zeit and staffing the training facilities for its personnel. To have his country firmly linked by alliances with Western countries was clearly the best way to achieve economic and technical progress, but in order not to become too strongly committed to one side if there were ever serious conflicts between the superpowers, he ensured that the other side was not neglected, and visited Moscow for the first time in 1959. He did not share the views of either side, viewing both with detachment and from a distance, as if they were interchangeable – two rival orders, neither of which was capable of being adapted to the purposes of the Ethiopian people. In one of his rare private conversations with a foreigner, during a weekend rest outside Addis Ababa in 1951, he made revealing comments. The subject was communism, which he said presented no danger to Ethiopia, however dangerous it might appear to be elsewhere. "Our people are different," he said, meaning that they were immune to communism because their very nature was averse to communist ways of thought.

It was his own conviction, he said, that patriarchal rule, combined with the principle of the ruler's service to the state, was still the most appropriate form of government for his country. In the Abyssinian war, when the country was faced by the greatly superior equipment of the Italian forces and was unable to buy arms anywhere, Hitler's Germany was the only state which actively supported Ethiopia. The first German grant of three million marks, given in July 1935, was spent on rifles, machine-guns, sub-machine guns, ammunition and hand-grenades from Germany itself and cannons from Switzerland. In addition, Hitler ordered the delivery of thirty anti-tank guns equipped with armour-piercing shells, and made some further minor grants. Three aircraft with volunteer crew were also sent, probably not for delivery to the Abyssinian forces as such but to parachute the less heavy material to units in the highlands engaged in warfare. Germany's strange participation in the Abyssinian war, involving covert action against its official ally, was based on its own political interests at the time. The episode is little known, although details of it were published in France as early as 1959. Even after the Italian victory and occupation of the country, some

German supplies were delivered to the patriotic forces still resisting the invaders. It was not the Emperor's habit to overlook or forget facts: small wonder that his personal views regarding dictatorship diverged markedly from enlightened opinion in the world at large. Furthermore his views were close to those of the Ethiopian population as a whole.

Did he follow the Japanese example? This might have been possible in Menelik's time, in the evolutionary spirit of the nineteenth century (a span of cultural history slightly out of calendar, lasting from 1814 to 1914), but this would surely have been impossible after two world wars had changed the rules of the game and replaced evolution by revolution. By now, too, other parts of his blueprint were devalued. Such idols as Frederick the Great and Napoleon, if they had lived in the twentieth century, would have counted not merely as autocrats but as war criminals, and this image would have been carefully fostered by the media. In some of the tasks he regarded as most urgent, the evolutionist Haile Sellassie stood alone, his position already overwhelmed by the revolutionary social theory and development practice of the time. He saw the only way to progress as being in not disturbing the existing institutions but in letting them adapt of their own volition to changing conditions (the changes to take place as fast as possible) and thus grow into the new order. Thus his task as ruler was to keep the balance – on the one hand not to force his people to adapt more rapidly than they were able to, and, on the other, not to lose time when he felt it possible to take a few steps further in a desired direction to achieve his goal.

His blueprint, made up essentially of fragments of foreign philosophy and historical knowledge, was an 'ideal' in the nineteenth-century sense. It accounted for the lifelong consistency of his endeavours and actions, and the concentration of his energy and abilities upon a single aim, not allowing for any waste. As an idealist, he shared the recklessness of most idealists: for the sake of a higher goal, every obstacle in his path had to be removed, and every sacrifice was justified – the sacrifice of comfort, the enjoyment of a private life, and time for rest and recreation and of the interests of others. If the obstacles happened to consist of individuals, they either had to yield or disappear – even being 'liquidated' if no other means was to hand. When considering the victims Haile Sellassie left in his wake – and there were rather more of them than is generally known – no instance has so far been revealed where the deed was done out of a selfish motive, such as personal gain or revenge; all the known

* cf. Manfred Funke, *Sanctionen und Kanonen*, Duisburg, 1971.

deaths were dictated by the political necessity of the moment. This kind of ruthlessness has added an extra dimension to the image assumed by Ras Tafari in the eyes of traditional Ethiopian society due to Menelik's curse, his involvement in the downfall of Emperor Yassu, and the circumstances surrounding the death of Empress Zauditu. Whether or not Ras Tafari had a hand in this, the fact that the Empress died at the very same time as the battle of Zebit struck the superstitious population as of sinister significance. This accounted for the reserve with which Haile Sellassie was always treated among his own people, and for the whispers that were exchanged about him outside his closest circle. But it also helped him to regain the respect and even the affection of his people, which he had once put at risk by being partly dependent on the assistance granted to him by foreign powers when he was still Regent. What they hated above all else were weaklings in high positions, and most of all one in the top position, and this at least could not be said of him.

Convenient though it was, the time of Empress Zauditu's death may easily have been no more than a lucky coincidence for Ras Tafari. None the less, within Ethiopian society the rumour that she was strangled has stubbornly persisted right up to the present day. Few travellers have adopted this version in their books, and historians stick to the official version, which in itself is not very convincing. By this account the Empress was attending the traditional baptismal ceremonies held at the festival of the Epiphany, and was treated with too much enthusiasm by the priests, who submerged her totally in water. The weather was extremely cold, and her lungs became inflamed, causing her death a few weeks later. But was it conceivable that the priests could have behaved in this way with any woman, let alone the reigning Empress? Exactly how she died will probably never be known, and it is now of little importance because it cannot change the streamlined image of Haile Sellassie's life, whichever version of the Empress's death one accepts. Apparently, there was no way that progress could be achieved as long as the way to the throne was blocked. If the decision reached in the victorious battle of Zebit could not be put into effect straight away, the other alternative – as experienced earlier in the case of Fitawrari Habte Giorgis – of waiting for one's opponent to die a natural death could have been too lengthy. There was always the possibility that during the time of waiting new enemies might emerge and old ones form alliances.

V. THE EMPEROR

No book has yet been written that throws light on the landscape of Haile Sellassie's mind: one can only single out a few features that recurred constantly in his actions throughout his life and reign.

In the matter of language, it is generally known that, having received a French education, he had a perfect command of French and always preferred it for audiences and conversations with foreigners. It is not so well known that he was also fluent in English, Italian and Arabic. The few instances when he undoubtedly spoke a short sentence in flawless German, responding exactly to an unforeseen situation, are not enough for it to be certain how much study he had given to that language, but he was certainly able to read it. His mother-tongue being Amharic, he also mastered the ancient ecclesiastical and literary language of Ethiopia, the Ge'ez. It has never been said which of the country's numerous languages he could speak, but probably he knew Harari, Galligna, Gurage and Tigrigna. His solid knowledge of Latin, which enabled him to pursue his secret medieval studies, has also strangely escaped his biographers' attention. There is a German saying: 'As many languages as you can speak, in that number of worlds are you at home.' To those who at some time interviewed Haile Sellassie and all those who have so confidently and loftily described, analysed and judged him, such niceties meant nothing: those people were only at home in one world, and because Haile Sellassie was a master at saying exactly what they wanted to hear or what fitted into a given situation, their one world could remain intact. There were times when he would listen in a most attentive and friendly way to a foreigner reporting to him on a subject of which he himself knew more than the reporter, but he would let that person leave his presence with the impression that his presentation had been a success. The same applied to the proceedings within his private cabinet and the Crown Council, where he would listen quietly to lengthy reports and arguments without ever entering into the discussion himself, and concluded the matter with a decision which was completely unexpected and stunned everyone present, and which he did not explain.

Haile Sellassie's ability not to reveal his inner self – his feelings, thoughts and character – was often noted. The impenetrable nature of his reserve becomes clear to anyone investigating the range of his linguistic skills. Nobody who had not heard the Emperor use a particular language could know which languages he was able to speak. The learned Ethiopians who assisted him in his private studies – often people who held inconspicuous and lowly positions – would not reveal even that they had access to the Emperor at all, let alone the exact way in which they had assisted him, or how great was the Emperor's knowledge in their fields of learning. Matters may of course have been different within the family, but nothing has ever been revealed about his conversations with his children, grandchildren and cousins such as Ras Imru and Ras Asrate Kassa.

The Emperor's family was large. The inner circle consisted of the children by his marriage to Empress Menen, whereas those born from the previous marriages of the Emperor and Menen were members of the family who were outside the line of succession. According to Ethiopian custom, his distant cousins, Ras Imru and Ras Asrate Kassa, along with their families, were also still counted as members of the imperial clan. Only two of Haile Sellassie's six children survived their father, but there were still seven princes among his grandchildren – and two more outside the line of succession. Some of the grandchildren were already married with children of their own. It was most unlikely that the line of succession, as Haile Sellassie had envisaged it, would fail in the foreseeable future.

Empress Menen had been married twice before, and she had already four children when she married the nineteen year-old Dedjasmatch Tafari in 1911. The orphaned Tafari had married very early – in a customary marriage by contract, not concluded in church; such alliances usually expired after a few years if the contract with the girl's family was not renewed. This was hardly a marital status befitting a provincial ruler. After the restoration of Dedjasmatch Tafari to the governorship of Harar, the rich and important key province in the young Emperor's political plans, Lidj Yasu saw to it that this was corrected: all previous marital engagements were dissolved, and Tafari had to marry Menen, Lidj Yasu's niece, and thus a grandchild of King Mikael of Wollo. Menen is said to have been a striking beauty, and she was very wealthy in her own right. The Emperor's long married life with her was harmonious and virtuous. Although the Empress had no political influence, she played a significant part in public life; she supported the Ethiopian Orthodox Church, enriched monasteries and adorned church buildings, and was active in setting up institutions of social welfare and in keeping them active. For this purpose she used a considerable amount of her own

Table 1
THE SOLOMONIC LINE
SELECTED DATA

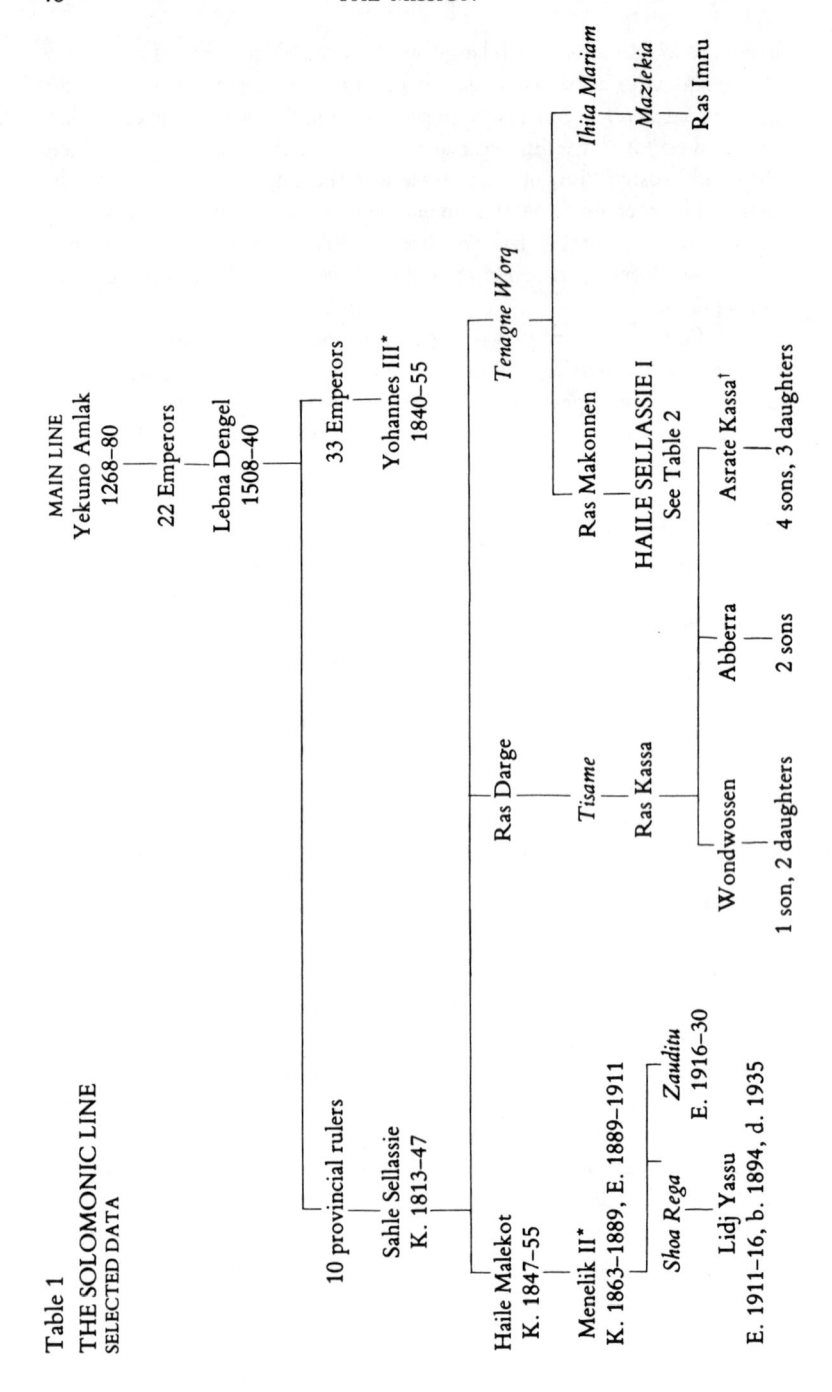

```
MAIN LINE
Yekuno Amlak
   1268–80
      |
  22 Emperors
      |
  Lebna Dengel
    1508–40
    /      \
33 Emperors  Yohannes III*
              1840–55
                 |
        ┌────────┴────────┐
  10 provincial        Sahle Sellassie
     rulers              K. 1813–47
                            |
              ┌─────────────┼─────────────────────────┐
      Haile Malekot                              Ras Darge
        K. 1847–55                                   |
             |                                   Tisame
        Menelik II*  —  Shoa Rega                   |
      K. 1863–1889,                              Ras Kassa
      E. 1889–1911       Zauditu                    |
             |          E. 1916–30        ┌─────────┼─────────┐
        Lidj Yassu                    Wondwossen  Abberra  Asrate Kassa†
     E. 1911–16,                      1 son,     2 sons    4 sons,
     b. 1894, d. 1935                 2 daughters          3 daughters

                         Tenagne Worq  —  HAILE SELLASSIE I
                                            See Table 2
                         Ras Makonnen
                              |
                         Ihita Mariam
                         Mazlekia
                         Ras Imru
```

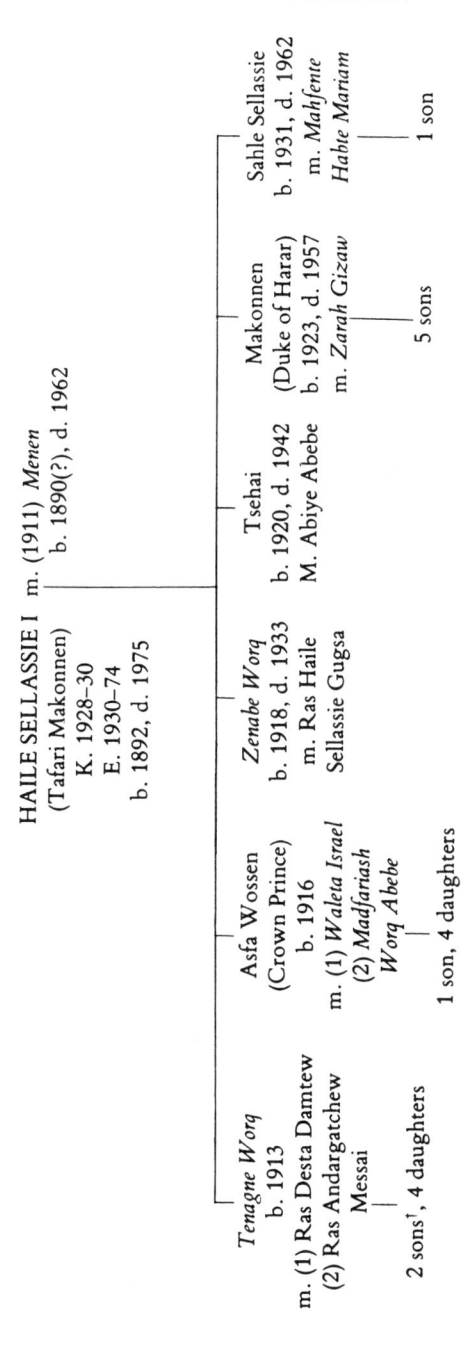

Table 2

HAILE SELLASSIE I m. (1911) *Menen*
(Tafari Makonnen) b. 1890(?), d. 1962
K. 1928–30
E. 1930–74
b. 1892, d. 1975

Tenagne Worq	Asfa Wossen	*Zenabe Worq*	Tsehai	Makonnen	Sahle Sellassie
b. 1913	(Crown Prince)	b. 1918, d. 1933	b. 1920, d. 1942	(Duke of Harar)	b. 1931, d. 1962
m. (1) Ras Desta Damtew	b. 1916	m. Ras Haile	M. Abiye Abebe	b. 1923, d. 1957	m. *Mahfente*
(2) Ras Andargatchew	m. (1) *Waleta Israel*	Sellassie Gugsa		m. *Zarah Gizaw*	*Habte Mariam*
Messai	(2) *Madfariash*				
	Worq Abebe				
2 sons†, 4 daughters	1 son, 4 daughters			5 sons	1 son

Key
Female names are italicised.
K. = King
E. = Emperor
* End of succession by male line.
† Executed by new government, Nov. 1974.

private wealth, without having recourse to state funds. A granddaughter by her first marriage married Ras Asrate Kassa, thus tying the bonds of allegiance of the Kassa clan, which had been by-passed in the line of succession by the young Tafari after the deposition of Yasu.

Haile Sellassie had one daughter by his first marriage, Romanaworq. She married Dedjasmatch Bayene Merid, a governor of Bale, who died as a leader in the fight against the Italians during the occupation. Two of his grandsons by this line played a part in public life: one of them, Lidj Samson Bayene, died in an accident in 1963, and the other, Dedjasmatch Merid, who served as a provincial governor, survived the revolution and lives in exile.

It has often been noted that his relations with the Crown Prince, Asfa Wossen, were uneasy, and this has been interpreted as alienation and even strong antipathy, resulting in many wild stories and dark rumours, which were either unfounded or irrelevant. However, there are more plausible explanations at hand. The foreign world had been a strong influence on the education and character of his younger relatives; they were children of their time and thus belonged to a particular span of cultural history. Lidj Tafari, on the other hand, had formed his views and the plan of his life in the spirit of the nineteenth century. The Crown Prince grew to adulthood after the First World War when the rules of the game had changed, and saw himself as representing the new democratic age; his part would merely be transitional, leading to the time when under the new constitution granted by his father, he would be a constitutional monarch, and the actual ruling would be done by others. The father was a builder, the son a representative. Differences between the two were already apparent between the wars, and the gap naturally widened after the Second World War, with all the turmoil it caused. To the solitary orphan Lidj Tafari, the life ahead of him had appeared as a tremendous challenge, requiring the concentration of all his skill and energy, without which failure would be unavoidable. No such challenge faced Asfa Wossen, growing up in a world with solid foundations, and where his future role was clearly defined. If, under the new constitutional monarchy, others were to have the real power, he would not be able to interfere with their task anyway, and therefore it would be pointless for him to work obsessively, like his father. In retrospect it is clear that Haile Sellassie's gifts were exceptional, and thus it is unfair to measure average people against him. One could rationalise further, but the obvious differences of background and character are enough to explain the disharmony that existed without looking for gossip. After his coronation, the Emperor bestowed on Asfa Wossen the governorship of Wollo, the fief once held by the Crown Prince's maternal great-grandfather, King Mikael – who, after losing the battle for the crown of his son, Emperor Yassu, had died a prisoner. If tradition had been followed, the Crown Prince would have been crowned King of Wollo – but Haile Sellassie, far from creating kings, actually abolished them: they might otherwise have become contenders for the throne, as in the past. The Emperor, having founded a new dynasty, was determined to use the resources of his own family and clan for the succession, rather than revert to the ancient rules of the Law of Kings.

His second son Ras Makonnen, who had a preference for the title 'Duke of Harar', was his favourite, and it was even rumoured that his father would have preferred the succession to pass to him. He was a good officer, and was also shrewd and imaginative as a businessman, dealing in export and import – often, it was said, at the expense of his foreign partners. By nature he was untroubled by ideological preoccupations, and thus knew how to take the best advantage of his high position, showing a marked predilection for beautiful women and fast cars. Occasionally the Emperor intervened, although this did not become public knowledge. Once the Duke was arrested by the police and brought in chains before an investigating committee after the Emperor had learned from his security agencies that he had received some payments through condoning a revival of slave-trading in a remote corner of his province. Another time, he was fined for using his large personal landholdings to grow *qat* as a cash-crop for export to Arabia and thus make fast and easy money: cultivating a drug-plant was not the kind of agricultural development the Emperor had envisaged for the province. More than once, the Emperor rebuked him to his face for his love affairs; he was a married man with many children, and required to avoid gossip. But despite these setbacks to smooth relations between them, the Emperor was attracted by his uncomplicated personality, down-to-earth pragmatism and independence: the Duke did not stand in his father's shadow. When, in 1957, he was killed in a car accident, the Emperor felt the loss of this favourite son keenly, and, as he walked behind the coffin in the funeral cortege, cried out in the words of King David, 'Would God I had died for thee, O Absalom, my son, my son!'

The Emperor's youngest and most talented son, Sahle Sellassie, differed in appearance from his brothers, and resembled his famous ancestor, the King of Shoa, after whom he was named. During his education in England, he embraced the spirit of contemporary art and literature.

He had no military ambition or any desire for an administrative career such as that of a governor. Because of his dissipated behaviour and poor health, he was removed from the line of succession and allowed to retire into private life. He spent all his time on his artistic and technical interests, and was occasionally seen accompanying his father on visits to exhibitions or to the theatre. The Emperor intended that he should somehow be held in reserve to play a part in the fulness of time, in the cultural development of the capital, but it was not to be: he too died relatively young, in 1962.

The Emperor used to have long and intimate conversations with his eldest child, Princess Tenagne Work, more so than with his sons. The Princess was Ethiopia's great lady in matters of public welfare, but he also used to seek her advice and opinion, concerning the rapid changes taking place in social behaviour – some conservatives saw the hand of Satan in many of these changes. For him, characteristically Ethiopian in this respect, a woman's viewpoint was valuable in what was still largely a male-dominated society. The princess had much influence in her own domain, and occasionally even in the appointment of certain officials in the administration. This influence did not extend to politics or the main sectors of economic development. At the end of her father's reign, she joined the circle of ministers, governors and generals who implored the Emperor to defend the crown and the country against the mutiny. She did all she could to dissuade her father from his stubborn refusal to order his loyal troops to fight, and from his decision to negotiate with the mutineers instead. Her pleas, too, were in vain.

To the outside world, Haile Sellassie expounded his practical goals in hundreds of public speeches. They give us at least some insight into what he thought, the work that engaged him, and what he knew. Although the speeches were often drafted by others, they corresponded to his directives, and he always revised them personally. They were delivered to serve particular purposes or to mark particular occasions, and because they were prompted by political necessities of the moment or adapted to prevailing trends in the foreign media, they would often not betray his real opinions and motives. A considerable part of the entire picture of his plans, methods and style can be pieced together by examining these speeches. Where the outside world was concerned, he knew that he was going against the prevailing tide and would attract no attention unless he made some foolish and obviously ridiculous statement, which would then immediately be picked up and become news. The Emperor meant his speeches chiefly to be explanations for his own people, and he looked upon them as an unavoidable adjunct to his duties. So that they could never be used by those intent on impeaching the dignity of the crown, he avoided the common public relations ingredients of humour, irony and polemic in favour of a rather solemn and uniform style. Thus the foreign media tended to overlook them and not bother to search for the significance of what he said. Only a few of his speeches, given on the more spectacular occasions, were ever reported abroad.

Already at the early stages of his ascent to the throne, as Regent, Ras Tafari kept his own counsel and hid his determination behind an appearance of mildness and obliging manners. However, this alone would not have been enough to give him a position of ascendancy over his rivals, since these were common features of Ethiopian society. People who talked too much were either of humble origin, uneducated, or otherwise not up to the standards which their positions required of them. The ability to treat any item of knowledge or information as an element of personal power which would be wasted if it were given away without sufficient cause is found at every level of society from the highest to the lowest, among servants and among illiterates. This national quality had always been a highly effective means of defence against what were perceived as influences threatening to dissolve the values and manners that constituted the people's way of life. Foreigners have often seen this as no more than a kind of oriental ruse, a needless trafficking in secrecy.

The weapon of structural defence of a society was suitably baffling because it was so remarkably efficient. At a time when the national economy was being developed, it led to strange situations. Foreign experts, eager to make their work conform to what the government required, felt frustrated because they had not been able to discover what these requirements were, and apparently nobody was interested in imparting that knowledge to them. Even the reports of those who had previously done similar work in the same field of activity were not made available. If such an expert should find one of these documents by chance, or by ferreting it out of the Ethiopian archives, he would be mystified as to why such important information had been withheld from him, and attributed this mystification to disorder in the filing system for state records. But in fact he was expected to obtain all such knowledge in advance, before arriving in Ethiopia, where no information would be yielded up voluntarily. People who failed to grasp this point in their appraisal of Ethiopia were all the more popular the less their views corresponded with reality. Even if they held unflattering views about

Ethiopia, and were known to express them publicly, they were allowed to live in their fool's paradise for as long as their skills were of use. Care was taken that all such visitors in the country should stand on their own feet, relying on what they themselves could find out, and on exchanges of views within their expatriate circle and their colleagues. Only if Ethiopians felt that their secrets had been seen through did the offending foreigner produce negative reactions, and come to be regarded as a potential danger. It would then be time for his contract to be terminated.

In earlier times, conscious of danger and following the national tract of reticence (which partly stemmed from it), an important man always kept his preparations for a journey secret, and when he suddenly disappeared with his retinue, it would be difficult to find out where he had gone. It was considered improper for his servants to divulge any information about it to other servants or to outsiders, and if they did so, this was considered a crime that deserved to be punished severely. Nobody should be given the chance to mount an attack with superior forces or lay an ambush in the vast and deserted highlands, which were always plagued by *shiftas* (gangs of robbers).

Ras Tafari could evaluate situations unemotionally and rationally, taking into account his strengths and weaknesses, and those of both his followers and his opponents, the country's internal situation and the political constellation abroad. He would use all the information he could obtain – whether it came from the circuit of information concealed in the mesh of Ethiopia's close-knit society or from friendly-disposed foreign secret services. From his analysis he would determine his course of action and his timing. He could wait quietly and inconspicuously for an opportunity, if necessary over a long period, and then at a given moment move quickly and decisively. Sometimes his adversaries likened Ras Tafari to a snake in the grass. His rational pragmatic attitude served him well in his dealings with them – his 'iron curtain' of reticence was an impenetrable defence.

Circumstances forced Tafari to stand on his own very early. He had lost not only his parents but also Abba Samuel, the outstanding figure among his tutors, who had drowned when his boat had accidentally capsized while crossing a lake. Tafari, already burdened, while still little more than a boy, with the tasks of government and of determining the fate of his fellow-men, was now deprived of this trusted friend and guide, for whom he had felt great affection. He now had to make the best of his talents alone. Apart from his capacity for clear thought, he had also developed unusual powers of perception with regard to the way people behaved and expressed themselves in speech. Some foreign advisers, after an audience with Haile Sellassie, had the uneasy feeling that the Emperor had been reading their thoughts – this was often said.

Ras Tafari intended to abolish the privileges of the feudal class, of which he was himself a member, and in the latter part of his reign as Emperor he did exactly that. Only he himself and the imperial family retained such privileges. As for all other Ethiopian citizens, there were no privileges fixed by law; any that still persisted in practice were illegal and could be contested in court. (Differences in wealth may have given the opposite impression.)

Ethiopian nobles generally were not the kind of exploiters they are now mostly thought to have been. There were admirable characters to be found among the provincial rulers and the rural gentry, who were regarded with respect and affection by their people to whom they stood in a father-like relationship. There were also exceptions: rulers and nobles who enjoyed little respect either from their people or among their peers, and these represented a risk of popular uprising. In Ethiopia little was needed to set off a revolt – the country had never been without internal dissensions – but in all periods the Ethiopian Orthodox Church had succeeded in making religion the common binding force for all layers of society, so that feudal rule retained an ethical and juridical basis.

But the resistance against which Ras Tafari always had to contend was not only due to rivalry and self-interest, although that did play an important part. Was he not the moderniser, obsessed by foreign ideas, the would-be destroyer of traditional values, in which lay the country's capacity to defend itself? Neither as Regent not later as Emperor did he take this kind of opposition lying down. Throughout his reign he did all he could to reinforce the position of the Orthodox Church, loyally observing its customary rituals and beginning every working day by attending mass. Occasionally he invited foreign missionaries to lunch with him, conversing with them on religious questions and trying to explore what part religion plays in modern society. His private studies of such authors as Thomas Aquinas were almost certainly prompted by his desire to restore this ancient link. In this he failed – the integration of religion with modern social theory remained a problem he never solved, but it is one nobody else has solved either.

The most striking gift of the Emperor, which largely eluded the attention of biographers and reporters, was his memory. As well as a vast quantity of administrative detail, he stored personal information about thousands of individuals away in his brain: he knew the names, faces, positions, functions, tribal connections and family relationships of officials, military officers or students. All of them he had personally appointed, promoted, transferred or dismissed, or he had supported their education; and reports on all of them had been submitted to him. It was said that he never forgot any conversation he had ever had and indeed from his early youth he had been trained to store everything in his memory. He avoided leaving any written records of his actions, and never took notes: only his final decisions went into the files. For the population it was a matter of course that the Elect of God should have supernatural qualities, but for officials it was deeply portentous, and it kept them constantly in a state of apprehension. Even when unexpected situations arose, the Emperor would be able quickly and effortlessly to recall accurate details of events which had taken place many years before without consulting files or asking his aides.

Sleep was an unavoidable interruption, which he limited to five hours. Whenever he could be seen by a human eye, he felt himself to be on duty and performing his royal office: not even a servant should ever be given an opportunity to see him in an undignified situation and be able to ridicule him behind his back. Because of the extent of the tasks the Emperor felt driven to take upon himself, he scarcely ever allowed himself even a few hours of private enjoyment or rest, to the despair of his physicians; and when he did, his rest was likely to be interrupted. For the time, such as it was, that he spent with his family, could not be regarded solely as private because in this particular capacity also he felt that he was serving as an exemplar to a nation structured on the lines of family clans. At the same time, he was taking care of his obligations as head of the imperial clan.

Discounting the time which he spent with his family, the Emperor's normal working day rarely consisted of less then twelve, or more than sixteen, hours. To keep himself physically fit, he lived on a strict diet, avoiding alcohol, tobacco and drugs. This did not accord well with traditional views: 'He is becoming lean and weak like a bird' people said; 'this is no way for a man to live!' All that the students were able to see was an old man struggling hopelessly for a lost cause.

The splendour and ceremonial of court life, and the monotonous praises heaped on the Emperor by the Ethiopian press, with such ritual phrases as 'Imperial Majesty', 'Elect of God', 'by the Grace of God' and so on, have been interpreted as reflecting personal vanity on the part of Haile Sellassie. In fact they had no other meaning than to honour the imperial crown, the symbol of the Ethiopian state. The Emperor himself was a servant of the state, so his subjects should submit their lives and work to it too.

Haile Sellassie ruled his country like a virtuoso soloist playing a concerto. Each day's work was like a theme of which he had to give an individual performance; he was not willing to tolerate any discordant sounds such as would be produced by an ensemble of amateurs. His keyboard may have had a limited range, but it was certainly greater than any that could be claimed by his collaborators or his critics. In the major keys he showed much of the ways of thought, of cold analysis and reason, that he had adopted from Europe, but he also mastered the minor keys represented by his own country, with a wealth of imagination, a weave of philosophy and history. The 'music' he played on the keys of his people was not yielded up to the listener on a superficial hearing. He was under unremitting pressure from his nation of individualists, all of them trying to build up power for themselves either by force or by subtlety with the help of their clans; old enmities blended with new alliances in ever-shifting plots and intrigues. Visible events had their roots in the tangled web of Ethiopian society.

Haile Sellassie sought the reconciliation of all contradictory forces, and the elimination of the local feuds and tribal wars which had been part and parcel of Ethiopian history throughout the centuries, for ever threatening anarchy and the disintegration of the empire. Two dangers had to be faced. One was that the country would fall back into the pernicious ways of the past – civil wars leading to slaughter, the destruction of material goods, and the institution of slavery. The other was the danger of revolution. The impetus for this could not possibly come from within the country; it could only be introduced from abroad and nurtured by the foreigners working in the country. But even if a revolution took place, Ethiopia would still have to be ruled afterwards by autocratic means, or it would vanish from the map as a political entity. Haile Sellassie retained his independent judgement, and developed a superior performing technique: to achieve balance without letting any other player join in. Up till his death, he remained the solo virtuoso.

VI. FIGHTING THE DESERT

There was much more solid achievement during the reign of Haile Sellassie than meets the eye. The most important problem of Ethiopia's development – the prevention of an ecological catastrophe – remained unsolved, as it still does today. Every year, an area previously covered by vegetation is permanently lost to the desert. The extent of such losses is hard to establish, because no measurements have ever been made, but it is estimated that in the period from the liberation to the revolution, an average area of about 1,000 square kilometres was lost each year, the total equally the size of Belgium. There is still no end in sight to the continuous shrinkage of the people's only natural basis for subsistence. The yearly gain of soil under the plough cannot redress the balance as long as the area covered with vegetation continues to shrink.

At the heart of all development activity in Ethiopia is forestry. If the country still had sufficient forest cover, as in ancient times, this would keep the balance between soil, humidity and climate, and make the recurrent droughts bearable. It would also defend the land covered by vegetation against desertification. Drought cannot be eliminated, since it happens at regular intervals – thought to be related to the eleven-year turning period of the sun and the incidence of sunspots – and it has taken its toll throughout Ethiopia's history. And in addition to their natural shrinking with the deterioration of the climate, the forests were recklessly squandered by the inhabitants. According to a reliable scientific report published in 1966, the yearly destruction of dense forest areas amounted to 2,000 square km. which would mean that an area twice the size of Belgium has been denuded in the post-war period. Seen from this angle, the change in the social order appears logical and even as necessary. The revolutionary government understood the gravity of the situation and immediately undertook large-scale re-afforestation programmes. However, these were frustrated by the famine itself and by the demands of the civil wars. If it should ever succeed in this, the revolution will have justified itself, and its countless victims will not have suffered in vain. But there is no possibility of it succeeding. The revolutionary leaders now face the same situation as faced the Emperor: namely, that the main determinants of a solution are beyond the remedy of any Ethiopian – and, indeed, of any African.

The ecological catastrophe in Africa is man-made, and it is a dangerous mistake to attribute it to some slowly-evolving geological development which no human power can arrest. Even if this were so, the state of scientific knowledge and technical know-how is more than enough to counter-balance adverse effects of that nature. The catastrophe is, above all, a fact of global history. For Ethiopia the range of options available is narrow, and none promises a permanent solution.

The Emperor was fully aware of the danger implied in the destruction of the country's forests, and that the doomladen prophecies of some British naturalists and foresters might prove correct. These experts, with unrivalled experience at that time in relation to East Africa and the Near East, had submitted their reports already around 1950. They foretold that a famine of previously unimagined severity would strike the country after about twenty years unless re-afforestation were started immediately. The prediction proved correct: twenty-three years later, the big drought struck and continued for several years. Hundreds of thousands of people died – and the world was given a justification for the Emperor's fall and the need to replace the old order.

A consensus of the world's press held that the Emperor, despite being fully informed, had kept his knowledge of the tragedy to himself, shamefully hiding the facts from the outside world. He had thus violated the duty inherent in his position. However, this interpretation is absurd. The world had its ear pressed close to listen to the heartbeat of Ethiopia. In the country were numerous reporters working either for individual newspapers or for the international press agencies, the staffs of the foreign diplomatic missions, experts from the United Nations agencies such as the Economic Commission for Africa, the Food and Agriculture Organisation, the World Health Organisation and the International Labour Organisation, and the many foreigners at the Haile Sellassie University in Addis Ababa. All knew of the tragedy unfolding in Wollo, and if there was a need to give the facts added publicity or inform the outside world more urgently, they were completely free to do so. Instead they preferred to collect and publish reports which were damaging to the Emperor's reputation, and attributed a 'duty' to him which was never his. He, rather, made the mistake of believing that with all the foreign experts and journalists as witnesses, this aspect of the country's public relations was in safe hands. Haile Sellassie's supposed failure to report the famine was compounded by another crime: the 'fact' that he had salted away billions of dollars in private bank accounts in Switzerland, thus robbing his starving country of its wealth: figures published in the German press estimated the amounts as high as $11 billion. Both allegations were inventions and contained no shred of truth, but as the years pass since the Emperor's death, world opinion has been fixed by these distortions.

Faced with a task far exceeding the technical and financial means of the state, the Emperor still thought that he saw a solution. We should consider his basic deliberations in this respect, since they illustrate his political stand in other contexts. We have already noted that the ecological catastrophe is man-made, but it has not been caused by the Africans themselves. If a continent occupying one-fifth of the earth's land area irresistibly deteriorates, it is the concern not of Africa alone but also of the whole world, especially when its population is expected to double within a single lifetime. Hence it is the world's task to solve Africa's problem and Ethiopia's in particular. A great responsibility lies with the United States and the Soviet Union, which, through their power, can exert decisive influence over the state of the world. Superficial changes notwithstanding, their ideological rivalry for hearts and minds in the developing world will not cease for a long time to come. Hence the present situation must continue, with the African countries being left to solve their own problems largely on their own. Africa, unable to get effective help from either side, slides ever deeper into crisis with each year that passes. Because the American and Soviet political models are both equally detrimental to the Africans, there is unlikely to be any relief if the two super-powers finally agree on a common basis: things might get even worse.

At the African level, Ethiopia never suffers alone when there is a drought. All the other countries in the Sahel zone, which spans sub-Saharan Africa from east to west, suffer too, and remedial action taken in one corner of the Sahel zone will not influence the situation much if all the other countries do not agree to act together. Neither Ethiopia nor any other African country has the means to take effective action. The problem is so vast that it has got out of hand and can no longer be managed with the means at the disposal of any ordinary state budget.

In this tangled situation, Haile Sellassie resorted to a stratagem once used with apparent success by Menelik when he engaged Alfred Ilg, a Swiss engineer who had gone to Ethiopia to assist in some technical projects, in an executive capacity, and even raised him to the rank of a minister of state. Soon Ilg had become indispensable to Menelik, assisting him in all his dealings with foreign governments, securing the frontiers of the new Abyssinian state, and defending the country against the ambitions of the colonial powers. The technical and commercial competence of this unusual minister was instrumental in realising a number of other projects such as the railway from Addis Ababa to Djibouti, and his lively interest in every other field of cultural development stimulated Menelik's imagination and spurred him to take initiatives of his own. Not surprisingly, Ilg's name has an honoured place in the annals of Ethiopian history.

Haile Sellassie thought that by using the same tactic of employing a pre-eminent tropical forestry scientist in an executive function, as an insider within the administration and not merely as a hired expert, he would have the same chance of success. If such a man were to share the attitude of Ilg, he would identify his own interests with those of the country. An expert in that position would see the imminent danger much more clearly, and be appalled by the non-availability of the means to fight it. The Emperor thought that the access which a renowned scientist would have to foreign governments and international agencies, as well as to the world press, would be sufficient to initiate major transcontinental projects, and the whole gamut of superior skills, technology and economic power which is only to be found in the rich capitalist countries would be thrown into the scales. Whatever could be achieved by the many scientists and forestry experts sent by the UN's Food and Agriculture Organisation (FAO) or by individual governments within the framework of their technical aid to Ethiopia, competent and useful as their detailed reports always were, remained only a patchwork and ineffective over the long term; the problem was not seen in its proper size and context, and thus the task was not dealt with by appropriate means.

For millennia, Africa's living nature was protected by the awe which humanity felt towards it. Plants and animals were the abode of spirits, and the fear that those spirits would avenge wrongs committed against them prevented men from helping themselves to more of nature's riches than they needed. For as long as man still lived by hunting and gathering, the protective shield of religion deterred him from abusing his power, In Africa, this sanction still accompanied man through the early stages of agricultural settlement. In Ethiopia, where Christianity had been implanted on African soil in early times, the Ethiopian Orthodox Church retained sufficient 'magical' ingredients – features derived from indigenous African belief – to protect living nature. This was gradually dissolved under the cultural influence that radiated from nearby Europe. There, nature was sufficiently safeguarded by the common sense of the solidly settled farming population, whose natural affective attitude towards animals had survived from prehistoric times. Even before the Middle Ages, the protective function of religion, which was no longer needed to preserve nature, had shifted entirely to social ethics.

As European missionaries swarmed over the continent, they started to remove the natural shelter, thus making Africa's natural wealth an easy prey to anyone able and willing to grab it. With the best of intentions, and unaware of the harm they did by their very presence, the Europeans set off the avalanche of Africa's devastation. The impact was felt at once. At the beginning of the sixteenth century, when there was a major influx of the Portuguese into Ethiopia, about two-thirds of the country's present area was covered by dense forest. Since then, in a single uninterrupted movement, the forest cover has receded, to the point where by 1960 it consisted of only 9 per cent of the area. And the process continues.

Never before in history had the devastation of the continent accelerated as it did with the 'development' that took place in the post-war decades. This was due to the Technical Assistance offered, the character of which was non-religious if not openly anti-religious, and due to the scope of its programmes, and the fervour with which they were implemented, they reached into every corner of the continent, and dug out the last hidden and forgotten tribes. Nearer to present times, an increasing part of Technical Assistance flowed into two branches: first, humanitarian aid, which cares for its own victims, feeding millions of uprooted Africans, who cannot be integrated anywhere, in camps where they gradually lose their natural resistance to hardship, and secondly, military aid to warring factions in civil wars. Meanwhile, Africa's ecological catastrophe rushes on with unabated speed.

The colonial powers also brought Africa new techniques for personal survival. Thus the second avalanche, of population growth, started to move. This movement too has gained considerable momentum in the post-war decades. Stabilised throughout the centuries at about 85 million up till 1800, the population has jumped to about half a billion at the present time and is expected to reach one billion within less than one human lifetime. Africa still has a sufficient agricultural area to support every living African and more, but in history the dynamic counts for more than the static. The two avalanches rushing towards each other are bound to meet and intermingle one day if they cannot be stopped in time. Where they meet, Africans will be afflicted by mass destruction, whether through war, famine or disease. Africa's many flourishing agricultural ventures, where Technical Assistance has been successful or where prudent policies pursued by African governments themselves have borne fruit, will not be enough to counterbalance the overall devastation: as an opposing movement, it will be too slow. Population explosions, here as elsewhere, cannot be halted by birth control. Thus nothing can be planned, and people must be left to solve their own problems. Stopping the other avalanche, the devastation of Africa, is undoubtedly possible, but it depends on conditions which in practice do not yet exist; much of the strength needed for that purpose is nullified by political deadlocks, and people furthermore are prevented by a maze of theoretical misconceptions from seeing the danger in its true context. Africa, as seen from the outside, is no more than the appendix to the unsolved problems of others.

And as seen by an insider? What if the insider in question were not an African but a well-known foreign scientist of vision? Might not such a person be in a position to ring the alarm bells world wide? The Emperor, his imagination fired by this idea of Menelik, broke his own rules for the Ethiopian government by installing a foreign expert as chief of the forestry department, a post normally reserved for an Ethiopian assistant minister. He was tentatively given the title of Director-General.

The incentive came from Britain, and it might have been wise to choose a British expert because, as a victor in the war, Britain would be less restricted in its policy than the Federal Republic of Germany. But Haile Sellassie calculated that Britain was still over-burdened by the obligations resulting from the dissolution of its colonial empire to wish to become involved in major ventures in developing countries outside the Commonwealth. He therefore called in the West Germans, rating this as a better prospect because Germany had no post-colonial obligations and was rapidly expanding its economic power. There were few options open. Where forestry was concerned, he distrusted Americans since they had not been able to control self-inflicted erosion in their own country. France was enmeshed in its own language-area of Africa in a way similar to the British. The Italians were ruled out as the country's former invaders and occupiers, although, other things being equal, they would not have been a bad choice in view of their previous experience there and the many forestry studies they had conducted in the past. The West Germans had only recently joined the community of sponsors of

Third World development, and were fully committed to the theoretical concepts generally prevailing: no new ideas touching the basic principles of Technical Assistance could reasonably be expected from them, and if there had been any, they would have been ignored.

The new director-general, Franz Heske, was highly satisfied with the exceptional status accorded to him in this novel environment – but saw only the honour itself and not the true implication, intended by Haile Sellassie, of making him an insider as Ilg had been in his time. There was no substantial German grant of Technical Assistance accompanying the project. Even if the unusual new Ethiopian official had become sufficiently enthused to encourage the government of his home-country to engage in a large-scale reforestation project in Ethiopia, West Germany's potential was not yet sufficient in 1957 for a decision to devote the necessary resources to an oversized project to be possible politically, since this would have meant withdrawing assistance from numerous other countries for which various amounts had been allocated, and re-allocating it to a single one.

The result was costly to the Ethiopian government, which could have obtained the same services at a much lower cost if it had continued to employ foreign experts in the normal way, as before. Eight years had now passed since the warnings from British experts around 1950 – how much time now remained to Haile Sellassie to take effective remedial action? Even if a large reforestation programme could have been started right away, it was already too late to have any major impact on the impending drought, but at least the population would have had some protection in the areas where the programme was implemented. To avoid a whole maze of disagreements with the Ministry of Finance, which would have hampered him in his professional work, the director-general declined the financial responsibility for his department. Instead he delegated it to an Ethiopian official, unaware of the special power (beyond anything known in European administrative practice) possessed by the keeper of the purse in any Ethiopian institution.

The German team carried out its duties conscientiously, within the budget provided by the state for the Department. In the eyes of the Emperor, this was a patchwork once again. The scientific report of the team leader, later published in extended form in Germany, was a solid and reliable piece of work that would have been useful for any successor who might be appointed to take the patchwork a stage further. The Germans had established tree nurseries and started some minor reforestation ventures, and according to the report, the recession of forests in Ethiopia could be stopped within fifty years, and subsequently reversed, if reforestation could be continued on a regular basis throughout the years ahead by allocating an additional 5 million Ethiopian dollars to the Department every year. But progress at that rate could not keep pace with the growth of the population – or with the Emperor's expectations. Haile Sellassie was disappointed, and when the German contracts expired at the end of three years, they were not renewed.

VII. ANIMALS AND PEOPLE

Haile Sellassie had a natural gift for handling animals, and early in his reign he used to go in the morning and feed the tame lions which roamed freely in his park. In later years he seemed to enjoy the friendly tameness of his two cheetahs, which followed him about and playfully leaped and rolled in his path. He found relaxation with dogs: his very small favourite one was often taken on drives and tours of inspection, and even accompanied the Emperor on more solemn official occasions. He also had a way with his horses, which neighed in recognition when he entered the stables. Not all those who gave the Emperor animals as presents were well advised; for example, a pack of greyhounds was given by the Australian government but somehow it could not be integrated, and the sport of dog-racing was never introduced. The beautiful animals ended up in the compound of the Pasteur Institute, shut up in cages and used for the production of anti-rabies serum, rabies being one of the scourges of Ethiopia.

The Emperor disliked hunting, and refused to take part in hunts himself. However, for economic reasons it was tolerated as a sport for tourists. During his reign, he issued a number of orders and decrees aimed at preventing senseless cruelties to domestic animals. The international movement for the creation of game reserves evoked his sincere interest and support. National parks were established, and laws were enacted for the protection of wildlife and natural resources. Haile Sellassie regarded the protection of the country's rich fauna and flora, very definitely, as part of his imperial task, along with economic development; it would preserve raw materials and at the same time encourage the tourist industry.

His attitude towards animals was unsentimental, defined not so much by emotion as by his search for the reality of life. Superficial appearances are deceptive – what lies beneath them? With animals he was able to relax; they could never deceive him, whereas a human being was always an enigma. Haile Sellassie constantly experimented in his relations with people; he would never take someone else's judgement of a person on trust, and did not even trust his own first impressions. His unaffected philosophical scepticism was often misinterpreted as a kind of pathological suspicion and distrust. Haile Sellassie raised a question-mark over anything he had not seen for himself or what he had not followed through in his own mind. This attitude was impersonal, and not directed against any individual.

During the rare hours he allowed himself at weekends for relaxation at a palace out in the countryside, he liked to occupy himself in observing his people. He would stand by a pinnacle on the roof and look through a telescope at unsuspecting groups down in the busy marketplace, or at passers-by in the road leading to the palace. Or he might retire to his mysterious small library of medieval Latin authors. Nothing that he did was ever without its particular purpose, and did not cost him effort. He seemed to be always restlessly exploring something new.

So does one have to regard Haile Sellassie as a voyeur and an eavesdropper? He had many telescopes and thousands of pairs of eyes incessantly watching out for him, and many ears pressed against walls. On his strolls through the park in the early morning before sunrise, he would be accompanied by officials of his secret services, who then gave him verbal reports summarising their latest findings. There were two such services, which worked and reported to him independently of each other. In addition there was a secret branch of the military, which did not report directly to the Emperor. This was a close-knit network of secret supervision, which functioned with remarkable efficiency.

This instrument was the personal creation of the Emperor, and it was among the stranger features of his reign. Its history has some dark pages. He has been accused of letting his informers spy not only on all the foreigners in the country but even on members of his own government, officials in the administration, and advisers. People's personal lives and the privacy of their correspondence were not spared – there were to be no exceptions. In contrast to much of what has been alleged in books and the world press concerning Haile Sellassie, the degree of control exerted by the secret services has generally not been exaggerated. The work of the supervisory agencies was simply part of everyday life in Ethiopia. Where foreigners were concerned, everything was considered of interest, and sometimes the most insignificant details were recorded: an individual's working habits, how efficiently he did his job, his conduct during working hours and off duty, social contacts, spare-time occupations, living standards, financial position, political views and general approach to life. What people said, whether on serious topics or casually, was faithfully collected and written down. And in addition to the official file kept by the administration on any foreigner working in Ethiopia, a second secret file was kept for use by the supervisory agencies, sometimes augmented by an album of snapshots taken of the unsuspecting subject. The second file was intended to present a comprehensive image of the person based on what had been observed by *Ethiopian* eyes. Material that gave a bad impression of a person's moral character was collected separately, and would not be used against that person provided he remained useful to the country and well-liked. But it could occasionally be used as a pretext if the government wanted to terminate someone's services, or for other reasons. Whenever the Emperor had to make a decision concerning the future of a foreign resident, the unofficial file had to be submitted to him. As a rule, information gathered secretly to serve the analysis was not used in its immediate context against the person concerned.

The existence of agencies that supervised the activities of foreigners in Ethiopia was often noted, but little is known of the service that existed in the Ethiopian administration itself, both in Addis Ababa and in the provinces. Its most important task was to monitor the use of government funds. Some cases of fraud and embezzlement were made public, and were duly cited abroad as typical examples of Ethiopian corruption, but almost every case of abuse of public funds was unearthed by the secret service and settled and atoned for in camera, usually out of court. Some civil servants had to work for years while their salaries were held back until the misappropriated amount had been earned. Some of those found guilty chose suicide instead – the actual means of the death were always concealed and passed off as a stroke or an accident. Death was accepted as a final and complete settlement of account, cancelling the debt and leaving the miscreant's name untarnished. No claim would be pressed against his family or heirs.

When the Emperor was angry, he was in the habit of lowering his voice. His face would remain expressionless, but when he spoke in a low voice, everyone was afraid. He not only destroyed careers; he could also destroy the people themselves and in a very small number of instances this is what he actually did. Challenges were occasionally presented to him, which he could not ignore.

If someone who had formerly been his confidant or with whom he had associated personally in any way turned against him and abused the inside knowledge so acquired to discredit him in the eyes of his people, that person might suddenly die or disappear without trace. Only a clear breach of trust would call down such severe penalties; he simply ignored the kind of slander which is the usual currency of political propaganda. Another point on which he would not tolerate any challenge was his position as head of the imperial clan. When a student leader, after becoming a member of the clan by marriage, overheard the warning and continued to organise and lead demonstrations against the Emperor, he was shot in the street by a security officer in full view of his fellow-students. Although Haile Sellassie had placed his own person under the law in the system he had himself introduced, he reverted in this case, where the essence of Ethiopian tradition was involved, to the ancient Law of Kings.

Ethiopia was an exceptionally backward country, as many scientists had found out, and as the statistics undeniably proved. In all the African countries which had been under foreign administration for eighty or a hundred years longer than Ethiopia, there had been more progress, according to such criteria as *per capita* income, gross national product and literacy (meaning the ability to read and write in a foreign language). They also had more schools, more students and teachers, and more roads – there was rather more of everything than in poor Ethiopia. The people had more money in their pockets, and knew more of foreign technology. This was claimed to be the fault of the archaic Ethiopian system, and Haile Sellassie came under attack for his failure to end the scandal.

International conferences on Ethiopia were held in Rome, Tel Aviv, Nice, Manchester, Lund and Chicago, as well as in Addis Ababa, and scholars from universities around the world travelled great distances to attend them. Ethiopian studies were 'in': many universities now had chairs and sections, and their courses attracted numerous students. Exhibitions of Ethiopian art and culture were put on in many countries, and collections of Ethiopian treasures were made in museums and libraries. Tourists flocked to Ethiopia's sacred places – Aksum, Gondar, Lalibela. Reporters extolled the country's merits in their papers, books were published, films were made, the cameras never stopped clicking; new hotels had to be built. There they were – the dignified old priests, learned in their country's literature, reading and writing the Ethiopian script, often surrounded by their pupils, who might be children but could also be groups of older men under instruction. Was this not the living past – something that had been done in the same way for centuries? Those who did not have the good fortune to come to Ethiopia could see it all in the week-end reviews in their homes in San Francisco, Sydney, Tokyo or Reykjavik. Was it not marvellous, colourful, unique? It was all those things, although it was not yet gentrified or included in statistics comparing Ethiopia with other sub-Saharan countries.

VIII. GENERATION GAP

In his time, Ras Tafari himself had been a representative of the protesting young generation in his intention to change Ethiopia, reeducate the people, abolish the feudal order, reform the state and modernise generally. In the later years of his reign, he took a relaxed attitude towards the endless series of revolts and student demonstrations against him: he used to say that he had once been young himself. He knew that there was still a lingering resistance to his reforming policy among some older representatives of the feudal caste. But the Italians had relieved him of many tasks that he might otherwise have had to face by destroying old structures which he then simply did not reinstate.

But he still did not command that one instrument which he wanted to help him to turn his dreams into reality: the younger generation of Ethiopians. If they, being able to understand the spirit of the age, would only share his enthusiasm for modernisation and follow him, he could then pass on the torch to them. An Ethiopian army of young administrators, judges, teachers, agriculturalists, foresters, engineers and technicians should go into every part of the country and help bring about its gradual tranformation into a modern state, capable of joining the world community of modern states. As the Emperor saw it, he himself, through his life and work, could serve as an example to the young generation, and right up till the time of his death, he never ceased to hope that they would finally receive and digest his message.

The imperial treasury – the exchequer of the Emperor himself – provided the 'black' money of the Ethiopian state, amounting to a second budget, parallel to the official one. In the early years after the liberation, it was applied to education. Scholarships and other educational facilities granted to Ethiopia were still scarce, and the Emperor personally selected those who were to attend schools, universities and military academies abroad. Because of the change from feudal rule to administration through a civil service, many a landlord of the former ruling class had suffered losses of property and power. As a matter of course, some kind of compensation had to be given to them, and thus their children were the first to be selected for education abroad. As for the schools and colleges within the country, applications for admission were well in excess of the places available, and so the Emperor saw to it that a mixing of pupils and students was achieved, that children from Tigre, Galla, Gurage and other peoples were admitted, and also that those from the middle and lower levels of society were adequately represented. After the first graduates had passed their exams, the mix also became increasingly noticeable among those sent for schooling or further training in other countries. The network of schools, colleges and training facilities within the country expanded continuously throughout the Emperor's reign. It is notable also that a growing number of Eritreans were now admitted to schools in Addis Ababa and subsequently to public office. Eritreans had been made more familiar than Ethiopians with foreign ways of living and teaching because of their comparatively long experience of colonial rule and the activities of missionaries in their country. Their children thus had a slight advantage which showed in their performance at school.

Most of the Emperor's arbitrary decisions and orders could not have been financed within the tight budgets of ministries and government agencies, and therefore a certain margin of financial freedom was needed to support the personal style of his reign. Although he derived a considerable income from his landed property and from investments in numerous business ventures in the country, this was not hoarded abroad but used by the imperial treasury for current expenditure. Where the line was drawn between private and public funds was decided by the Emperor himself, according to his needs and plans. His private deposits in foreign banks were always on a modest scale. On the eve of the revolution, determined to face it out instead of either resisting it or going into exile, he transferred his accounts to his heirs.

When Haile Sellassie returned from exile, after the Italians had been forced to abandon the country, education was given priority over all other areas of internal development. No minister of education was appointed in the first years; Haile Sellassie assumed the task himself, and it was he who laid down the guidelines for the emerging school system and who set the curricula in motion. In this he used British advisers, one of whom warned the Emperor against adopting the methods and programmes of contemporary English and American schools. Such a course, he advised, would breed a revolution; he recommended instead a return to the curricula that had been used before the two world wars. This man immediately fell into disgrace and had to leave the country with his contract uncompleted. The Emperor had already seen this challenge, and was not prepared on any account to side-step the controversy with the progressive Ethiopian youth, since he felt confident of his ability to convince them of the rightness of his own views.

He frequently went on tours of inspection of the country's schools.

He asked for searches to be made among boys in the lower grades for the best achievers in school-work and those who showed exceptional natural talent in other ways. The Emperor had these pupils presented to him when he visited their schools, and if his impressions were favourable, they would be given further help through secondary school, the University College in Addis Ababa or the military academy at Harar. Some were later selected for further studies abroad, and on their return they quickly rose within the administration, the army or the imperial bodyguard.* In this way, some Ethiopians had already started 'dream careers' when they were at their elementary schools.

An example was Lieutenant-Colonel Workineh Gebeyehu, who for a short time was the most powerful man in Ethiopia after the Emperor. As a boy possessed of spectacular ability, he had been hand-picked by Haile Sellassie during an inspection trip to Gondar. He then finished school early, and after becoming one of the youngest officers ever commissioned at the Harar military academy, was sent during the Korean war of 1950–3 to serve in a responsible capacity in the Ethiopian contingent fighting with the United Nations forces. Having passed this important test, Workineh was appointed chief of internal security in the Ministry of the Interior, chief of the secret services, and vice-chief of staff of the imperial private cabinet. In each of these posts he was officially the second man, but in fact he wielded greater power than his superiors. He had unrestricted access to, and enjoyed the unrestricted confidence, of his master, who revealed to him all his ideas and plans for the future. The day was not long enough for the Emperor's schedule, which always continued well into the night, and in order to be available whenever his presence was required, Workineh was commanded to occupy an apartment in the palace. Their long nocturnal talks became more frequent. Never before or afterwards was Haile Sellassie ever known to share his thoughts with another human being – it seems that Workineh Gebeyehu alone was privileged in this way. Unobserved by the host of diplomats and other foreign residents in Addis Ababa, Workineh had achieved something which previously had been almost unthinkable: while not the chief functionary but merely a head of department in the Ministry of the Interior, he had by-passed the most powerful man in Ethiopia next to the Emperor himself – Ato Makonnen Habtewold.

Makonnen Habtewold – his brother Aklilu served for a long time as

---

*This élite unit consisted of the country's best-trained and best-equipped soldiers, and came under an independent command.

minister of foreign affairs and was the last prime minister of the imperial Ethiopian government – had emerged from the middle class, which was then still sparsely represented in government. Starting his career as a scribe, he had already risen to rank of minister of economics and business before the Italian invasion. The Habtewold brothers (there was also a third, Akalework) owed their careers entirely to the favour of Haile Sellassie, who thought that through them he would gradually replace the nobles who held public office, and introduce a new type of civil servant on the Prussian model. It was his deliberate intention not to grant a rank to any of the three, and indeed they were men of unquestioned integrity, loyalty and devotion. They all shared Haile Sellassie's five years of exile in England.

Makonnen Habtewold was minister of commerce and industry (for a short time immediately after liberation this was called 'commerce, industry and agriculture') and later of finance. At the same time, he controlled the Department of Information within the Ministry of the Interior, and later became Minister of the Interior. People became used to regarding him as the Emperor's right-hand man. Being in charge of information, he went to even greater lengths than the Emperor himself in imposing a rigorous control of the press, and it was he who introduced the practice of censoring foreigners' mail. Students saw him as a reactionary: nevertheless he tried, albeit in vain, to bridge the gap between his more conservative ideals and those of the Ethiopian progressive youth by heading some of their newly-formed associations. Makonnen Habtewold was a hard worker. He was also tight-fisted: as minister of finance, he ordered officials to live within their means, and indeed he lived frugally himself. He saw to it that salaries in the administration were kept low; right to the end, imperial Ethiopia remained a country where civil servants were modestly paid, and even the highest ranking ministers received lower salaries than foreign experts sent by the United Nations agencies or by their governments.

Whispering started as soon as it became known and confirmed that Workineh Gebeyehu was able to ignore and overrule ministerial decisions. The man in the street took notice. Such freedom could only be given by the Emperor's own hand: what did it mean? Workineh's private home looked more like an embassy than an ordinary residence, and he drove expensive cars: where did the money come from? Because he had a second office at the palace in addition to that in his ministry, it was rightly assumed that the Emperor found it necessary to confer with him at night! Soon it was rumoured that Jan Hoy – His Majesty –

intended to give the young officer one of his granddaughters in marriage in order to bring him within the imperial family. According to rumour even the size of the princess's dowry was known: it would be a million Ethiopian dollars! There could be no doubt that Jan Hoy had selected a dream successor, and by degrees was preparing the young man to take over the crown as his successor.

What the Emperor's actual intentions were regarding Workineh Gebeyehu has never been revealed. The line of succession to the throne was established by law, yet he could have toyed with the idea of pulling the rug away from under the feet of the would-be revolutionaries by offering the country an Emperor from the people, selected because of his talent and prepared for the throne in the fullest possible way. Such an Emperor would be popular and strong enough to hold the empire together until the people had become mature enough to live under parliamentary rule. Even then, a strong central government would be necessary to ensure Ethiopia's survival.

Workineh Gebeyehu clearly understood the meaning of the signals being conveyed to him, and his reaction was that on no account would he become Emperor of Ethiopia. From a peasant's hut to the throne? Such fairy tales were a thing of the past. Those who wield power had to enjoy the world's approval – but an Emperor in the modern climate of opinion aroused the world's disgust, and the whole world would be against him. At the very best it would pretend to tolerate him and laugh behind his back. This was not something Workineh could tolerate.

IX. THE COUP

Workineh Gebeyehu was the initiator, mastermind and leader of the palace revolt of 1960. All the other figures who seemingly emerged as leaders were mere instruments carrying out roles assigned to them. It was Workineh's deliberate purpose to appear as an incidental participant who was merely joining in the action of his friends; this would serve his purpose after the coup when he emerged as the country's uncontested revolutionary leader. He knew the revolutionary potential of the Ethiopian intelligentsia, and he also knew the liberal leanings of some members of the imperial family; from all these he could select the best brains. The Neway brothers were especially close friends of his. Mengistu Neway, commander of the imperial bodyguard, had been his tutor at the military academy in Harar, and Girmame Neway had particular intellectual and literary gifts which fitted him to serve as the theoretician of the revolutionary government. His political allies were two older generals: Mulugeta Bulli, minister of community development (a ministry newly created by Haile Sellassie) and at the same time chief of the Emperor's private cabinet with Workineh himself as his deputy, and Tsigue Dibou, head of the police, whose effective power had been greatly increased with the help of Western technical aid. He assessed that the Western powers would become more interested in the country once it had changed its social order – which might have proved correct had it not fallen so completely within the Soviet Union's sphere of influence.

Workineh enjoyed excellent relations with the Soviet embassy, and was a frequent guest there. Having received part of his military training at the Frunze Academy in Russia, according to the Emperor's plan, he had an insight into the working of the Soviet security services. He knew what revolutionary cells there were in the army and in government institutions and agencies, and was confident that the students at Haile Sellassie I University (till 1960 the University College) in Addis Ababa and all the other colleges and secondary schools would come out on his side. As the Emperor's closest confidant he saw the picture in its totality – all the strings came together in his hands. During the period of preparation, the lives of all the conspirators were at his mercy. Nobody could harm him, because if there were any dispute, there could be no question as to whom the Emperor would trust: the others would die.

According to popular rumour, the Emperor wavered for a time over which of the two favourites he would prepare for the throne. Mengistu Neway was more mature and a stronger character than Workineh, but he had the handicap of being descended from the feudal class. It would not be out of the ordinary for a nobleman to ascend the throne, outside the usual order; there were several well-known precedents. But then the intended message to the rebellious students – that talent and performance were all-important, and that every Ethiopian 'carried the crown in his napsack' – would not come into play. The fact that Workineh came from a poor family had tipped the scale in his favour.

The coup failed because of the arbitrary interference of Mengistu Neway, who did not follow the instructions given him by Workineh but acted prematurely. Possibly it was not a mistake but a deliberate ploy by the Neway brothers to downgrade the initiator of the plot. According to Workineh's instructions, the town's telecommunications network was to be disconnected as the top priority, followed immediately by the arrest of the ministers, the chief of staff of the armed forces (a son-in-law of the Emperor) and the other military leaders. Mengistu Neway, aware of the dissatisfaction of the rank-and-file soldiers and the revolutionary activists among them, was confident that the army would side with him or at least that it would split apart, and the minority who still supported the crown would be won over. Workineh, schooled by his frequent talks with the realist Haile Sellassie, knew that in the army, as everywhere else in Ethiopia, leadership was of crucial importance. If he held the army's leaders, he would hold the army itself – otherwise, the success of the coup would be threatened. But the interruption of phone communication happened about half an hour too late – which gave the military enough time to receive information that some extraordinary and alarming events were taking place at the imperial palace. With astonishing speed, and while it was still dark, the officers reached their posts and were with their troops, and loyalists were in the various headquarters, at the war ministry and in the garrisons. Possibly they had received some warning from the military security service, which was not under Workineh's control.

At this time, the Emperor had yielded – reluctantly – to the urgings of Workineh Gebeyehu to go on a state visit to Brazil. As far as the political reasons for accepting Brazil's invitation were concerned, he had no confidence in the theory that a bloc of non-aligned nations could ever act as a counterweight to the might of the superpowers – and had said so on appropriate occasions. Even less did he think of Brazil, though allegedly a rich country, as a potential source of Technical Assistance. He never undertook journeys that did not serve a clear purpose.

However, since returning from his war-time exile, Haile Sellassie had envisioned a plan to found a new city on the shores of Lake Tana, in the north of the country, and then transfer the government and thus the capital to it from Addis Ababa. The climate was more favourable, there were plentiful sources of hydro-electric power and a rich variety of mineral deposits and other raw materials available in the area, and furthermore the lake itself provided a cheap means of transport. In times of drought, famine or war, Lake Tana's abundance of fish and animal life could replace other sources of food for a large urban population. The Emperor may even have been influenced too by Empress Taitu's old plan to move the capital to a place (Gondar, as in medieval times) that was better protected than the site of Addis Ababa before the Southern territories were incorporated in the empire, and nearer to the heart of Ethiopia's ancient culture and the sacred sites of the Orthodox Church. British firms had devised plans, built a model and submitted cost estimates. Construction had already begun, and parts of the new city, Bahr Dar, had actually taken shape, housing some important institutions such a large technical college jointly sponsored by the Soviet Union. The project of establishing the central government there aroused mixed reactions among the country's foreign advisers, and in any case was ruled out during the Emperor's lifetime due to its prohibitive cost. The city needed time to grow into the surrounding lands and adapt itself to the existing infrastructure: roads, a railway and full telecommunication links needed to be established first.

Of all the countries in the world, Brazil alone seemed to have achieved the seemingly impossible feat of planting a modern capital in the wilderness, straight from the drawing-board. The Emperor's cherished plan had been the subject of controversy for years, but he finally decided – in spite of his belief that this was not the opportune moment – to go and inform himself on the spot how the Brazilian experiment had worked out – how it was financed and how the new capital actually functioned and the people lived. This was his fundamental reason for the visit, but he also added some political items to his agenda. No public announcement of his destination was made till after his departure, and most people in Addis Ababa were under the impression that it was not Brazil but Brazzaville, capital of the Congo. By skillful persuasion, Workineh had prevailed on the hesitant Emperor to go to a distant country on a visit from which no immediate return was to be expected. The moment for action had arrived.

On 13 December 1960, ministers and dignitaries of the imperial government were summoned to the palace at an unusual hour, close to midnight, on the pretext that the Empress was critically ill. Then, at midnight, they were arrested, and even those whom the conspirators had counted on as allies were taken into custody as a precaution until they committed themselves irrevocably to the coup. Then, only hours after their arrest, they were presented as members of the new government. Three hours before his own arrest, the Crown Prince, acting as Emperor in his father's absence, met his distant cousin Ras Aserate Kassa, away from their homes or offices on an abandoned building site in Addis Ababa (a foreigner saw them there, walking to and fro for a long time, engaged in earnest conversation). Some officials had not been called to the palace, and worked in their offices throughout the next day as usual.

Ras Aserate Kassa remained at liberty, acting as a negotiator between the two camps. Foreign powers were inevitably interested in developments, and the United States ambassador in particular offered his services as a mediator. The Emperor's staunchest supporters, who were incapable of changing sides, were held captive in the so-called 'Green Saloon' at the palace, where they were killed two days later (see below, page 79–80).

But not everything had gone according to plan. The general staff had not been arrested owing to the delay in disconnecting their telephones; short though the delay was, it gave the army time to prepare. When Workineh himself entered the stage, the psychological moment had already passed. Shying away from immediate involvement in a street battle, he tried by negotiation to persuade the army to surrender to the new government. However, the army conceded only a limited truce for negotiations.

By the following day, the imperial bodyguard was covering all offices and banks, major squares and other busy traffic intersections, and of course the railway station and the airport. Police units were posted in the city's outskirts at checkpoints erected on the ring-roads. Tanks and armoured cars patrolled the streets. Yet, in other respects life appeared to be going on as normal. Offices and shops were open, and people were going about their daily business. At noon, news of what had happened was broadcast to Ethiopia and the world. The composition of the new government and its programme were announced. The Emperor had been banished, but the Crown Prince was still nominally head of state, acting as figurehead for the new regime.

Paralysis and stupefaction, bred of disbelief, struck the people of Addis Ababa. Had those special favourites of the Emperor, whom he had showered with honours and every advantage, really overthrown Jan Hoy, declaring him a public enemy and condemning him to exile? Had the imperial bodyguard, the police and the security services – those men to whom Jan Hoy had particularly entrusted the protection of his person and the crown, and whose essential duty was to watch out for all revolutionary machinations – revolted and deposed their master in his absence?

The Crown Prince, deputising for his father as the repository of imperial power, read a proclamation conferring legitimacy on the new government. He announced that he himself was a salaried employee of this government, and he promised that it would make reparation for all the evils and injustices the people had suffered in the past three thousand years. He spoke of the tractors that would be used to plough the state-owned lands in the future – did this mean that property rights would be abolished? Had the Crown Prince, as head of state *pro tempore*, ordered the arrest of his father's most faithful and respected ministers? Other revelations contained in the proclamation were equally baffling. Ras Imru was stated to be prime minister – as the Emperor's cousin he had belonged to the retinue which had regularly travelled with Haile Sellassie on his foreign journeys. He had served a term as ambassador to India, and had recently been appointed ambassador in Moscow, but he had not yet set out for this new assignment and so was still in town. General Mulugeta Bulli, the new commander of the armed forces, was one of the progressive officers whom the Emperor had especially favoured; he had served as head of the military academy, as minister of community development, and as a member in the private cabinet of selected ministers. Furthermore, as a member of the previous government he had been given the chance to put his ideas into practice on his own initiative. The Crown Prince had announced that General Merid Manguesha, hitherto commander of the armed forces, and General Kebede Gebre, commander of the territorial army, were both discharged from their posts and demoted – but as everyone knew, the two men were still at liberty; they had not been dismissed and were still carrying out their duties. The territorials were the reserve of the armed forces; they formed an overwhelming majority in numbers, but were poorly trained and equipped. In war, they were as devastating as a plague of locusts, and in addition they were known and feared for their bravery in action. If they had been called in to crush the revolt – which proved unnecessary since the standing army were able to manage above – the urban people would have faced a terrible situation. Much argument was now going on in the huts all over Addis Ababa. The young people – students at the University and in the colleges and schools – were taken by surprise. Easily aroused, they flocked into the streets and, full of enthusiasm, marched along as spearheads of the revolution, carrying posters and banners, and singing songs to which they had composed revolutionary lyrics themselves.

Tension was building up. Ordinary daily life continued normally into the second day, but many shops now decided to close, and fewer cars were seen in the streets. Army units had taken up their positions: the truce was coming to an end. Exactly at three o'clock on Thursday afternoon, all hell broke loose. Shooting began simultaneously in all parts of the town. Beggars sitting in the main streets were killed in the crossfire. Foreigners on their way to work hastily turned their cars around and then, seeing their way home also blocked by fighting, fled for the nearest shelter. Some received gunshot wounds. Close to the war ministry, some mortar-shells exploded in the street and killed passers-by. Stray shells smashed into hovels, killing their occupants. The United States Information Service (USIS) building had better luck; a direct hit damaged the frontage, but did not penetrate the solid concrete walls. The firing continued without a break for two days and nights. The two sides tacitly agreed to spare the residential areas lived in by foreigners, only a few of whom were accidentally killed. However, several were wounded when stray shots pierced the clay-brick walls of their houses.

It soon became clear that the rebels were in a hopeless situation. Elite they may have been, but they were no match for the superior strength of the army. Reinforcements from other garrisons were flown in, and one captured position after another, including the airport, was re-taken. Air force planes showered leaflets over the city, containing proclamations staunchly supporting the crown issued by the army high command and the Metropolitan of the Ethiopian Orthodox Church. By Friday afternoon, the outcome was decided. The army's tanks stormed the palace, where the rebels were holding loyal ministers captive in the 'Green Saloon', and the Crown Prince, along with his prime minister Ras Imru was residing on the first floor. General Tsigue Dibou, the chief of police, was killed in the action. Workineh Gebeyehu, the rebel leader, had already escaped, and was soon to be followed by the Neway brothers who made sure, as they fled, that the captive ministers could not be rescued and were killed by firing with automatic weapons.

It was not a part of Workineh's plan to have the captive dignitaries killed. They should only be prevented from interfering in the events of the coup, and kept as hostages during the negotiations with the parts of the armed forces still faithful to the imperial government, in case a split appeared in the army after the arrest of its leaders. Due to the initial failure to arrest the military leaders, there was not a split in the army, and the attitude of its leaders was adamant during the negotiations, which continued till noon on the second day and in which even the American ambassador tried to play an intermediary role before they broke down without result. For the captives to be used effectively as hostages, it was essential that they should not be rescued by force. Only in case this were tried did the guards have orders to kill them rather than let them go.

When the attack on the palace started, Mengistu Neway tried to halt it by announcing through loudspeakers that the prisoners would all die if new negotiations were not resumed for their sake. This was a grave mistake, committed in the heat of events: being familiar with the rules of conduct in his society, he should have known in advance that there was no possibility of anybody heeding his threat or offer. Now he was obliged to kill his colleagues rather than suffer dishonour himself. Apparently, the Neway brothers became aware of this obligation after having already retreated before the firing from the palace, and they now returned to the attack. There were guards on duty there who had remained faithful to their commanders, but because none of the prisoners had any intention of leaving – they stood quietly in the Green Saloon waiting on events to come – there seemed to the guards no point in shooting at them. Thus to force them to obey their last-minute orders and open fire, Mengistu personally had to start shooting on his own: the waiting group was riddled by the bullets from all the automatic rifles. No time was left to identify the dead; because the army would arrive within a few minutes, everyone had to disappear from the scene, using a back door of the palace. A pre-arranged route for their escape was necessary because the palace grounds were extensive, and the stone walls surrounding it, and the exits through them, were not yet controlled on the outside throughout the full length of their perimeter – some 2 kilometres. This was still so, even when the army's tanks were breaking through the front gate.

Two of those attacked with concentrated gunfire in the Green Saloon survived by throwing themselves to the ground and pretending to be dead; they were then buried under the dead bodies of the others. It is not known what happened to General Mulugeta Bulli. The Crown Prince had proclaimed him as a member of the new government, but his name later appeared among the victims in the Green Saloon. His body was found outside the palace, but whether he was killed in the affray or killed himself remains a mystery.

In his flight, Workineh Gebeyehu tried to hide out in the very extensive compound of the Soviet embassy, which contains a wood, but this refuge had to be denied him. There was no way that he could escape from the capital, and eventually his pursuers hunted him down and stopped him on a hill-side in the outskirts. 'He went on shooting to the end, and saved the last shot for himself' – on this point all reports were agreed. Shortly before his death, friends tried to persuade him to surrender – the Emperor would surely pardon him even if he refused to pardon anybody else – but he answered sadly that he would never see the Emperor again. Then, with his last words, he referred to Theodoros, the Emperor who had taken his own life in preference to being taken prisoner after his defeat, when the mountain fortress of Magdala was surrounded by the British expeditionary force and there was no escape. This was the model he would follow. Others have said that he was eager to know whether the ministers had been executed, and whether Ato Makonnen Habtewold was definitely dead. Receiving an affirmative answer, he exclaimed: 'So we did not live in vain – Ethiopia will never again be the same!' The very same last words have been attributed to Mengistu Neway. In any case, the three leaders of the revolt were later to become legendary figures among the students as their revolt steadily gathered momentum.

Prince Sahle Sellassie, the Emperor's youngest and most gifted son, who had retired from public life and indulged in activities as various as writing film scripts and experimenting with radio, was urgently asked by his mother, Empress Menen, to send out a radio message about the coup in the hope that it would reach the Emperor. Although he had misgivings because of his sympathy with the revolution, he nevertheless relayed the message during the night immediately following the start of the revolt, and it was immediately picked up by another radio amateur in England, who in turn relayed it, as the message requested, to the Ethiopian embassy in London. Thus the Emperor received information that a revolt was under way before the revolutionary government had even broadcast its announcement of the coup from Addis Ababa –

which of course was also conveyed to him. Significantly, the name of Workineh Gebeyehu was not mentioned in the information the Emperor received.

Haile Sellassie immediately cancelled his programme in Brazil and flew home. But by the time the plane carrying him and his party had reached Fort Lamy (now Ndjamena) in Chad, one of its engines had broken down. It seemed there was nothing for it but to wait for a repair to be carried out on the plane – something which could take several days, but the Emperor would not even consider the possibility of a delay. He asked his retinue and the crew, 'Whose life is it you are trembling for, yours or mine?' Thus the same aircraft continued its journey over the vast stretches of the southern Sahara, in defiance of international air-traffic regulations, until it reached to Khartoum, where another Ethiopian Airlines plane was waiting. He used the break of less than an hour between flights to talk with the representatives of the Sudanese government who had come to welcome him at the airport. He arranged to have messages broadcast from Khartoum telling the world that there had been some minor irregularities in Ethiopia during his absence, but that all of them would soon be resolved. When he arrived in Asmara, he was received with the usual royal pomp. Life there had remained undisturbed by events in the capital.

During a council he held in Asmara with his ministers and governors, the Emperor told his dismayed audience that they had no reason to worry, since Workineh Gebeyehu had all the means necessary at his disposal to crush the revolt, and he had been given full authority to do so. The uneasy silence that followed was broken by Ras Mesfin Sileshi, a fuedal lord known for his courage, who told the Emperor that Workineh Gebeyehu was the ringleader of the revolt. The Emperor rose and quickly left the room. He appeared to keep his composure; but nobody dared to follow him.

On the evening of Friday 16 December, all the key positions in Addis Ababa – the headquarters of the bodyguard, the palaces, the ministries, the airport and the railway station – were in the army's hands. The battle was won, but still fighting went on throughout the night, as some minor strongholds of the bodyguard refused to surrender and were continuing to resist. Towards morning, the firing seemed to cease; it re-started on Saturday but at less frequent intervals. Some scattered and beleaguered outposts still held out; in others, the defenders surrendered to save their lives. All over the outskirts of the city, groups of people – the common people – banded themselves together and, using spears, sticks, stones and whatever came to hand, attacked and pursued the rebels who had brought so much carnage and misery into their peaceful lives. They were not capturing any of their victims: anyone they could lay hands on was killed outright with whatever means were to hand. Many of the inhabitants of Addis Ababa owned firearms: some of the bursts of gunfire that were heard during that afternoon were summary executions. Many young soldiers of the imperial bodyguard had fought till they were completely exhausted, some for two days with no sleep and almost no food, only to fall victim to this sudden eruption of rage from the citizens of Addis Ababa, whose city had been turned into a battlefield. Hundreds of civilians had died, in the crossfire and many more had been wounded; the countless flimsily built huts that were their homes had offered almost no protection.

Who were the guilty ones? Undoubtedly they were the members of the bodyguard, those special servants of the Emperor, favoured and exalted by him above all others, who had betrayed their trust and become agents of death and destruction almost as soon as their master had turned his back. Had not Jan Hoy called Mengistu Neway and Workineh Gebeyehu to him before his departure and handed them money with the words, 'I leave the country in your hands'?

Ethiopians believed strongly in the virtue of obedience and took pride in it. It was axiomatic that servants could be trusted. Through service, a man could rise in the hierarchy: for a slave it marked out the way to freedom, and to a warrior it brought honour and distinction. Dedjasmatch Baltcha had worked his way up by serving in Menelik's army to become a noble and a provincial governor, yet he had started life as the son of a slave. Most inhabitants of Addis Ababa still followed their customary ways, and what had happened was far more serious than the usual fights, uprisings and intrigues, in which certain basic rules were still observed. If the employees of all the banks had closed the doors and shared out all the money among themselves, no greater indignation could have been stirred up than was felt now. The split between the vast majority of the people and the educated minorities had been revealed, and the hurt was keenly felt.

Late on Saturday afternoon the gunfire abated, and by dusk it had ceased altogether. Now one could hear shouting and wailing from those who were mourning their dead. As the evening advanced, there came a sudden silence, and then from the direction of the airport, far away, a peculiar sound could be heard, faint at first, but resolving itself, as it became louder, into a mass of human voices. As it came nearer, the wave of sound rolled over the town. Everywhere, on all sides, came cries and shouts from the huts and houses. The men's voices united in a hollow roar, interspersed by women's high-pitched yodelling, the traditional Ethiopian sound of jubilation. People came out of their homes, the masters of wealthier households along with their servants. While those lining the route from the airport cheered the Emperor as he passed, he himself sat in the open car stony-faced. Some actually prostrated themselves on the ground, praying and thanking God as the motorcade, with its escort of armoured vehicles, sped past. Their minds were still dominated by religion, mixed with superstition, and attendance at church or mosque formed a regular part of their existence. They were not yet awake to the demands of the new age, and their sheer overwhelming number counted for nothing; others were speaking and acting in their name, and now bloodshed and horror were the result. However, Jan Hoy was back, and peace had returned to their huts and streets.

Haile Sellassie had been received at the airport by the Patriarch, the army commander, and ministers of his former government. The Crown Prince was there too, carrying a stone on his shoulder* – the traditional sign of submission in Ethiopia – and prostrating himself before his father. Haile Sellassie ordered him to stand, and dismissed the gesture of the stone. The Crown Prince, he was told, had acted under duress, with a gun in his ribs. But nobody could manipulate Haile Sellassie. According to a popular version, he replied: 'And you didn't know that your last hour had come? You have not learned how to die like an Emperor.' The relationship between the two men was still the same as before: there had been a gulf between them then, and there still was one now.

After the coup had ended in failure, there were investigations and punishments, but these were only pursued in the most unavoidable and pressing cases. Sons and grandsons of the Emperor and other members of the imperial clan, ministers, vice-ministers, governors, army officers, heads of government agencies and other officials, senior members of the University and those involved in the cultural life of the capital – all of them had been on friendly terms with Workineh Gebeyehu. Many of them could now be considered as conspirators before the coup or collaborators after it. At the very least they were sympathisers who, consciously or unconsciously, had helped Gebeyehu in his preparations. To

---

* The gesture is designed to appeal to the fairness of the victor. A rather heavy flat stone is generally used, supported by the bearer with one hand.

some extent they had been his partisans. Haile Sellassie knew this, and did not need or want to know more. The obvious involvement of a number of particular individuals, among them high-ranking officials, was deliberately overlooked. They continued in office as if nothing had happened.

The Neway brothers – and a few other members of the secret revolutionary committee, who were counted as the most guilty because of the high positions they had previously held as vice-ministers and heads of government agencies – succeeded in getting away from Addis Ababa, but none escaped altogether. The frontiers were too far away, all roads were guarded, and rewards were out for their capture. Everywhere ordinary people joined in the search. The would-be escapees hid during the day and moved at night. There were few people in the countryside whom they could trust, and they were thus unable to obtain food, water or mules in the villages. Therefore they could not travel far. One conspirator managed to reach the heavily-guarded border, but he was caught before he could cross it and later hanged. A week after their escape from Addis Ababa, the Neways were spotted by farmers, the population were alerted, and soon they were surrounded by police. They used their firearms to defend themselves, and continued firing up till the last moment, when Mengistu Neway shot his brother dead and then tried to kill himself: the shot blinded one of his eyes but was not fatal. He was taken to a hospital, made fit to stand trial, and then sentenced to death by the civil high court at Addis Ababa and hanged. The trial was scrupulously fair and correct: the atmosphere was impartial, every right to which he was entitled as a citizen by the legal codes of Ethiopia was accorded to him, and he was protected from assault by those intent on exacting vengeance for fellow-clansmen who had been among the victims. In court he pleaded with dignity, taking on himself as much responsibility as he could and exonerating other conspirators by saying that they had done no more than obey his orders, and that they had not been informed of his plans in advance. Because at the trial he did not reveal the part played by Workineh Gebeyehu, he gave every appearance of being the original leader of the coup. He died with composure wearing uniform but with his insignia of rank stripped off.

X. AFTERMATH OF THE COUP

In the centre of Addis Ababa is Menelik Square (in fact a circle), containing a bronze equestrian statue of Menelik the Great. At one side of the Square the hangman's tree formerly stood, and now the bodies of three men were hanging from newly-erected gibbets, two suicides and one who had died in the battle. They were displayed there to announce to the people that justice had taken its course. Their heads had been carefully groomed, with all traces of blood and dirt wiped away, and they had been dressed in clean clothes. The body of Workineh Gebeyehu was clad in an immaculate new uniform, again without insignia. The handsome young man, in his well-pressed trousers, swung gently in the wind like a puppet. A few days later a fourth body, that of Girmame Neway, was added. Every day for a week, the spectacle drew curious crowds, including foreigners and especially press reporters and photographers, who mostly made a point of being there at the times when Haile Sellassie passed on his regular visits to various parts of the town. Many watched in silence but there was also muttered conversation and whispering among the crowd. What had Jan Hoy imagined he was doing when he searched out the most talented boy in the country, gave him the best education possible, sent him abroad to England, France, the Soviet Union and Japan, and treated him like his favourite son? That new leader whom Jan Hoy had searched for so assiduously, representing all the best qualities the country could provide, the very essence of a modern man, was now hanging here before the crowds. The people waited patiently, though some grew agitated at times when it was expected Haile Sellassie would come and visit the spot. He did not come.

The breach of faith committed by Mengistu Neway, the third leader of the coup, had left in its wake about 2,000 people dead or wounded. Trusted ministers, forming the core of Haile Sellassie's government, were murdered – among them Ato Makonnen Habtewold, who had served him selflessly for more than a decade and always supported him faithfully. Mengistu Neway took part himself in the slaughter of those defenceless people whom he had lured into a trap with lies. Haile Sellassie had felt a justified pride in the establishment of a modern administration and legal codes, and had seen in this the fulfilment of a major part of his life's task which he had set himself. He had brought the country under the rule of law, and he would leave behind an inheritance that would benefit any successor-government, whatever its nature. Did this imply that leniency should be accorded to Mengistu? In the people's eyes, such a concession would have destroyed his life's work at a single blow and made him a laughing-stock. If existing laws were not obeyed now, none of the other modern laws could any longer be considered valid. The only way left to him was the way of duty.

Of the twenty-five members of the secret revolutionary committee, a further three were sentenced to death, while others received prison terms. Some minor officials were dismissed from the public service. The imperial bodyguard, betrayed by its leader, had borne the heaviest losses. More than 500 men were dead or wounded, and more than 300 still missing: they would either be dead or at large. A further 700 of the guard were being kept in detention for several weeks until all investigations had been concluded: here too, one officer was sentenced to death, a few more were condemned to terms in gaol, and others were stripped of their rank and dismissed. Yet most of those who had been involved in the action and who had survived got away unharmed. Students were summarily forgiven, without any punishments being imposed, and inquiries into what part they may have played in the days of the short-lived revolutionary government were dropped. All the Emperor wanted now was for the whole crisis to subside as quickly as possible and for life to return to normal; he wanted to limit the consequences of the revolt, shorten all procedures and avoid complications. This chapter in the history of his reign should be concluded and then forgotten.

The shock was indeed soon past. The Emperor's days were filled with the same duties as ever. He would rise in his usual way, well before dawn while his subjects were still asleep, and continue working till late at night, and the effort and fervour he put into it were greater than ever. The rising challenge had to be met. He did not repeat the mistakes he had made in the first half of his reign. He switched his priorities. No longer would he interfere with the work of the ministry of education or the university; foreign policy and agricultural and industrial development would now take first place.

The search for talent among the underprivileged in society, neglected tribes or the children of freed slaves was left to the safer and more conventional methods of the ministry of education. Let them conduct tests, count scores, compute results, quarrel over budgets and approach the foreign missions in Addis Ababa or universities abroad for scholarships and training facilities. He would no longer devote his time to these problems, and the available resources of the imperial treasury were earmarked instead for items falling under the responsibility of other ministries. They would not be used to support ordinary careers under the auspices of the two major educational institutions. He would be satisfied in future if he were merely informed of whatever the education ministry and University were planning or had actually carried out. However, if he was dissatisfied, he would still dismiss the ministers and senior officials involved. At graduation ceremonies he himself would act as the representative of the state: dressed up in the robes of his own honorary degrees, he would solemnly distribute scrolls and certificates.

So to this extent the revolt had achieved results: the Emperor was now delegating more of his power – a step that was long overdue because the burden of his daily tasks was overwhelming. His working days were never long enough, and he needed some respite. Other measures followed. The Emperor renounced his privilege of appointing the mayors of the hundreds of villages that had grown into small municipalities, and the administrators of all the countless small provincial sub-districts. In this respect, the powers of governors were increased, and in many places, mostly remote ones, social units continued with their former practice of having leaders who reflected the preferences of the population, or returned to that practice where it had been abandoned.

The Emperor also gave up some other tasks. In a significant step, he conferred the authority he had exercised over some minor institutions in the capital to the Crown Prince, who was thus entrusted with a ruling function at the centre for the first time. This, of course, was distinct from his personal fief, the governorship of Wollo, of which he had been the ruler ever since his father's coronation in 1930. The task of reforming Wollo was enormous, and indeed any innovations, let alone a programme of agricultural rehabilitation, were hardly possible in that half-eroded and deserted country without a massive budget. Still, the way in which the Crown Prince had quietly resigned himself to the situation, waiting for Wollo's intractable problems to be solved by the future democracy in which he was willing to play the role of constitutional monarch, had disappointed his father. The Emperor had intended that Wollo should be the test of his successor's ability to rule. Had he not himself, when no more than a boy, twice ruled over large provinces, and struggled with all his force to achieve results? But at that time Tafari had still commanded his own feudal army, and possessed a tangible dynastic power. He had also been much richer than the Crown Prince was now, and had learned very early the valuable art of encouraging foreign investment. The latter was now more freely available, but all of it was channelled to the Emperor – what potential investor would give a thought to Wollo? In the current situation, the task was an impossible one to fulfil – whatever means might be used. On the other hand, the challenge of the apparently impossible had always been a powerful dynamo for the Emperor, capable of re-charging his energy.

XI. DEVELOPMENT AND ASSISTANCE

In the far south of the country a hill had become overgrown with wild lush vegetation. A few old men sat in their huts, sadly remembering the time when it had been a bustling place, full of life. A great number of people had somehow been crowded into that small area, and all had made a living from the hill and the small surrounding plain. From the fertile and intensively cultivated soil, and in particular from the terraces built with great art into the side of the hill, an astonishing quantity of crops had been produced. Many animals were raised there too. But this had now been abandoned, the people had gone away, and the forest had taken over.

The plain surrounding the hill had been exactly divided into three concentric circles. Each circle had a different function: the outer one was common property, the inner one consisted of land that changed from one private owner to another, and the centre was permanent private property, and its ownership never changed. Anyone living on the hill spent a part of his life in each of the three areas, moving between them at times determined by intricate rules. But now some had emigrated in groups to neighbouring states, some were scattered in the south or west of Ethiopia, and yet others had gone north, to swell the numbers of the urban poor in Addis Ababa and other cities. This, said the old men, was done by Haile Sellassie. The men he had sent were devils who had driven the people of the district away.

Could the strange traditional structure of the people on the hill be integrated easily within a uniform system of administration and taxation? Were the government administrators to be blamed, bound as they were by the new laws and administrative rules which had been created for the sake of justice to all and promulgated by the Emperor with the intention of placing all citizens in the state on an equal footing? The Emperor was far away in the capital, but if he could have seen or known what was being done in this name – as a governor early in his career he had been in charge of one of the most ethnically diverse provinces in Ethiopia, and had thus seen much of that kind – might matters not have been different? But he was assisted by foreign advisers and experts – people from the United Nations, the FAO and other bodies – who had studied the people, and knew what they were doing. These experts coolly decided what had to be destroyed in order for their plans to be realised, but before it disappeared from the face of the earth, it had to be preserved by ethnologists, depending on its nature, in either museums or libraries for further research. There was a division into two clear categories, the ethnological and the sociological. The advisers, the practical people, were sociologists. The ethnologists had to mind their own business – they should not even attempt to interfere with development policy – yet in extensive regions bordering the deserts, nomadic tribes had lived since time immemorial in a strictly democratic order, without immoveable property of any kind. To have distributed the land in these regions would have condemned the inhabitants to starvation.

There were regions of Ethiopia covered by small private holdings, where a land reform would scarcely have been noticed, since what was now desired as a new order had been in existence there since before the Emperor's reign. But there were other regions where a land reform would have resulted in the collapse of the population's means of subsistence. In the countryside there was not just a single agricultural or social order, or a single system of land tenure; there were at least sixty such systems. To have enforced a uniform order from the centre without delay would have benefited a small part of the population, driven others out, and worsened the situation of the majority. In a country containing about fifty different ethnic groups, each speaking its own language, where so many religions were practised and such a rich variety of customary structures existed, it was unrealistic to think of rapid and radical change. The consequences of such changes would have been unforeseeable and uncontrollable. There were other questions too that would need to be solved before any action was taken. The task of measuring and registering the newly-distributed land was far beyond the financial resources of the state and the capacity of the available technical personnel. But of course, in addition to this, there were numerous other technical matters, and there were legal questions concerning titles of ownership. Who, according to the newly-introduced legal code, should be compensated when property was appropriated? Who were holders of land as fiefs that could be withdrawn (a form of land tenure which lasted up to the end of the Emperor's reign)? And how was the money to be found for those being compensated in a country where, before 1960, the state's total annual budget had never reached the equivalent of US$80 million?

On returning from his exile after the Italian occupation, Haile Sellassie had included land reform in his working programme. But he knew that he could not compensate the existing landholders who would be dispossessed, and that the resources to finance the other necessary expenses involved in such a reform were not available. He therefore took another course. By not fully restoring the rights of former owners to their heirs, and by not renewing temporary fiefs which had been abolished by the Italians, he kept a considerable amount of land in the possession of the crown and members of his family. By that means he would have a resource ready to hand as soon as the other preparations were concluded. Once he set the example, the feudal lords would follow, and they would be all the more willing to do so since by that time all their children were foreign-educated and many of them would already have taken over control of their family holdings.

Haile Sellassie had withdrawn the economic privileges of the landlords, as well as many of their former duties, in favour of his new administrative system. Levies which the farmers previously had to pay to the landlords over and above the taxes payable to the government were abolished. Limits to the farm-rent to be paid by tenants and sharecroppers had existed before, fixed by custom, but these were now more appropriately determined by law. This left the landlords with a regular but reduced income. They had also lost their traditional ruling functions within the local context: their military, judicial, protective and representative functions and privileges were transferred to officials and administrations of the central government specially trained for the task. A minority among the Ethiopian nobles were opposed to the Emperor's plans and distrusted the new order. Resentfully they stayed in their country strongholds. They saw him bringing about the destruction of Ethiopian ways and values, and would have no part in it. So they preferred to stay on, even with reduced material means and the gradual loss of their social functions, now to be transferred elsewhere.

Most nobles, however, were convinced that Ethiopia had to be modernised and that the new order would benefit the country as a whole. During the occupation, the Italians had taken many irreversible steps in this direction. They had created technological marvels – for example their network of all-weather roads, surpassing in their scope and size anything done in that respect before, or what could subsequently be done right up till the revolution. Most of the institutions of the imperial government functioned till the very end in buildings erected by Italians, and many of the private houses of foreigners and Ethiopians alike, as well as hotels, banks, factories and so on, owed their existence to the Italians. The few new office buildings that were built during the Emperor's post-war reign, such as the municipality of Addis Ababa and the new headquarters of Posts and Telegraphs, were all planned for the modern state of the distant future; they were mostly too big for their existing staffs. The economic prospects for landlords who stayed in the countryside were dim; most were better off working as state functionaries although salaries in Ethiopia were low. Even the most senior minister earned no more than the head teacher of a secondary school in a developed country. The modern-minded landlords had appointed some of their servants to act as managers in their absence and had flocked to Addis Ababa to be close to the Emperor, who alone could appoint officials above the middle rank, at least up till the end of the 1950s. In the 1960s, more power was delegated to ministers who could now promote people to be directors of ministerial departments, and minor townships could elect their own mayors. The highest functionaries of ministries and other government agencies, along with their deputies, were always appointed by the Emperor himself; he personally selected more than 1,000 of them throughout the empire. It seemed that he could not shed his sense of a ruler's obligation towards the aristocracy in a feudal society; yet at the same time he was able to pursue his plan to include modern trained bureaucrats and technocrats in the administration, including some who had risen from the lowest social levels, who were from peoples other than the Amhara or Tigre, and even those belonging to confessions and religions other than the Ethiopian Orthodox Church. The Emperor never ceased to pursue his aim, and the share of those people in administrative posts, including the highest ranks, was steadily increasing. At the end there was no government institution which did not have a Galla heading one of its subdivisions, with educated people from all social levels among the other staff. To comply with the need to place all the candidates waiting, modern as well as traditional, the Emperor needed a vast number of vacancies to achieve the best blend in the composition of the administration. As the inventor of the new order, he was responsible for it, and now had to prove to the doubting population that such a blend was even possible at all.

No doubt, the nobles were well fitted for high positions due to their cultural background and their experience of exercising command over people. As for natural talent, they were the best resource the country had to offer – at least, this was the view of the Emperor who as Lidj Tafari had been of their number and therefore knew that each one of them felt himself a potential emperor. Most could even prove their possession of the traditional legitimation: Solomonic blood, however diluted it might have become over the generations. This would be carefully hidden, being revealed only if a specific occasion arose. Solomonic genealogy – if traced through the female line, as happened with Haile Sellassie – is a hydra, the ramifications of which nobody has yet explored. There were probably hundreds of people in Ethiopia who could have claimed Solomonic descent in that way, some without a title and living as ordinary citizens.

Since Ethiopian society is impenetrable, possibly the nearest that an outsider can come to understanding what was going on in the minds of Ethiopians in the time of Haile Sellassie is by means of a simple illustration. The Ethiopian cake was sliced horizontally, with the same pattern being repeated on each layer. Percolating through layers, determining the cake's quality, was religion. Haile Sellassie had made a change by slicing the cake vertically, each segment consisting of a different subject: thus religion became such a subject in itself, merely a slice of the cake, having changed places with reason, which now spread over and covered and percolated everything. The Emperor had to find out into which specialised post any of his nobles would fit best by virtue of individual talent and qualities. He tried to do that by continuously moving all his higher officials around – making the same person successively a governor, a minister or an ambassador, and chasing his ministers through many posts, dismissing them and re-appointing them later elsewhere, or transferring them directly from one ministry to another. He continually kept track of the performance of the various institutions of government and studiously compared results. He exerted control by reading reports – both of Ethiopian officials and of foreign advisers seconded to ministries; by making personal inspections without warning; and through the agents of his secret services who had to find out whether any irregularities had been covered up at the lower departmental levels which might not otherwise be detected. Even his most trusted men had to pass through at least three posts on the same level – not counting the previous appointments which could be seen as steps on a ladder. To chose one example out of many, the career of Balambaras Mahteme Sellassie was typical. Serving as Minister of Agriculture in the early 1950s, Minister of Finance in the latter half of the decade, Minister of Education and Minister of Public Works in the 1960s. After being released from ministerial duties, he moved up to the Crown Council. Arrested after the revolution, he remained a prisoner through the 1970s and died in jail in the early 1980s.

The Emperor had a second reason for the frequent changes he made when using official posts as ability tests for individuals. No individual, however able, is equally strong in every respect: unavoidably, any weaknesses in the leader of an organisation would lead to corresponding weaknesses appearing at the lower administrative levels as well – at least, this was the common Ethiopian view. Because two men's weak points are not quite the same, frequent changes of personnel were needed to create equilibrium in an institution; for one man to be permanently in its charge could mean that his ministry would have a permanent defect in structure and working capacity. Haile Sellassie always had the two aspects – control of the individual and the working capacity of the institution – in his mind when making appointments.

To return to the case of the feudal lords, the Emperor estimated that because of the insufficient number of civil servants to serve the needs of this new field of activity, they could act as arbitrators in minor quarrels within the community, and mediators if there were differences with the outside world. They could also deal with planners and, with their superior technical knowledge and good connections at the centre, give guidance and protection to the emerging community of new landowners. The main problem would be how to find a way of persuading the feudal lords to leave Addis Ababa and return to the countryside: they had previously flocked to the capital, drawn by the prospect of careers in the Emperor's gift, as well as by the urban life-style, which seemed infinitely easier than the harsh conditions of their rugged homelands – a distant echo of the court of Louis XIV of France. It was now a long time since Haile Sellassie started the gradual process of replacing them in the ministries and other central offices with his new kind of official. For these posts he wanted modern bureaucrats and technocrats, but he still preferred the feudal lords as governors of provinces; a long time would still have to pass by before bureaucrats became available to whom such responsibilities could be entrusted – whereas his nobles bore them with ease. The nobility were also effective in ambassadorships, but for these there were now other candidates available. The Emperor hoped that by giving them a ruling function in their home territories, adapted to the changed conditions, they would have sufficient incentive to return. In this way they could at least retain the respect and affection of their people.

This plan would quite possibly have been feasible, but in fact it was doomed to failure because, in order to succeed, it would have involved a revival, rather than abolition, of the archaic structure of feudalism – it was ironic that the reformer Haile Sellassie now had to be regarded as its champion. In development practice, the changing of the social order had priority over every other objective of development, and in this the abolition of feudalism was the most important immediate objective. Any thought of achieving land reform through cooperating with the Ethiopian feudal nobility was ruled out: no foreign adviser could contemplate such a course and still hope to be taken seriously by his peers. Seeing that he could not hold the line on his own against foreign influence, Haile Sellassie used a strategem: he let his cousin Ras Imru distribute all his land, and thus show the world that the Ethiopian nobility were prepared to cooperate in land reform throughout the country. But this message was not taken at its face value. Instead it was immediately reported that the Emperor was angry with Ras Imru for not waiting his turn, and trying to teach his master a lesson.

Social discipline being very strict throughout all levels of the population in Ethiopia, such an action by Ras Imru would have been a clear affront to the Emperor and he would have been banned from court for it. He could not possibly start land reform on his own, but had to wait until the Emperor had started it. But because he did not fall into disgrace, it was clear to the people that his action had indeed been prompted by the Emperor, and intended to woo the foreign world to cooperate in his version of land reform. Typically and significantly, the Emperor's message to the world was turned against him: the progressive-minded Ras Imru has tried to push the hesitating monarch towards land reform. This version gained currency among the foreign experts in Addis Ababa, and made its way into the press and literature.

This affair did not have any influence on the principles of technical assistance as applied to Ethiopia. Already before the coup, it was clear that the Emperor could not make any further progress along this road: he dropped his original plan, accepting its failure as a defeat. The coup finally gave him an opportunity to switch to an improved version. He could not possibly have done this earlier, because the great number of young Ethiopians whom he was able to employ in the second phase were not yet in place. Some of the same basic features remained. The essential resource – the land retained by the crown and the imperial family – remained undiminished, and the feudal lords still cooperated, though in a less conspicuous way. The Ethiopian nobility constituted a reserve of talent, and the Emperor wanted to draw on it. Only a few older landowners had taken up a defensive position in response to the world's anger at their very existence. Most of them took a more relaxed attitude, especially those who had virtually settled in the capital and did not intend to return to rural life straight away: they were looking out for their chance.

Immediately after the coup, a committee of land reform was created, an interministerial institution assisted by subcommittees of foreign advisers. Later, in 1966, based on the preparatory work and the recommendations of that committee, the new ministry of land reform was set up, staffed by members of the new élite of graduates returned from studying abroad. Planning sections, specially designed to cooperate in land reform, were also set up in other ministries, to operate within the context of the usual responsibilities of those ministries. This was particularly the case with the ministry of agriculture, where there was a large development section that worked with remarkable efficiency, and the ministries of community development and the interior. All these newly-established and newly-staffed units had a definite task and clear orders: quickly to conclude all the necessary technical and administrative preparations, and then start putting the reform into effect as soon as the necessary preconditions existed. The land to be distributed was there and waiting. The former planning board, hitherto the domain of Yugoslav experts and advisers, was now renamed the ministry of planning, and somewhat more ethiopianised: however, its orders remained the same as before. It cooperated reluctantly, fearing that all the wind might be taken out of its sails. In the case of the ministry of education and the University, it was left to their discretion if – and, if so, how – they would cooperate. The Emperor, in this second phase, had ceased to interfere with their work, and left them full freedom of action. The ministry of education cooperated insofar as it began preparing layouts and budget estimates for primary schools in newly-settled regions, but the curricula of schools and teacher-training institutions were unaffected by the new development. The University limited its role to part analysing the Emperor's plans and actions. Some of its criticism was constructive and, when requested, it cooperated with the staff of the newly-created ministries of community development and land reform, who were young and appropriately trained. However, there was an increasing trend of destructive criticism directed at the person and actions of the Emperor – despite the fact that he had personally been eager to create these two ministries, and had selected and appointed the progressive young staff.

All the graduates of the agricultural colleges whom the Emperor could get hold of were now employed in the new bureaux created for speeding up land reform (they were no longer under his direction but under that of the University, which continued to send some abroad for advanced studies). They swarmed over every province, reaching the remotest corners. Everywhere they made sample surveys and collected data, measuring, counting and comparing whatever could be measured, counted and compared. They compiled reports and studies which were soon piling up in the planning offices, there to be amassed into larger works, which in turn began to fill up shelves in the libraries. The larger items were printed in book form, and hundreds of copies of each one accumulated in warehouses. Carloads of them went to the palace, where they ended up in the Emperor's archives. Those considered the most essential, the best of the crop, landed on his desk. Clearly the new staff were working hard!

The Emperor studied some of this literature, but no human being could read it all. He busied himself rather with reading the reports and recommendations of advisers from the ECA (the United Nations Economic Commission for Africa) the FAO (Food and Agriculture Organisation) and other bodies. The related fields of economic and social development were not neglected, and there was a large output of reports on these subjects also. But his reading could not be confined to the topics currently being given priority. Administrative, legal and judicial matters and correspondence with foreign governments also claimed attention. Parliament now had increased authority to initiate and pass laws and decrees. Yet no law or administrative regulation could be proclaimed or put into effect which had not first crossed the Emperor's desk. He allowed the great majority of less important matters to pass through without bothering himself with them, but if an item provoked his interest, he would read it carefully and often return it to parliament for textual revision or for reconsideration of the substance. Such items included the statutes of private associations* and commercial corporations which could not become legal entities before they had been sanctioned by the highest authority, at least in broad principle. Nevertheless, there existed a host of flourishing private corporate bodies – such as student, teacher, alumni and parent-teacher societies and some professional bodies – which were able to pursue their activities unhampered, but they were not empowered to conclude contracts or negotiate with government departments.

Judicial appeals to the Emperor had to be attended to, and the numerous petitions presented to him personally on his journeys by the humblest people were never overlooked: often a decision was needed from him personally to settle the matters at issue. The hours of the day were filled to overflowing with other matters. His reading was concentrated into the evening hours and continued till late into the night; conse-

---

*Examples are the Wildlife Protection and Natural History Society of Ethiopia, the Horticultural Society of Ethiopia, the Society of Friends of the Institute of Ethiopian Studies, the Ethiopian Women's Welfare Association, the Ethiopian Social Services Society, the Christian Fellowship, and the International Women's Club.

quently, he slept less and less, as is often the case with the old. There were the fixed hours when he met his personal entourage, ministers and court dignitaries, and when he sat with his private cabinet and crown council; also when he disbursed funds from the imperial treasury – the additional budget. There was always a mountain of applications to be worked through, and audiences to be given to foreign ministers, diplomats, advisers and experts – anyone of any importance. They were introduced to him on their arrival and often awarded decorations on their departure. And there was a fixed time too for receiving people of less weight – reporters; groups, whether of Ethiopian women or children, or of foreign tourists; and scientists, researchers or representatives of churches holding international conferences in the capital.

The remaining hours would be spent moving around in and out of town, covering the same range of activities as before, but with some slight modifications. Reflecting the shift in his priorities, less time was devoted to general education. He still occasionally made surprise visits to schools and colleges to ensure that this sector did not slip wholly out of his grasp, but they were becoming less frequent; instead, he would shuttle between development ventures, agricultural pilot projects, experimental stations and training centres. There he would be shown round and, after listening to reports, would ask questions and speak briefly. The hours before sunrise remained unchanged; they were devoted to attending mass, conferring with the secret services, and enjoying the company of his animals. Exceptional conditions prevailed when foreign heads of state or royalty came on state visits, and when the Organization of African Unity (based in Addis Ababa) held its summit conferences. The whole day would then be filled up with the pageant of official business and social events. Called upon as a matter of course to open, attend and address the meetings, he would be the focus of world attention. Performing all these tasks – and indeed everything he undertook – with natural ease, and ever aware of the inevitable and irreversible changes that were taking place around him, yet adapting to them with his habitual composure, he was the artist of power. That this should be so was not surprising, observers remarked, in a man so rich that he could do anything he wanted. Others had to do the hard work; he could merely enjoy the fruits of it.

XII. THE NEW AFRICA

Through the initiative and personal authority of Haile Sellassie, Addis Ababa had become the political capital of the whole of Africa. The seat of the ECA and the permanent secretariat and headquarters of the Organization of African Unity (OAU) were there, and it was the venue for numerous pan-African gatherings and for international conferences of all kinds. Numerous big hotels had sprung up in the city, some of the highest international standard, to serve the needs of important guests, the retinues of visiting heads of state, and the armies of press and television reporters who tail them – technical facilities were installed for the latter. Queen Elizabeth II and Presidents de Gaulle and Pompidou of France, Lübke of West Germany, Tito of Yugoslavia (repeatedly) and the Presidents of Poland, Czechoslovakia and Romania all came on state visits in the period after 1960, following in the footsteps of the many who had come earlier: the King of Greece, the Queen of the Netherlands, the Shah of Iran, King Hussein of Jordan, the President of India, and others. Sometimes not the head of state but a deputy made the journey: United States Vice-Presidents Nixon and Humphrey, the Crown Prince of Japan, and Premier Chou En-lai. In this final period of the reign, the Emperor continued to make state visits of his own and conducted negotiations in person. He went to the United States and the Soviet Union (twice each), the People's Republic of China, West Germany, France, Italy, Spain and (as frequently as President Tito visited him) Yugoslavia. Of course, he visited African countries too: Egypt, Morocco, Kenya, Malawi, Zambia and Mali among others. In foreign policy as well as in the related area of development policy, he strove for an equilibrium between East and West on the one hand and North and South on the other to foster competition between diverging forces in technical assistance, and abate the revolutionary pressure being exerted on imperial Ethiopia from outside. By so doing he hoped to gain the necessary respite for laying the foundation of his constitutional monarchy. The empire could be kept together under the crown, while the old order and traditional forms went through a steady and orderly process of transformation into something new.

Thus the Emperor himself stepped out into the foreign world, and made a bid for a leading position at the heart of the political forces that were intent on destroying him. The spirit of the age demanded its tribute, and Haile Sellassie was ready to pay it. The reason why he intensified his flirtation with President Tito of Yugoslavia was in order to become a cornerstone in the building of the Non-Aligned Movement. He also assumed the posture of a pan-African leader, becoming involved personally as a mediator where African states were in conflict with each other. In this he scored successes: not least, he managed to secure once more, by political means, Ethiopia's controversial borders with Somalia. It was at his urging that Ethiopia joined the small group of states which brought South Africa to the International Court of Justice in The Hague to defend its occupation of the former German colony of South West Africa (Namibia). The Lion of Judah went as far as to break off its diplomatic relations with Israel, although Israel had cooperated in Ethiopian development programmes, and sometimes given aid. Who was responsible for these actions? Was it still the young idealist Tafari, or was it the aged realist Haile Sellassie? Was it a political pragmatist, or a modern man who had lost his way? This has to remain an enigma.

After his coronation in 1930, the lack of funds and trained personnel prevented Haile Sellassie from doing much to continue Menelik's technical projects. What he was able to do was extend the networks for electric light, piped water and (on a large scale) the telephone; improve the condition of streets and roads, import here and there cars, trucks and bicycles, and introduce wireless telegraphy. He also went ahead with equipping the army. The Italian occupation, whatever its political and social implications, pushed the whole country, especially the capital, a big step forward technically. With their large-scale investment and some spectacular efforts, the Italians saved decades of post-war technical development, and enabled the Emperor to start afresh at a considerably higher level, and make more efficient use of the means of Technical Assistance that were to be offered in the development age just opening, than might have been the case otherwise. Thousands of Italians stayed behind in the country. After the liberation, many Ethiopians took revenge by attacking and plundering them, but one of the Emperor's first decrees after his return was to forbid any unlawful acts against Italians – transgressors were threatened with capital punishment. He meant what he said, and after a few offenders were hanged, the Italians were able to carry on living and working in peace. Many of them now fell in the social scale, but this did not worry them. Haile Sellassie's perception of the matter had been correct: industrious, adaptable, inventive and technically and artistically imaginative, they became the indispensable foundation of all the future technical work in the country. The Italians had reshaped Addis Ababa, putting up numerous buildings, laying out new streets and a network of arterial roads, and introducing scores of technical innovations and new, more advanced trades. It is difficult to imagine how Addis Ababa could have been kept going and in any state of repair without Italian artisans, and how all the manpower needed in garages, carpenters' shops and so on would have been found if the Italian labour-force had not been available. They soon became liked by the Ethiopians, intermarrying easily and making good family men, and their humanity and good-nature helped to make the town a colourful place. Among foreigners they were the least respected – by other foreigners because they were not wealthy and by Ethiopians because foreign experts on contract had more influence – but they were always the most useful. This, however, was in the early days, and many rose to wealth and a higher social position in Haile Sellassie's Ethiopia.

The last phase of the Emperor's reign saw the transformation of Addis Ababa into a modern city, with towering glass-clad blocks, imposing squares, broad avenues flooded with cars and illuminated throughout the night, filling stations, elegant private houses and bungalows in parks and gardens, and of course airports.

In contrast to the extraordinary mastery he possessed in political science (in the literal sense), the humanities, jurisprudence and economics, the Emperor's understanding of technology was, by European standards, in the lower range. Much more than in other fields, he had to depend on foreign advisers, but his shrewd perception and sensitivity enabled him to select the best people, whom he would then trust. It was therefore all the more necessary for him to abide by the principle of encouraging technical and industrial ventures by displaying his own personal involvement. Hardly any office building or major modern structure was built in the capital, or a new industrial plant of any significance in the surrounding suburbs, or a major venture like an electric power-station, a dam, a bridge or a new stretch of all-weather road begun anywhere in the country, however far away from Addis Ababa, without the Emperor personally visiting it. He laid foundation-stones, unveiled commemorative plaques recording his presence, cut ribbons, and listened to reports on the spot by the responsible administrators and technicians, to which he would often give a short address in reply. When he could not perform that particular ceremony, he would come and inspect the site later. In the first years after the liberation he even inaugurated some central filling stations to emphasise the need to develop motor traffic.

But what truly aroused his natural instincts and interest was anything that concerned living nature and man in nature: agriculture, forestry, cattle-breeding, veterinary science, wildlife reserves and national parks. He visited all sorts of agricultural projects and related endeavours, agricultural schools and training facilities, and forest nurseries; there he would symbolically plant some trees himself, to encourage farmers to support the government reforestation programmes by taking their own initiatives.

After the coup he withdrew from his close involvement with the work of the University, and confined himself to work of a representative nature – to receiving certain members of the staff in audience and showing around visiting heads of state and royalty. This was partly to demonstrate his recognition of its academic freedom, and partly also because he could no longer spare the time needed for close involvement. The University was generously staffed and in every way equipped to take care of itself; thus his presence was superfluous. There was a much greater need for him to show an interest in related ventures outside the University, such as the Archaeological Institute (this was a government department, but supported by France and largely staffed by French scholars); the Pasteur Institute, which had been there since before the Italian invasion; and the National Library. He repeatedly visited all of them. In addition he kept a close watch, all through his reign, over the work of the large number of government offices and agencies in Addis Ababa, often arriving on visits without any previous warning. He attended and opened other international events, such as the festival of the International Red Cross in Addis Ababa, and in particular the ceremonies held by the Haile Sellassie I Prize Trust in Africa Hall, seat of the ECA. As the Trust's sponsor he would preside, accompanied by the Crown Prince and sometimes also by his small dog, and distribute prizes to foreign scholars of international and Ethiopians of national standing. And there were national events to be attended, such as track and field competitions and inter-school sports at the Imperial Racing Club. He received Olympic gold medal-winners and gave them decorations and promotion; he watched the national soccer team's matches and gave receptions afterwards in the palace for the participants. At military parades he would take the salute, standing like a pillar for hours on end; likewise the ceremonies at the Military Academy at Harar in which officer-cadets received their commissions were extremely taxing. Religious services, continuing sometimes for three or more hours, were another matter again; and he would go on pilgrimages to distant destinations, always walking and never riding on horses or mules, let alone in cars. In particular, he favoured Kulubi, a shrine dedicated to the Archangel Gabriel, who was reputed to bestow the blessing of fertility on childless couples. Huge crowds would converge on to the place from all parts of the country, and some pilgrimages lasted for weeks, since the miraculous benefits of the Archangel were only granted to those who went the full distance on foot. Every year, the Emperor joined the pilgrimage on a certain holiday around Christmas, starting his symbolic participation from the nearest town, Diredawa, which was about 12 miles away. He used to walk with astonishing speed, getting his entourage out of breath and showing no sign of exhaustion himself; also, the date of his appearance would never be postponed due to excessive heat or bad weather.*

In his drive to act in a representative capacity and as his country's great reformer, Haile Sellassie definitely failed to achieve his aims for the economy, for education, for changes in the constitution, and in both his cherished ventures of land reform and reforestation. There were of course numerous industrial ventures, roads, public buildings and major engineering projects such as dams, ports and power stations which would remind later generations of his life and work and be of benefit to any future governments. But he achieved two great innovations which will provide a solid foundation for Ethiopia, whatever form of government it may have. First, he placed the whole country, uniformly, under the rule of law. By codifying the laws and adapting judicial practice accordingly, he made all Ethiopian citizens equal in a legal sense. Secondly, he created a modern administration, ridding the administrative process of class privilege and tribal distortion. Haile Sellassie's work threw the career of an administrator open to any Ethiopian. The basic principle, as well as the institutional network spread throughout his empire, will continue to benefit all Ethiopian citizens.

Most Europeans, living with others under the same law and in the same order as a matter of course, lack the perspective to grasp the magnitude of these two achievements. In Ethiopia, there was not just a single social order to be changed, but countless ones. Apart from the two great bodies of the Ethiopian Law of Kings – developed by the Orthodox Church in the Middle Ages and not adaptable to modern conditions

* For further information, see Edmund P. Murray, *Kulubi* (New York: Crown Publishers, 1973). Although in the form of a novel, the book contains much factual detail and excellent observation on the traditional population in its lower strata, as well as on modern educated people.

– and the well-defined legal practice of Islamic law, there were also numerous tribal and customary structures.* They had nothing in common except for the fact that their background was religious. In the belief of the people, the judges – whether kings or tribal chieftains, clan elders or priests – were either endowed with supernatural wisdom or they had been charged by their gods to watch over the order of life. To change the foundation of law from religion to legal theory was a revolutionary act – almost a futuristic one. It would take time for the peoples and tribes to become used to the new order, and for trained judges and other agents of the legal process to become available in sufficient numbers to serve every part of the empire. A new serious attitude towards matters of state had to grow out of the increasing economic interchange between the country's regions and its different social levels, the network of schools and government offices, and the mixing caused by military service, based on the common legal order.

At the time of Ras Tafari's Regency, the Bank of Abyssinia had actually been owned by the National Bank of Egypt in Cairo and was an integral part of it. Tafari succeeded in buying it and relieving it of its debts by forming a joint stock company, investing part of his own fortune in it, and urging both his followers and his enemies to do the same. The latter was something that Ethiopians would be certain to find difficult because they had traditionally despised merchants. In modern times they still distrusted them, and were themselves unwilling to become involved in commerce. However, the Emperor had a firm grasp of economics, even though he had only a limited understanding of technology. After the liberation he encountered the age-old resistance in his people when he tried, using every possible means, to persuade them to invest their hard-earned savings in commercial ventures. He did so because he believed this to be the best way of creating a solid middle class as the foundation for the constitutional monarchy. Time and again, he

---

* All the Christian orthodox areas in Ethiopia had in their judicial practice important common features, based on their medieval code, the Fetah Nagast or 'Law of the Kings' (already referred to on p. 6), a manuscript codex found copied in an identical text in many churches and monasteries, and still copied by priests up to the present day: translations and commentaries by Western scholars have been published. Islamic law and legal practice is more diversified according to locality, owing to the variety of Islamic sects and their greater ethnic diversity, whereas variations in the Christian areas were slight. Also based on religion, Islamic law and legal practice are essentially the same everywhere. This is not the case with African animistic religions, since they are not book religions.

had to channel funds from the imperial treasury into companies to keep them afloat. Those who followed his example were mostly the Greeks, Armenians and Asians, rather than his own people.

The only success here was scored by foreign news reporters. Here was a sure sign of Haile Sellassie's insatiable greed: not satisfied with being the country's biggest landowner, he now owned breweries, bus companies and shoe factories as well, while his people were allowed to starve. This was not the Emperor's only sin: the vast majority of the inhabitants of Addis Ababa still lived in their tukuls, low mud huts made (as they had been since time immemorial) of chika, a hardened and water-resistant mixture of clay and straw. However, the Italians, in the name of progress, had replaced traditional, skillfully-made conical straw roofs with flat sheets of corrugated iron; thus the shape of the tukul ceased to be round and became square. The tukuls now had a sad look; they had lost their original character without changing the customs and habits of the people who lived in them. However, those people now at least had some protection from the rains that beat down mercilessly for about four months of the year. (The rains also opened up deep cavities in the asphalted streets, where a foreign contractor had failed to provide adequate foundations beneath the apparently immaculate solid surface, and washed a vast volume of fertile soil down from the Ethiopian highlands into the artificial lake of the Aswan dam – once it had fertilised Egypt, but now phosphates had taken its place.) The old straw roofs had not lasted long in the rains, and laborious repairs were continually in progress. Iron sheets were easily fixed and repaired, lasted longer and cost less. The square tukuls were easier to build, and it was also simpler in the evening to divide up the sleeping areas between parents and children, relatives and guests, by means of curtains. From the air, it looked as if a great quantity of metal sheets had been scattered over a wide expanse of not very densely planted eucalyptus forest. Some were larger than most of the rest, and a few were conspicuously large; this was because, with few exceptions, all the luxuriously appointed houses and bungalows and some of the large buildings in the city centre were roofed with the same material, although the larger roofs were pitched and not flat. The victory of corrugated iron was all but complete. The aerial view of the centre – the markets and the business areas – showed these sheets forming solid rows. Most of the bungalows of the foreign residents were also built of chika, though more carefully planned and crafted. The wall surfaces were smoothly plastered over and then chalked or painted, which made them shine brightly in the sunlight. After the rainy season, this brightness would have faded somewhat; they all needed to be frequently replastered and repainted – at the cost of the tenant, not of the owner.

Housing had become a flourishing business, and indeed was the main industry of Addis Ababa. The post-war period had seen a rapid and steady growth in the number of Ethiopian urban landlords, the tukul-owners, who had previously lived in rented tukuls and now owned small chika houses, into which square tukuls could easily be transformed by the addition of more rooms. The owners of the bungalows that were rented out to foreigners often still lived in tukuls. Foreigners in Ethiopia were generally not permitted to own property, but had to rent it. The few exceptions were the owners of industrial premises and those whom the Emperor had personally authorised to have property transferred to them as a reward for outstanding service or merit. Embassies and other foreign missions with extra-territorial rights held their compounds as property only if there was a mutual agreement to that effect.

Any Ethiopian citizen owning a patch of ground in Addis Ababa apart from his own tukul – and there were many of them, although more than half of the metropolitan area was still owned by members of the imperial family and the nobility – could obtain a bank loan and use it to build a bungalow of dressed chika or a more conspicuous house with solid stone walls; it would then be rented out, the bank would be repaid and the owner would thereafter enjoy a high regular income. Maintenance and repairs, the laying out of gardens, and the addition of facilities such as swimming pools and garages, were not their concern; they would be the tenant's responsibility, but of course would revert to the landlord and become his property when the tenant left. If, on the other hand, the terms of the letting contract made them responsible for such things, they would merely increase the rent as much as was necessary. Foreigners tended to feel happier with the former situation, which left them free to shape their homes according to their own taste and needs, without negotiating each alteration with the landlord. When their employment contracts expired, they would leave the country, and the next tenant would then, quite reasonably, be charged a higher rent because of the improvements made by his predecessor.

Amortisation took about twelve years for solid stone houses, while bungalows of dressed chika could be paid off in half that time or less. With chika, building costs were low since the necessary materials were available in abundance: the clay was the subsoil of the town itself, and the reeds used as a straw were the natural cover of the vast neighbouring plains. The eucalyptus tree had the remarkable quality of being fully adapted to Ethiopian conditions. From the stump of one that had been cut down, ten new trees would immediately grow and become usable within only a few years without needing to be tended in any way. The tree, introduced by Menelik from Australia, was a blessing for Addis Ababa; the town could be said to be situated in a sparse eucalyptus forest bordered by a dense one, which was constantly expanding. Thus there was never any shortage of wood for burning or for the traditional kind of building; however rapidly the city's population might grow, the eucalyptus would grow still faster. While it causes impoverishment of the soil for other forms of cultivation wherever it is found, it none the less improves the climate.

With the building of houses to let becoming Addis Ababa's major commercial activity, even the less fortunate, who owned no land other than the small patch on which their own tukul stood, or no land at all and were obliged to rent a tukul, were able to benefit. In most such cases the landlord would be a non-Ethiopian merchant who had become a citizen of the country, like many of the Greeks and Armenians; or he could be a high-ranking Ethiopian or even the Emperor himself. Within clans, groups were formed for cooperative enterprises; with money they saved, they would buy a piece of land from the big landlords and thus enter the property business. Soon the tenants of rented tukuls became owners, and after a few more years they would be receiving a steady income, even if quite a small one after being divided into many fractions. Then, as we have seen, the transformation of the tukuls from round to square had increased their utility since they could easily be expanded into regular houses. The growing number of people with radios in their tukuls, who were thus in touch with the outside world, were now lured by the government into forming cooperative units outside their clans – something unheard-of earlier. The adventurous acted accordingly, and were rewarded with a proud name: they were now members of registered bodies such as the Mortgage Company, the Home Ownership Association, and so on. The rules of the free market dictated that a tremendous rise in the price of urban land had to follow, but these rules did not yet have validity here. Higher prices were charged to merchants and foreign investors, but Ethiopians could still buy land at very low prices.

Within the little-noticed and unpublicised sector of urban land reform, some of the nobility who owned large tracts of land in Addis Ababa could easily cooperate, since they were not hampered by the hostility of the outside world towards them. In this they followed the example of the Emperor, who had begun secretly selling off his urban land. Once they had moved into a bungalow of dressed chika and built a few fine stone houses to rent out, and thus secured themselves a sure income, the rest could be disposed of. They could enjoy a tenfold profit and more if they stayed in the business, but here was a problem. Such an activity was something compatible with the status of a merchant, but not with the dignity of an Ethiopian of rank: an aristocratic engaging in such activity would be trading away his natural inherent authority with the common people. Because of the repercussions that might follow from this, it was probably not really such a good business proposition as it seemed; and furthermore they would be risking the Emperor's displeasure – something clearly ill-advised.

Urban land reform had this inconspicuous quality because no foreign money was employed or needed, transactions among Ethiopians remained private, and took place almost without any hint of them being given to foreigners. Landlords could cooperate without the interference of the foreign, outside world. The Emperor's plan to achieve land reform by using the feudal structure of society was frustrated by foreigners, by their hostility towards the feudal structure, because for them the change of the social order through abolishing the feudal structure had the highest priority, taking precedence over every other objective of socio-economic development.

The double standard is immediately apparent: everyone expected land reform from the Emperor, but no foreign expert ever presented a workable plan to achieve it on a country-wide scale. The Swedes made some remarkable steps in this direction, with their pilot projects on a small regional scale, to which there was general agreement in the country, even from the Emperor. They conducted hundreds of scientific studies and spent vast sums of Technical Assistance money to achieve what they did. Nobody ever explained to the Emperor that the money needed to do the same throughout the whole country might be hard to raise. The hostility of all foreign developers to the Ethiopian nobility was evident everywhere, e.g. in the total indifference of the world's press when the best among them were murdered during the revolution.

Thus, with the radical change in urban landownership, the Emperor had succeeded in one of his principal objectives: the formation of an Ethiopian middle class. He had tried this from so many angles, using educated people, but it had finally taken root among the common people – the majority of the people of Addis Ababa – who still lived traditional lives.

This was both a healthy and a rapid growth, which the Emperor had overseen from its very beginning, although much of the economic impetus came from foreigners. He had done all he could to make Addis Ababa an attractive capital and a supranational centre for the whole of Africa. With so many foreigners coming to Addis Ababa, the demand for housing was bound to rise steadily. The luxury hotels were already there.

But the more splendid the new metropolis of Addis Ababa became, the more would foreign observers, especially journalists, be appalled at the contrasts that were emerging at the same time. No one with a social conscience could any longer tolerate the blatant contrast between rich and poor; palaces, luxurious homes, towering hotel and office buildings alongside slums where people existed in filth and misery; the magnificent automobiles flooding down the avenues and the thousands of beggars, lepers, blind people and those with missing limbs who lined the same avenues, and prostitutes beckoning to clients through the bead curtains hanging in the entrances to their tukuls. Festivals, balls, receptions and parties – the amusements of foreigners – succeeded each other endlessly, and only came temporarily to a halt in the rainy season; then cars had to struggle through water and mud, and as torrential rain hammered down on the corrugated iron roofs, the music was dampened and hosts and guests had to raise their voices to be heard; all would be shocked into silence as lightning struck nearby. Most foreigners took their home leave or travelled outside the country at this time, and returned at the beginning of 'the season', in other words the remaining eight months of the year, all dry except for a short period of light rain. But even in the rains more than two thousand boys loitered in the streets hungry, emaciated, without shelter, without schooling and without work – they were lucky to earn a few coppers cleaning a foreigner's shoes. Disease, ghastly and unconcealed, was everywhere – at the same time as the festivals were taking place, with dance bands playing and people drinking and enjoying themselves. These contrasts provided plentiful ammunition against the Emperor.

What were perceived – naturally, perhaps – as the slums of Addis Ababa were actually rows of tukuls, which represented the customary way of life of Ethiopians. Anyone imagining that it was easy to wean them from their customs should have tried it. Tukuls were inevitably low because of the usable lengths into which the eucalyptus-wood wall supports could be cut and the instability of longer poles. Progress was being made in building chika ceilings to increase water-resistance in the wet season and warmth in the cold nights of the dry season; most houses now had them, and those that did not would soon do so. Also the combining of tukuls into a single small house gave better protection, because pitched roofs had already begun to appear on these constructions, and were becoming increasingly prevalent.

Tukuls did not have attractive colours; they blended very much with the ground on which they stood, and of which they were largely composed. Nature had given protective colouring, adapted to the surroundings, to its living creations out in the highlands, and thus there seemed no reason why tukuls should now be coloured pink. As we have seen, their fronts were occasionally painted – with a cheap pigment made of coloured chalk, – and this made them look cheerful and bright in the dry season, but would mostly be washed off in the next rainy season. This special decorating was done for 'reasons of state' – for example, if the Emperor was returning after a long absence, state visitors were being shown around, or the start of a summit conference was imminent. The people had no strong feelings one way or the other about painting their houses.

There was one thing which perplexed those without close knowledge of the country: there were no emaciated, malnourished people in Addis Ababa. The only exceptions were those recently arrived from one of the drought-ridden regions to save their lives: there were always great numbers who starved out there, since lack of water was the curse of Africa's Sahel zone all the way across from the Atlantic to the Indian Ocean, and had claimed victims in Ethiopia throughout history, as in other regions on that latitude. But otherwise the poorest men, who carried loads for a living, might be seen chatting and laughing, and looking healthy enough. The street boys – doing odd jobs such as shoe-shining, but also begging, stealing and much other mischief, often organised in gangs – were also healthy. Most of them were children who did not yet belong to a clan, and who had literally escaped death by coming to town. Either they were fugitives from a drought which had already killed their parents, or they had come from the highlands, where they were the children of freed slaves; in the latter case, the parents had lost their subsistence and protection, and they could not work for money for their former owners who could no longer have afforded to pay them, nor could they remain slaves without defying imperial orders and published laws. Hordes of such children had flooded the town in earlier periods, and nobody knew what to do with them. However, the Emperor had built a non-residential school especially to integrate them and a number of welfare institutions and associations were patiently and consistently dealing with the task of taking the boys off the street into schools and training establishments to turn them into skilled artisans.

There was still much disease in the country – and here again it was strange to see how some writers blamed the Emperor for the very conditions which, having identified at the beginning of his reign, he was particularly determined to change. The people themselves were as fully conscious of the value of health as the Emperor and public health made spectacular progress under his rule. There were now many hospitals, several of them caring for poor people without payment, run by the Ethiopian government or in joint ventures or by foreign governments, by churches, missionary societies and international agencies. Hundreds of foreign doctors worked in these hospitals after the war, and at the same time an indigenous medical profession was coming into being. Well trained, competent and conscientious Ethiopian doctors, dressers and nurses were conducting a vigorous campaign against disease at many levels. The World Health Organisation organised wide-ranging programmes to destroy disease-carrying organisms, malaria and other endemic diseases: many were now in retreat and a few, like smallpox, had been entirely eradicated. These medical skills were also channelled into research institutions such as the renowned French Pasteur Institute, which had been in operation there for several decades, and remains highly effective right up to the present; to the numerous colleges and training centres for public health; to school feeding programes; and to large scale ventures for the rehabilitation of lepers and the blind. A large part of foreign Technical Assistance went into public health. Haile Sellassie made hundreds of visits to hospitals, to show his interest and encouragement.

In Ethiopian eyes, health is the most valuable of all possessions. If his health is good, the poorest man can improve his condition, and he is to be envied more than the powerful man who is not similarly blessed. The common Ethiopian greeting *'Tenayistilin'* means 'May God give you health for my sake'. This phrase happens to illustrate the fact that sometimes as many as seventeen words are needed to convey the meaning of an Amharic word in English. The meaning of this Amharic word, as literally translated, – 'Is God to be seen as my servant acting on my orders, or on my behalf?' – is obscure. Thus in English the inner meaning of the word *Tenayistilin*, which is neither spoken nor written, must be added: 'Since I am praying to God for your health . . .' Almost any compound word or phrase in Amharic has an inner meaning as well as its direct sense: the language is highly differentiated, with an unrivalled wealth of forms describing action and attitude, and reflecting the subtlety of the Ethiopian mind.

The highlight of Ethiopian life was a marriage celebration, which always had to be carried out with style. Large tents had to be used – they were available in any size, and could be hired with the seats and tables. A huge number of people would be invited – all the bridal couple's clan members, godfathers, friends and patrons. This obligation extended even to the poorest man, who would be willing to incur debts that could only be paid off over the rest of his life, rather than be found wanting in the duty to stand host at least once. If he fulfilled this duty, he could be sure of being invited to sit in tents as a guest many times subsequently. The hospitality and entertainment were usually sumptuous. For rich man there could be no better way of being happy than eating and drinking exactly according to his wish, enjoying the pleasures of the flesh to the full. He might have many such opportunities for gratification. The poor man only had few, but for both there would be feasting and beating of drums all through the night when the occasion arose.

The other great occasion highlighted by custom was death. Dignified and impressive ceremonies in honour of the dead followed a burial, and, as with weddings, tents had to be hired. An Ethiopian considered it his duty to attend the funeral ceremony of any member of his clan (clanship being wide-ranging) or anyone among his friends or colleagues. Ministers have cancelled important official engagements to attend the funeral of a minor employee, and servants have been dismissed from their employment because they insisted on taking part in the obsequies for a relative in some far-away part of the country. After the Empress died, official mourning lasted a full year. Haile Sellassie himself walked in procession behind a coffin many times, even when the dead person was not a member of the imperial family. Nobody followed his coffin.

XIII. REVOLUTION: THE YOUNG GENERATION

In all the fields of social and economic development, the Emperor laboured to be the first to reach its goals, and so forestall revolution. Seemingly alone in his resistance to the flood-tide, he felt ever more weighed down by the vastness of his task. The country's future was in the hands of the progressive elements in the younger generation. His differences with the students and the vain attempts he made to woo them are the most significant feature of his last decade in power. The Emperor and the young people were pursuing the same goal - their views differed only about the timing. The protests of the students against him continued relentlessly and were repeated with stereotyped uniformity. The Emperor, too, always put forward the same arguments - that the students would be able to do all they desired, with their own hands, but in good time: they first needed to acquire the necessary knowledge and skills. The state was paying for their education, and therefore he asked them to conceive of their duty to the state as being to prepare themselves for their examinations, rather than be for ever slandering the state. As time went on, his requests became more insistent: he pleaded with the students to obey him. In this contest the scales were in fact tipped in his favour, but outsiders stepped in to keep the student rebellion on the boil and prevent it from collapsing from sheer inertia. The organisers of student revolts received salaries, and those who took part in demonstrations were paid by the day and provided with meal tickets which could be exchanged in the hotels of Addis Ababa for as long as the government, as a countermeasure, kept the University campus closed. Student magazines were subsidised and there was a steady flow of propaganda pamphlets. Intermediaries in the mayhem were caught carrying large amounts of money, and some foreign embassy officials were asked to leave the country - but it was to no avail. Right up till the end, payments continued to be made to rebellious students through undisclosed channels, through embassies and other missions, through Ethiopian officials, and other dignitaries and a network of sympathisers - as the popular rumour had it, even members of the imperial family and the Crown Council were involved. Support came from countries of both the Eastern and Western camps.

Haile Sellassie's attempts to win over the young had been particularly ill-starred. The most brilliantly talented young man he had ever known - whom he had treated as a son and made his closest confidant -

had turned against him, murdered his ministers and deprived him of his most reliable and faithful supporter Makonnen Habtewold. He would never believe that Workineh had been the true initiator of the abortive coup; surely Mengistu Neway had been the ringleader. Several times in the palace the same spectral scene was repeated: the Emperor, waking suddenly in the night, would ring the bell and order the terrified servant to summon Colonel Workineh Gebeyehu.

It was generally expected that after the Emperor's death a new era would begin. Power would pass to the parliament, and the new Emperor would act as representative of the state. Adherents were gathering round the Crown Prince: he had his friends among Ethiopian officials, among the students, and within the circle of foreigners in the country, and inevitably also those who were thinking of their own future careers. He also had personal contacts with foreign embassies: he was used to negotiating with both Eastern and Western representatives, and was on good terms with all. He lived in comfort with his family – not for him his father's frugal life-style and obsession with work. Indeed, there was no reason why he should work like his father, because his tasks were of limited scope and could be easily supervised. In his province of Wollo he could exercise his rule merely by appointing the governors, and latterly a minor department within the central administration, headed by a minister but without political significance, had been placed under his control: this seemed like a first step towards a closer involvement in the functions of central government. Quite often he accompanied the Emperor on official business, and occasionally deputised for him when exhibitions had to be opened or foreign guests received. What would become of Ethiopia after Haile Sellassie's death? Patiently, the Emperor would refer curious questioners to the constitution: the succession was pre-determined. He allowed no reference to be made to the tension that was supposed to exist between him and the Crown Prince. As Emperor, he had his own way of doing things, his own style: his successor might do them differently. He wanted everything at least to look smooth on the surface.

But beneath the surface his worries increased. He had been successful in his aim of creating an urban middle class. More Ethiopians now owned property and had savings, and were involved in business and industrial ventures. The number of officials and employees in the public service had grown and was continuing to grow. Thousands of Ethiopian graduates and trainees had returned home after study abroad, and most had been absorbed into the administration and its agencies, or into the institutional network – banks, hospitals, colleges, the University, the various training centres, and the larger construction and engineering projects, at the same time. And many, by their own initiative, made their way into professional life seeking independent status. Even the numerous servants in the households of foreign residents were eager to study how their masters lived in order to copy them later; most saved up their earnings in the hope of being independent themselves some day. There had been a remarkable growth in the number of banks, and in the number of deposit accounts held by them. A healthy economic growth could be seen from the bottom up. In the capital, the balance had started to tip towards democratisation. However, the vast majority of its inhabitants still lived according to age-old custom and tradition, unwavering in loyalty to the Church and the crown. If free elections were held, they would be certain to nominate the elders and the most respected men within their clans – who could be trusted to represent them in the most appropriate manner.

Town-dwellers formed only a small fraction of the empire's population. The great majority lived in the countryside at subsistence level, in patriarchal and tribal orders dominated by religious conceptions, and blended in a variety of ways with the superimposed administrative network of the state. In the highly diversified country, there were few regions where any sort of rural middle class had existed for any length of time. Although several ventures designed to promote the formation of a new type of farmer engaged in profitable business had been started here and there and were working quite successfully, this was still a far cry from Haile Sellassie's aim of a true middle class. With premature democratisation, the multi-ethnic empire would break up into its component parts, followed by a series of civil wars that would continue for decades until a new order was finally consolidated. Menelik's creation would then, most likely, disappear from the map, and a number of smaller states would take shape in the Horn of Africa.

Apparently land reform, as a precondition for the emergence of a rural middle class, had to come before any other measure aimed at democratisation of the people out there in the countryside, and in a last effort the Emperor concentrated his energy and most of his working time on speeding it up. All the young progressive agriculturalists trained at the country's agricultural colleges were thrown into the service of the ministry of land reform and the cooperating ministries of community development, planning and the interior. The Emperor was now in a race against time, the evolutionist trying to outstrip the revolutionaries.

Among the numerous students sent into the provinces, there were many whose enthusiasm was genuinely fired, and who did much more than merely record statistics. After toiling throughout the day, they would continue working till well into the night on their reports. These were the very kind of young people the Emperor had longed to have as his disciples and successors, but there were too few of them, and they had come too late. The sun of imperial Ethiopia was already setting behind dense clouds. For a brief moment, it spread a rich glow across the whole landscape, before finally dipping below the horizon and leaving the earth in darkness.

The unrest among the young continued as the Emperor's efforts went unnoticed. The students kept up their monotonous demonstrations, and indeed their aggressiveness increased; they were now developing a hostile way of behaving towards foreigners. The cars of Ethiopian dignitaries and of foreigners working for the government were stoned as they passed along the streets by crowds of students and school pupils, assisted by street-boys. Time and again, they repeated their chief demand: land reform now and an end to corruption. The conscience of the world was focused upon them.

XIV. REVOLUTION: CRESCENDO

The worldwide press campaign against the Emperor was gathering momentum. It was enough that the students were up in arms and slandering him. The silent majority of his people, with the internal order on which they relied still intact, did not count. The stratum of the educated spoke and acted in their name; arbitrarily, perhaps, they had made their choice between the world's two opposed ideological camps. The soldiers were discontented with their low pay, and pressing for more; and, parallel to these, cells of resistance and political agitation against the imperial government had begun forming in the army. There was ample evidence of foreign countries having a hand in it, of their money flowing in, and of arms, propaganda leaflets and other material supplied by them being distributed. The foreign teachers and experts in the country merely fanned the flames. The world, East and West alike, had dropped the Emperor and was looking forward to the democratic Ethiopia that was about to dawn. The United States, after its disastrous involvement in the Vietnam war, had abandoned its military base in Eritrea, unwilling to risk a repetition of that experience by becoming involved in another internal conflict in the developing world.

In the decisive year 1973, Haile Sellassie made a last effort to stabilise the quaking empire. He went in May on an unofficial visit to Washington – as a petitioner, seeking to win President Nixon over to the idea of continuing and reinforcing the United States military presence in Eritrea by extending its contract on the Kagnew base near Asmara. The agreement had existed for twenty years and was due to expire in 1975; but the base had already been partly evacuated, leaving only some token installations in place up till the very end. As Haile Sellassie saw it, the Americans, who brought money into the country and provided work, and were therefore popular among the local population as a source of prosperity, could have helped by their mere presence to bring about a peaceful solution to the Eritrean conflict. If the military base could be expanded, and a programme of technical assistance were earmarked for the province of Eritrea at the same time, this would halt the insurgency and bring peace to the region. He was fully aware of the significance which a strong stand on the Horn would have in the eyes of the United States, in view of the high-profile political role Ethiopia played in Africa as host to such pan-African institutions as the OAU and the ECA, and its strategic position at the entrance to the Indian Ocean, close to some of the world's biggest oilfields – and biggest troublespots. But President Nixon was just then fighting for his own survival, and in any case the decisive power lay with the Congress. For politicians and world public opinion alike, Vietnam and Watergate were of far greater importance than the Horn of Africa. Thus the Emperor's last political bid was frustrated.

The Federal Republic of Germany enunciated clearly the new tendency among Ethiopia's friends. An official letter from the Bonn government informed the imperial Ethiopian government that its Technical Assistance would henceforth depend on the degree of progress made in social development, and that no more funds would be forthcoming unless there was an immediate change in the social order of the country. This document caused great perplexity as well as distress within the ministries and departments. For more than fifty years, Haile Sellassie had been changing the social order of Ethiopia and was still doing so to the very limit of his knowledge and power – but apparently the West Germans did not consider that the rate of progress being achieved was rapid enough. What exactly did they expect? Or had the letter that caused such consternation been intended for a different government, and come to the wrong address?

Then an urgent invitation was extended to the Emperor to visit Moscow for a personal meeting with the Soviet leaders. He was asked to bring only a small retinue. Immediately, the suspicions of traditionally-minded Ethiopians were aroused. Popular rumour in Addis Ababa is a remarkable phenomenon. It travels across the great rambling city with miraculous speed – its source unknown and its content unverifiable – purporting to represent information that had not yet found its way into the media. The Soviet leaders were said to have presented Jan Hoy with an instrument of abdication for his signature – wasn't the downfall of his regime imminent anyway? If he agreed to sign, he would be guaranteed not only a safe conduct out of the country, with his property and his servants, but a pleasant place of retirement in any one of the Communist countries. They even offered him a castle in the Crimea! Or, if he preferred to retire to a Western country, he would not be hindered in any way – nor would he be molested when he got there. So great was the respect and admiration with which Jan Hoy was regarded by the Soviet government and among the Soviet people, so he was told, that they were all deeply worried lest he should come to any harm as the result of the present difficulties in his country. But Jan Hoy had not even considered acceptance of the offer, and immediately left for home.

Even today, it is still not known whether the subject of the talks in Moscow was in fact the possible abdication of the Emperor; the official communiqué only stated that the traditional friendship between the two countries, based on their common fight against colonialism and imperialism, had been renewed. The very existence of such a rumour, and the wealth of speculation surrounding it, show how well aware the common people were of the tension building up in the last four months before the revolution.

After returning from Moscow, the Emperor seemed relaxed, as if he would let matters follow their natural course. But the situation in the capital quickly worsened. Not only University students and school pupils went on strike, but their teachers as well. Motor traffic came to a standstill as the result of a strike organised by the CELU – the Confederation of Ethiopian Labour Unions. There were sporadic strikes at industrial plants in different locations, and jobless people formed units to infiltrate the demonstrating crowds, workers and students. There were now excesses in which people resorted to violence against rich and high-ranking Ethiopians and against foreigners. Police fired shots at offenders, creating the first victims of the unrest: the government admitted three deaths, while rumour claimed nine. The Emperor promised anti-inflation measures, lower food prices and higher pay for soldiers – but it was to no avail, and the unrest only increased.

The CELU – fully recognised by the government – acted on behalf of numerous small labour unions in the various branches of industry, trade and public services, which were still to weak individually to form separate legal units, which required the standard procedures such as a published constitution approved by the ministry of the interior, regular meetings, board elections, annually published reports of activities, and published annual audited accounts. There were also other corporate bodies in Ethiopia, but they were unregistered and thus could not act as legal persons (e.g. negotiating with the government or concluding valid contracts). The associated unions were not yet obliged to follow the directions of the CELU; for example when, during the time referred to above, the CELU ordered a general strike, only a minority obeyed. The demonstrations were fully organised, by the CELU, the students and their teachers and by agencies of foreign governments.

It is worth mentioning here that for cultural and psychological reasons, the phenomenon of jobless people demonstrating spontaneously on the street was virtually impossible in Ethiopia. It was too alien to the Ethiopian mind, the way of thinking, feeling and doing things: as an onlooker, no member of the common rank of society (unless foreign-educated) could have understood its meaning. That this phenomenon appeared shortly before the revolution is proof in itself that all those jobless demonstrators were hired. The agents who went among them were Ethiopians, foreign-trained especially for that purpose, not to motivate them but to act as stage-directors, showing them how to act on such an occasion. Such care was superfluous, because the jobless illiterate youngsters – the street-boys – were keen observers who adapted themselves easily to any situation. They understood at once what was expected of them. They performed perfectly, imitating the organised demonstrators.

Ethiopia's was a feudal society and imbued with aristocratic values, from top to bottom, from the Emperor to the last servant (hence its impenetrability to the modern mind). This was mirrored even at the very lowest level – represented in Addis Ababa by about 2,000 boys, mostly the children of liberated slaves, who roamed the streets. They spontaneously organised themselves into gangs, with privileged leaders naturally emerging, to whom the other members had to pay a tribute. Discipline within the gangs, the internal rules of behaviour, were quite different from those they applied to the outside world, where putting on a performance, deceptions and all kind of mischief, including minor thefts, were allowed. On reaching adulthood, they disappeared from the streets. There were no adult jobless people in the European sense, except for beggars who were physically handicapped – the numerous lepers, blind people and cripples – and those who had fled from regions afflicted with drought and famine to stay temporarily in town, returning home when the rains returned.

XV. REVOLUTION: FINALE

Revolutionary cells, with foreign support, had formed within the Second Division of the army sent to Eritrea to control the rebellion, and secret preparations for a full-scale mutiny were well under way. Agents of the secret military intelligence network had picked up the warning signs fully six months before and the secret services of foreign powers had obtained more substantial evidence of arms centering the country to aid the coming mutiny. Members of the diplomatic corps in Addis Ababa gave the Emperor unofficial and confidential warnings – at great risk to their career. His last visit to Moscow should have removed any lingering doubts he might still have had up till that point. Tension among the population in the capital continued to grow: what would the Emperor do next? The revolution had not taken him by surprise: he had had more than enough time to consider the situation and decide on his final stand. He made his will and made his accounts with foreign banks over to his heirs. His English property in Bath, where he had spent his years of exile, was already sold. Nobody should have occasion after his death to point to his investments in real estate abroad.

The storm, after gathering for so long over Eritrea, finally broke with the mutiny of the Second Division. The mutineers placed their commanders, the governor of Eritrea and other high Ethiopian officials under arrest. The commander-in-chief of the Navy, a grandson of the Emperor, escaped to Djibouti. Diredawa, a town on the railway line between Djibouti and Addis Ababa, was captured, and in an airborne surprise attack the mutineers succeeded in seizing the Air Force headquarters at Debre Zeit, near the capital. The Air Force thereupon joined the mutineers, and declared their solidarity with the rebellion. The well-armed and well-supplied rebel forces advanced on Addis Ababa, where the inhabitants were beginning to realise that at last the great showdown was upon them: now, surely, *Jan Hoy* would act! The feeling of confidence and hope quickly turned to horror. Unbelievable events were unfolding. The Emperor was refusing to fight for his crown, or to allow the advancing rebels to be opposed by the army. Instead he had ordered negotiations. Negotiations with whom? With mutineers? Could *Jan Hoy* still be in his right mind?

Firmly, Haile Sellassie declared that he did not wish to see the shedding of blood, and that he would never again give orders that could have that result. Everyone felt agonised at what he was demanding. The military stormed at him: he could rely on three divisions that would definitely take his side, and there was also the enormous army reserve of 'territorials'; he would be safe with the support of such forces. His horrified ministers and aides, and all the members of the imperial family besought him: there were cries of rage and despair. If the armed forces were not to be allowed to fight now, they would be forced to join the rebellion. But the Emperor quietly and adamantly repeated his decision: there would be no bloodshed, but negotiations instead. Was he not able to see that bloodshed would certainly follow a revolution and that he was not only putting his own life at stake but sacrificing all those who had served him faithfully for so long? 'It is no longer a matter for me,' Haile Sellassie said. 'They wanted it this way.' Then he was asked, 'What is our destiny?' According to popular rumour, his answer was 'Pray to God, He will forgive you.'

The people of Addis Ababa were in a state of anguish. Every church in town was crowded. Prayers were said in the huts too, and many hut-dwellers were thinking that God's punishment had fallen on Ethiopia, and that Menelik's curse was about to be fulfilled. It seemed as if Haile Sellassie was thinking only of the salvation of his own soul, and no longer cared about the salvation of his people. The Cabinet immediately resigned. Some dignitaries started making desperate preparations for flight, but most returned to their homes to await their destiny, whatever it might be.

By his refusal to fight, Haile Sellassie placed his own life and the lives of all the key figures in the regime entirely in the hands of the mutineers. In February 1974, power passed to the army, and the negotiations ordered by the Emperor became mere empty manoeuvres. Was Haile Sellassie overthrown by the army? Was he vanquished by the revolution? Just as the rise of the young Tafari was shrouded in mystery, so also was the Emperor's disappearance from the scene. He was not overthrown by the army and he was not defeated by the revolution. While still in possession of power, he surrendered without a fight. This was a battle he did not want to win.

The next three months were filled with hectic activity – negotiations between the Emperor and the army (now headed by the Provisional Military Revolutionary Council), and the implementation of various reforms including the drafting of a new constitution and changes to the country's laws. The Emperor acted as if he were still ruling: he worked incessantly, and made speeches and read proclamations, and changed the composition of the cabinet of ministers. The mutiny had been settled by negotiation, according to the Emperor's vision, and the negotiations continued after the rebellious troops had returned to their barracks. Because he was still nominally in power, he was trying to settle the part to be played by the former government in the new state – in which actual power was held by the PMRC. To the legalistically-minded Emperor, any change in administrative practice – and such changes he acknowledged to be inevitable – required a legal basis, involving changes in the previous laws. And such changes had to be negotiated. Feverish activity continued in the palace, in the cabinet and in Parliament. But this was no more than shadow-play: the country was actually ruled by the PMRC, and even its membership was being kept secret. Nothing the Emperor did now would have any effect; he could make no more mistakes, and he could not save his ministers or his family. The shadow-play continued up till the Ethiopian new year in September. The country was then officially declared a republic, and the Emperor was arrested.

Diplomats who were accredited to Addis Ababa at that time later claimed that the enigmatic Emperor's most incomprehensible decision was a sign of incipient mental collapse, a mistake such as might be expected of a man more than eighty years old. But the Emperor knew about the impending revolution many months before it broke. He had had ample time for deliberation, and had spent spent many nights pondering the manner of his exit from the world's stage before deliberately laying his head on the block to await the fall of the axe. Historians will have to accommodate the difficult fact that his decision was made deliberately.

The army had been Haile Sellassie's pride, and a large part of the resources of the imperial treasury had been spent on building up and equipping the armed forces and on military education and training. He could have given the order that could have suppressed a mutiny in one division. But could he also have defeated the forces that were behind the mutiny? Being in possession of the Red Sea coast, the mutineers had unlimited access to supplies from abroad. No Western power was now in a position to intervene on his behalf, even if it wanted to. By avoiding the trap of a new Vietnam on the Horn, Haile Sellassie had thrown away all the logistical preparations that had been going on for years, and ensured that the mountain of assorted weaponry piled up far away, waiting and ready for its transportation to the Horn of Africa, would remain idle at the one moment when it was needed. He knew this quite plainly. A few years later, in 1977, this situation was to be echoed when the country's army, in spite of putting up a brave fight, could not keep the fragmenting state together any longer – and the world was stunned by how quickly and efficiently the Soviet Union was able to deliver by air a vast amount of military supplies, exceeding in material value all that Haile Sellassie had ever received from the West, including the United States. Menelik's creation had been saved once again – for the last time? – by a superpower. Should he have bled the peoples of the Horn to death to serve as pawns on the great-power chessboard? The Emperor did not see this as his mission. By refusing a fight, Haile Sellassie had shown for the last time his superior ability to evaluate a political situation.

But there were other significant indications as well. At eighty-two, the Emperor's life had come full circle: he had completed his task. He was proud of what he had done, and satisfied with his individual achievements: it was now for others to take care of his legacy. There was nobody around who had either the capacity or the desire to continue: the days of patriarchal rule in Ethiopia were finally over, and the reason for that was the lack of a succession. The solitary figure of the Emperor was now abandoned by all but a few of his early followers, who had faithfully dedicated their whole lives to his service, and a few doomed feudal lords of the old school. For an Ethiopian of rank, flight was not an option. The country's assertive, academically-trained youth, his chosen instrument for the realisation of his dreams of development, had turned away from him; his wooing of one of their number as his possible successor had been a miserable failure.

Nobody was prepared to see things in the same way as he did. Any idea that his students might succeed in reconciling the real, organic life of their country with modern thought, bringing Church and crown into harmonious co-existence with the theory of the new Ethiopian state, had been hopeless. None of them seemed able to see the world in any context other than that of the flat and fruitless East-West ideological conflict. The path which Japanese students had once taken – of adopting a foreign culture without sacrificing their own – was one which his students were apparently incapable of following. Were Japanese workers so much more efficient in their working practices than workers in other countries? Of course they were not, as any productivity test of European and American against Japanese workers shows, and as Haile Sellassie learned by investigating reports on the subject. But there was the phenomenon of Japanese workers praying for their firm at the beginning of every day's work, seeing its success as their own, and feeling at home in all the activities of their workplaces – where else in the world could anything like this be found? Workers with such motivation were in a class of their own.

It was Haile Sellassie's dream that something of the same kind might be created in Ethiopia. But what did Workineh Gebeyehu see when he was sent to Japan, and what did the students see? They reported that Japanese workers slept in rabbit hutches and had nowhere to go after work, which was why they were permitted to hang around their work places after the normal closing time in order to prevent them from being infected with bad ideas, and from assembling together outside the workplace, which would have created unrest. A similar unsurmountable gap in understanding was evident everywhere.

The Emperor had now been abandoned by both East and West, and was being generally slandered in the media. The last pillars – the officers and ordinary soldiers – were about to fall. Suddenly everyone knew better than he how to perform the offices of state. Had they only been right! Haile Sellassie still wanted to see how the new democratic state of Ethiopia would shape up: he was prepared to face anything. But he would hold on to power until he was sure that the reins of government would not be handed to civilians: the chatterers and speech-makers. They could not possibly save the state, and if Ethiopia broke into fragments as his reign ended, then his life's work would, incontrovertibly, have failed. It was not for this that, so many decades ago, he had deposed Yassu the rightful Emperor, reached out for the crown in open revolt, and taken Menelik's mission upon himself. The soldiers would not let Ethiopia die: they would fight.

Already before the deposition of the Emperor, the arrest of officials and dignitaries had begun, and the process continued on a large scale. Some governors, nobles and officials from ethnic minorities escaped to the countryside. They went either to their estates to try and assemble there the remnants of their former dynastic power and so form pockets of resistance; or to their tribal areas to join up with small groups of insurgents; or to the larger fronts of those fighting for Eritrean, Tigrean or Oromo independence. Some, accompanied by a few followers, went into hiding in the highlands. The media exhorted them to submit voluntarily to the justice of the people: they were assured a fair trial. A very small number escaped abroad or attempted to do so. Most of those already abroad, either for their work or for study, did not return home and tried to make new careers and homes for themselves in exile.

In November, sixty of the most senior functionaries and dignitaries of the old imperial order – among them two prime ministers, the president of the senate, and ministers, governors, military leaders, judges and members of the imperial family – were executed. Some had been in the Emperor's service for as long as forty years. Their landed property and bank deposits were disappointingly small, because they had not accumulated personal wealth. But among those executed were also young ministers, representatives of the liberal intelligentsia, one-time members of the silent opposition who had seen the role they were playing as transitional, but who now found themselves, seemingly by accident, on the wrong side. There were also representatives of a still younger generation who, after thorough training abroad, had offered themselves unreservedly for the Emperor's service and had carried out their duties conscientiously and irreproachably. Some of these victims were members of the feudal nobility with great landholdings. Among the sixty there were a few, certainly, who had abused their power, but the convenient accusation of 'corruption' had no foundation. The government's call to face the 'justice of the people' had not been without effect; a few had accordingly put themselves at the people's disposal. One such was Ras Mesfin Sileshi, governor of Shoa, and his reward was to be peremptorily put to death without any judicial inquiry or legal proceedings whatever. The killing was carried out during the night as the prisoners were being transferred from one gaol to another. An officer and a sergeant in the escort accompanying the prisoners – probably unaware of the true extent of the operation – refused to obey the sudden order to fire on them, and were themselves shot on the spot as mutineers. There was satisfaction throughout the world at the news that corruption in Ethiopia had been brought to justice. The details of the affair remain unnoticed.

The old Emperor was not affected by these events, which were no longer his business. If this happened to be what the victors had striven for, he had no part or share in it. Haile Sellassie had now become entirely detached from his life and task, letting the world take its course. In this extremity he turned to prayer. But as he was being held captive in a house in the grounds of the so-called Menelik palace, and was still surrounded by his servants, he had not changed his habits or his way of conducting himself, and filled the idle periods of the day with reading. He read all the daily papers regularly – something he had not done since his exile in England.

The stars of the great outside world that had shone so brightly for the young Tafari – Frederick the Great, Napoleon, Machiavelli, Voltaire – had lost their lustre. Only Thomas à Kempis now remained. He had returned home to repentance and a cross. He acknowledged that Menelik's curse had been fulfilled. In the earliest written version of it occur the words: 'The earth shall refuse itself to him.' Nobody would now know the resting-place of his body. And indeed it is possible that he never had a grave: that, instead of being buried, his body was burned and the ashes thrown to the wind, or perhaps it was fed to wild animals: few bones, if any, are left after hyenas have consumed a human body.

The closing of a circle was evident in other ways: the liberal philosopher-monarch, son of a military leader and architect of an army which was later to destroy him, gave up power refusing to cause bloodshed. It is remarkable that his ascent to power occurred just at the time of the First World War – a war of an altogether new type. And his whole active life and reign were interwoven with world war and its consequences: revolution, genocide and civil war that have raged intermittently ever since he first rose to power and are likely to continue. He in his turn was devoured by them.

The world is well-informed about the last Emperor of Ethiopia, of how his people suffered, and how he piled up millions of dollars in foreign bank accounts. The truth of the matter – that Haile Sellassie had no fortune abroad – is immaterial: ideological preconceptions outweigh facts. History will be the final judge.

XVI. EPILOGUE

It was in January 1951, and it had been a stressful day. I returned to my hotel feeling tired and disappointed, and sat in my room pondering what steps to take next. The people whom I had succeeded in seeing had been obliging and friendly. Nowhere had I been exactly rebuffed; everyone had appeared interested in my plans and willing to support them – but there had been no substance behind the words. Perhaps, maybe – if not right away, then possibly in the future; they would do whatever they could, but unfortunately that was not much. Had I seen so-and-so? Then it was recalled that this gentleman was abroad and would not be back for another fortnight. I was sent from one desk to another. This was probably the Ethiopian way of saying 'no': they did not want to give offence, but they also did not wish to commit themselves. It was a fine and cultivated way of behaving, but it was of no help to me at that moment. Unless one had already secured the backing of some persons of influence, writing an application to any public authority was useless. Answers might be deferred not just for months but perhaps for years – in other words, indefinitely. I could only stay in my hotel for a few more weeks.

On this particular day, a Swede had told me that there had already been several foreign applicants for the vacant post in the National Library, and one of them had stayed at my hotel for ten months before giving up hope and returning home. Any chance that I might work here in my profession seemed slim; hope was fading – what should I try next? But on the bedside table in my room I found a letter. It was in Amharic and consisted only of a few short lines. The letter-head was an official one. I found one of the hotel staff who translated the message; it was a request to appear at a particular room in the Ministry of Interior the next morning at ten o'clock. Was this part of the process of keeping a vigilant eye on foreigners? I imagined the sequence of questions and answers that might occur, and wrote down my answers on a piece of paper in the country's second language, English: as a precaution I did the same in French, because there were still some Ethiopians who preferred the traditional language of diplomacy. My visa was valid, and I had registered on arrival with the authorities. What could they want of me?

At the ministry, I entered a large room where an official was sitting at a grandiose desk and several minor employees and scribes occupied small tables. The official rose, greeted me with a handshake and offered a seat.

With great politeness he expressed sorrow at having disturbed me, but there was a minor detail in my papers that was not clear, namely my nationality. I claimed to be German, but had I not been born in Riga, which was in Russia? When he learned that my parents had also been born in Riga, he said that I must be Russian – but I had to point out that I was not, adding that I could not even speak the Russian language. Where had I been to school? Also Riga? At that time, I explained, it had been the capital of Latvia, an independent country. The fact that my citizenship had then been Latvian created more confusion. Even when I told my questioner that Riga had been founded by Germans as long ago as 1201, and that they continued to live there for many centuries, he remained sceptical.

Why had I come to Ethiopia, and what did I want in the country? The answer to this was that I had a special interest in the Imperial National Library. At once a happy atmosphere pervaded the room: work at the small desks stopped, and all the employees followed our conversation attentively; two of these humbler functionaries even left their places and came a little closer to us. The official spoke in a gentle and friendly voice: so I must have a contract? If I had not even been promised one, had I been sent to Ethiopia by the United Nations or by some other institution such as a university? Who had provided my affidavit, who was my backer, where did I propose to live? When he learned that I had come entirely of my own accord, and alone, a shadow seemed to fall over his face and he became solemn. But as he began to speak, he was immediately interrupted. A messenger boy had rushed into the room, bowed deeply and blurted out a few words. All faces registered shock. Each employee was at once back in his proper place, rapidly putting his desk in order; the official who had been interviewing me stooped down to open a drawer, took out a file and placed it on the desk. He said to me in an agonised voice that I must leave the room immediately and go to the waiting room at the end of the passage and wait for him to call me back. I was doing as I was bidden, but it was already too late. The Emperor had come into the room, followed by an officer who took his stand by the door. All rose from their seats and bowed. I quickly stepped to one side and stood by the wall.

The Emperor went to the official's desk, a short erect figure in military uniform, his back at this moment turned to me. Apparently he was in a happy mood: his voice was friendly, and the official sounded natural and self-assured as he reported to the Emperor – I could not understand a word of what they said. The tension in the room had markedly decreased. In answer to a brief question from the Emperor, the official pointed at the file and made as if to open it, but the Emperor made a gesture to show that this was not necessary. He appeared satisfied and turned to leave. His glance then fell on me and I bowed. He asked the official another short question, half turning back, and was given a short answer, the sense of which I assumed to be that it was a routine case of public business. The Emperor asked another question, and this time the answer was longer and given somewhat hesitantly. I could recognise some proper names, and apparently they were referring to the tangled problem of my nationality. The Emperor nodded: possibly he had some knowledge of Eastern European history, and it was a fact that before the Italian invasion some Baltic Germans had worked in Ethiopia. He turned to me.

The military drill I had learned many years before as a young recruit came to my rescue: I automatically stood to attention. Did that other basic rule – that one should look one's superior straight in the eyes – apply here? Was it permitted to stare directly at the Emperor of Ethiopia? But after my eyes had met his, I found myself automatically lowering them. I knew that it was not permitted to speak without being addressed, or to say more than the precise answers to his questions.

There was now complete silence in the room. After a moment's silence, he spoke in a cool voice in French: 'Your profession?' I answered, and after another silence he asked, 'What do you want to do?' The crucial moment had arrived. I replied that I would be happy to be able to serve at the National Library in an endeavour to build it up along the lines of the national libraries of Europe, and thus contribute to the development of librarianship in the country. The sentence I had prepared in advance for the official sounded more natural and less elaborate in French than it would have done in English. The silence that now followed was much longer. I stood as if nailed to the wall. Finally I heard his words, spoken quietly and firmly: 'You will do it. We command.'

Bowing deeply, and raising myself again slowly, I was struggling within myself to find an appropriate form of words to express my gratitude, but the effort was unnecessary. The Emperor was already leaving the room to continue his inspection elsewhere in the building.

The official who took me to the National Library the next day looked out of humour and discontented. Scarcely uttering a word, he merely threw me despairing side-glances. Subordinates seldom agreed with the Emperor's erratic decisions, but they could not be changed. Finally he said, also in French, 'I think you know what you have to do!' What did

I have to do? 'You have to *please*.' This time I had to know exactly what was meant: in what way did I have to please? 'One must be loyal,' he said.

Had I been face to face with the Emperor for three or for five minutes? During most of the time there had been silence, with the Emperor saying only a few words. I had spoken too much, making promises that I could not keep. A library working along the lines of the great European national libraries, those ancient, intricate treasures of mature nations, built for a distant future – who needed such an institution here in Ethiopia? Could they afford it? And how could the expense be justified? Most of the users of a national library are not yet born. In such a country as this, all available wealth and every scrap of human effort have to serve daily needs acquiring practical knowledge and keeping development projects going – and there was never enough money even for that. And what world should this library represent – the Western world? All the printed literature that had found its way here was from the West, and the new literature originating in the country somehow mirrored the Western spirit.

As for Ethiopia's own world, its independent culture, its ancient language and literature, I had only the faintest conception of them – little more than I had read up in reference works before leaving Europe. How could I, in good conscience, accept the Emperor's offer or carry out his order? He had asked no question about my professional competence and experience, or about my ideas as to what I might do. He had only said what I *would* do. The vital parts of the exchange had been left unspoken: You are not able to do it? Then do what you are able to do. Anyone can do something.

'*Vous le ferez. Nous donnons l'ordre.*'

'.... *Il faut être loyal.*'

APPENDIX
SELECTIONS FROM THE SPEECHES OF HAILE SELLASSIE I

SOME BASIC PRINCIPLES AND GUIDELINES

Harmony of development

It is axiomatic that development in any country must proceed simultaneously in all areas of its life. As a country advances economically, equivalent progress must be made in the creation of more highly developed social and political institutions as well. Any attempt to retard advancement in any single area will inevitably retard the development of the whole, and will create serious distortions in the overall fabric of the nation. This principle we have always recognised, and in our actions we have been guided by it. The emphasis which we have given to education in our country has stemmed from our determination to eliminate ignorance and to prepare our people for the changes which Ethiopia's emergence into the modern world would bring upon them.

It is also axiomatic that change begets change, that each step forward leads logically and inexorably to the next, and the next. Once unleashed, the forces of history cannot be contained or restrained, and he is naive indeed who says 'thus far will I go and no farther'. This principle, too, we have recognised and followed.

'The Emperor on ministerial responsibility', April 14, 1961, *Ethiopia Observer* (hereafter *EO*), vol. 5 (1961), no. 2, p. 98.

Risk of development

When, decades ago, we turned Ethiopia's face in the direction of progress and modernity, we were secure in the knowledge that in so doing we best served our country and its people. We recognise then, as we do today, that once embarked upon this course there could be no turning back. Ethiopia was committed to the future and to whatever it might bring. Man may, at the outset, control the direction which events take, but once his choice is made, events soon escape his control and history proceeds by its own force and momentum.

'The Emperor's Coronation Day speech on Nov. 2, 1961', *EO*, vol. 5 (1962) no. 4, p. 287.

Priority in development

The ultimate resource of a nation is its people. Unless this resource is employed for the benefit of the nation, unless the latest good which it represents is exploited to the maximum for the common good the nation will languish, poor in spirit, lacking in achievement. But no people can make their full contribution to the life of the nation to which they owe allegiance unless they possess and enjoy those few fundamental prerequisites indispensable to rendering their participation in the affairs of their country both possible and significant. The growth of a people is complex and interrelated. Man must be educated: he cannot come to grips with or cope with or understand the modern world unless he has been taught about it. He must be assured of a minimum economic security: he cannot concern himself with matters going beyond the day-to-day satisfaction of his physical needs unless he is fed and clothed and sheltered, nor can he acquire a sufficient degree of social consciousness to be able to subordinate his own personal interests to the good of the nation and the development of its society. Freedom, liberty, the rights of man – these mean little to the ignorant, the hungry, the ill-clothed, the badly-housed.

All of this we have, from our earliest days, recognised, and in the years during which we have guided and directed the destinies of the Ethiopian people and nation, we have endeavoured to accommodate and give due consideration to this basic truth.

Ibid. p. 290.

The cultural aims of development: The Japanese example

We have always had great admiration for Japan and for the achievement of the Japanese people in preserving their traditions, and while *acquiring the best of the new, successfully reconciling it with the best of the old*. During our visit to that friendly country we were impressed by the enthusiasm and hard work the Japanese people are giving to achieve their progress. At the same time our admiration and high regard for the Japanese people was greatly increased by our experience of their courteous manners and great kindness.

'The Emperor's speech on his Eastern Tour (broadcast over Radio Addis Ababa on December 10, 1956)', *EO*, vol. 1 (1957), no. 4, p. 115.

The essence of power

The power which you possess is but one side of the coin; the other is responsibility. There is no power or authority without responsibility, and he who accepts the one cannot escape or evade the other.

Each one of you and each servant of the Ethiopian nation and people would do well to ponder these words, to take them to his heart, and to guide his conduct in accordance with their teachings.

This is the challenge which faces you today. Let your labours here during the coming year demonstrate your capacity to meet it.

May Almighty God guide and assist you in your work.

To Parliament, Coronation Day, Nov. 2, 1966 (closing sentences), *EO*, vol. 10 (1966), no. 3, p. 169.

Practical aims of development

Our concern is with the many and not the few. The benefits of education must be enjoyed by every Ethiopian. Health facilities must be made available to all who require them. The ownership of a plot of land must be brought within the capacity of everyone who so desires. The benefits of an expanding economy must be enjoyed by all.

Ibid., p. 167.

Role of the individual in development

No man chooses his own parents. But in the last analysis, a man's ultimate worth is, in the modern world, determined by his accomplishments and his service in the cause of his nation and his countrymen.

To Parliament, Coronation Day, Nov. 2, 1973, *EO*, vol. 16 (1973), no. 3, p. 127.

Speed of development

We believe in the adaptation of modern economic and social theories to local conditions and customs rather than in the imposition on Ethiopia's social and economic structure of systems which are largely alien to it and which it is not equipped to absorb or cope with. We believe in a progress which does not strain beyond capacity the social fabric of our nation or destroy what is the most precious in Ethiopia's traditions and way of life.

This is not to say that we do not ourself recognise that the programmes upon which we and our government have embarked do not involve changes in attitude, in approach, in method, which are in themselves revolutionary. Quite to the contrary, we are dedicated to securing the advance of our nation at the fastest possible rate. But the experience of other nations where over-ambitious programmes have been announced only to be later abandoned in failure, where impetuosity and reckless over-optimism have been substituted for maturity and sound judgement, persuades us of the essential validity of our views on these matters.

To Parliament, Coronation Day, Nov. 2, 1962, *EO*, vol. 6 (1963), no. 4, p. 298.

Solemnity of style

On this auspicious occasion as we open the 1965 E.C. [Ethiopian Calendar, i.e. 1972] session of Parliament thanks be to the Almighty God, the fountain of all wisdom and strength, for His bountiful blessings in enabling us to witness in our life-time the manifold accomplishments of our endeavours during our reign for the progress and well-being of our country and our beloved people.

To Parliament, Coronation Day, Nov. 2, 1972, *EO*, vol. 15 (1973), no. 4, p. 198.

Emperor and people

What we seek is a new and a different way of life. We search for a way of life in which all men will be treated as responsible human beings, able to participate fully in the political affairs of their government; a way of life in which ignorance and poverty, if not abolished, are at least the exception and are actively combatted; a way of life in which the blessings and benefits of the modern world can be enjoyed by all without the total sacrifice of all that was good and beneficial in the old Ethiopia. We are from and of the people, and our desires derive from and are theirs.

Can this be achieved from one dusk to the next dawn, by the waving of a magic wand, by slogans or by Imperial declaration? Can this be imposed on our people, or be achieved solely by legislation? We believe not. All that we can do is provide a means for the development of procedures which, if all goes well, will enable an increasing measure and degree of what we seek for our nation to be accomplished. Those who will honestly and objectively view the past history of this nation cannot but be impressed by what has already been realised during their lifetime, as well as be awed by the magnitude of the problems which still remain.

Annually, on this day, we renew our vow to labour, without thought of self, for so long as Almighty God shall spare us, in the service of our people and our nation, in seeking the solutions to these problems. We call upon each of you and upon each Ethiopian to do likewise.

Ibid. (closing sentences).

Above all, Ethiopia is dedicated to the principle of the equality of all men, irrespective of differences of race, colour or creed.

As we do not practise or permit discrimination within our nation, so we oppose it wherever it is found.

As we guarantee to each the right to worship as he chooses, so we denounce the policy which sets man against man on issues of religion.

As we extend the hand of universal brotherhood to all, without regard to race or colour, so we condemn any social or political order which distinguishes among God's children on this most specious of grounds.

To Parliament, Coronation Day, Nov. 2, 1966, *EO*, vol. 10 (1966), no. 3, p. 168.

STATE VISITS

It became a custom for the Emperor to broadcast to the population at large on Radio Addis Ababa after his return from state visits abroad. These addresses were naturally in Amharic. The following excerpts are from the published English translation of a broadcast on August 28, 1959.

United Arab Republic (Egypt)

In particular, we are most satisfied that we were able to make personal acquaintance with President Gamal Abdel-Nasser and to hold frank and friendly discussions with him regarding matters of common interest to our two nations and to have been able to reach complete understanding. [. . .]

From the many important achievements of our visit, one which has given us great satisfaction was the successful completion of the agreement regarding the relation of our two Churches. During our reign we have spared no efforts to attain the greatness that is due to the Ethiopian Church which has been an island of Christianity in the Continent of Africa. We are most thankful to Almighty God to have witnessed the fruits of our efforts during our reign by the elevation of an Ethiopian to the Patriarchate of the Ethiopian Church.

The Soviet Union

In the talks which we had with the leaders of the Soviet Union concerning our two countries in particular and world peace in general, we reached full understanding. Moreover, we were able to make personal acquaintance with Mr Voroshilov, the President of the Presidium of the Supreme Soviet, and Mr Khrushchev, the Prime Minister of the Soviet Union, and we had frank and friendly exchanges of views on various matters and reached full agreement on all of them. As the result of our talks, agreements have been signed between our two Governments for economic co-operation and the widening of the scope of our cultural and commercial relations. Apart from this, it is a measure of satisfaction to us all to have obtained a long-term loan of four hundred million (400,000,000) roubles at low interest to finance Ethiopia's Five-Year Plan and the various other projects designed for the economic development of the country and the raising of the standard of living of our people.

Ethiopia has abundant natural resources. However, because of lack of capital, it has not been possible to develop these natural resources for the benefit of the people. It is to exploit these natural resources and to carry out the Five-Year Plan for the benefit of our people that we have acquired credits from friendly countries such as the United States, Yugoslavia, the Federal Republic of Germany and Czechoslovakia.

We believe the assistance we obtained from the Soviet Union will greatly expedite the exploitation of our natural resources and the development of our economy.

Czechoslovakia

Just as we have discussed and exchanged views with other leaders of the countries we have visited, we had a fruitful exchange of views with President Antonin Novotny on matters of common interest to our two nations, as well as on general matters that concern world peace.

The Czechoslovak Government has expressed its willingness to help us in our effort to develop our nation's economy and to raise the standard of living of our people by making it possible for us to purchase from that country industrial and agricultural equipment by way of credit, which will greatly assist us in the implementation of our economic plans. [. . .]

Belgium

After our visit to Czechoslovakia came to an end, we visited for three days the Kingdom of Belgium with which Ethiopia has maintained friendly relations for a long time. [. . .] We are pleased to have had an opportunity to meet King Baudouin in person and to have been able to exchange views on various subjects. [. . .]

France

After the conclusion of our visit to Belgium, we stayed in Paris for two days. [. . .] Not only did we renew our friendship with General de Gaulle, President of the Republic of France, which we had cultivated during the time when our two countries were under hard trials, but we also conducted fruitful discussions concerning economic, commercial and cultural relations existing between Ethiopia and France. [. . .]

Portugal

On the invitation of the President of Portugal, we visited the Portuguese Republic from July 26 to July 31. Portugal is one of the countries with which Ethiopia has had contact since the end of the fifteenth century.

The spontaneous and friendly welcome accorded to us during our visit by the Government and people of Portugal has left a deep impression on us. We had discussions with President Admiral Amerigo Tomas and the well-known Prime Minister, Mr Salazar, concerning relations between our two countries and international peace. A cultural agreement was signed. [. . .]

Federal Republic of Germany

During our short stay in the Federal Republic of Germany we were pleased to have had the opportunity to meet the President, Professor Heuss, and to discuss with him matters of common interest.

Yugoslavia

Continuing our visit to friendly countries, on the invitation of our great friend, H.E. Marshal Tito, we visited the Federal People's Republic of Yugoslavia from the 15th to the 23rd of August.

As you know, we have, during a period of five years, visited Yugoslavia twice, and His Excellency Marshal Tito has, in about the same period of time, visited Ethiopia twice. This is proof of the firm and friendly ties that exist between our two countries. Yugoslavia has not only granted Ethiopia a loan for the realisation of the programme initiated for the economic development of Ethiopia, but has also extended assistance in the form of experts in the field of medicine and various other technical matters. These aids have shown fruitful results to the greatest satisfaction of both sides. Even though the two countries have different economic and internal political systems, these dissimilarities have not been obstacles to mutual understanding and co-operation and to working together in a friendly spirit. This, we believe, is exemplary.

No hint on the objectives of his visits to three colonial powers in the final days of colonialism in Africa is given, beyond the exchange of friendly commonplaces. Frequent contacts with his 'great friend' Marshal Tito were sought by the Emperor, and were motivated partly by the Technical Assistance offered by Yugoslavia, and partly by the desire to make Ethiopia the African cornerstone of the block of non-aligned states, of which Tito and Haile Sellassie had been co-founders. In his usual manner, the first part of the Emperor's broadcast, describing his actual experiences abroad, is followed by a popular discourse in a different style on numerous aspects of Ethiopian life and development. The following is the end of the second part of the same radio message cited above. The headings are supplied by the *Ethiopia Observer*.

Value of thrift

One should realise that thriftiness is the basis for the accumulation of wealth and the economic growth of a nation. One seldom minimises the value of money earned by the sweat of the brow, however little it may be, but for the extravagant even a huge amount of money is worthless. Know how to use your money wisely and effectively. A habit once formed becomes an established second nature. Therefore utilise your wealth for worthwhile objects and avoid employing it for harmful purposes and for momentary pleasures. What are the things you possess? What was your objective in acquiring them? Learn how to spend wisely and the increase of your wealth will eventually be your guide.

Use your savings where they will pay you most. The hoarding of money does not yield dividends! If you wish your savings to pay you higher dividends, join then with those of your fellow citizens. It is through hard work, 'know-how' and patience that you will be able to increase your capital. The foundation and essential characteristics of a healthy society are mutual trust and confidence. Unless man undertakes the improvement of his society in co-operation with others, his striving for wealth becomes mere wishes. Do not be the victims of temporary contentment and petty satisfactions. Aspire for worthwhile aims that will be ideals for succeeding generations.

Individual and nation

The prosperity of each individual constitutes the wealth of our nation which will eventually enable us to expand the schools and hospitals we have established for the welfare of our people. The expansion of public health services will decrease the mortality rate and increase our population.

Just as a farm that is not taken care of cannot be free of weeds, so is also the development of a society. It cannot be denied that there are some people who have scrupulously or unscrupulously attempted to acquire or have succeeded in acquiring wealth. If the wealth of a person is not for the general welfare, what will he gain for himself and his offspring but grudging and hatred? The fruits of one's sweat and mental labour are always rewarding, not only to oneself but also to succeeding generations. Be resolute in your work and attempt to complete whatever you undertake; if you face failure, try again and persist in your determination to attain your aim. Develop a healthy pursuit of life and do not limit your efforts to satisfying your selfish desires.

Our youth, in particular, must be steadfast and take advantage of the benefits of modern civilisation. Do not fall a prey to idleness, for it will be a curse to you and to succeeding generations. You must set yourselves up as examples of determination and hard work. Plan your time and use both your physical and mental powers purposefully and productively.

We must remember that man's achievements in the field of wireless communications, aviation, medical science and many other fields have been accomplished through the ages by patience and hard work, diligence, perseverance and tenacity. It is in the light of these facts that we urge our youth to struggle constantly and unceasingly to achieve their aims.

Capital and labour

The fact that medical doctors, engineers, pilots, cadets in the various military academies, nurses, teachers and the many other professions, have been successfully trained in the various schools that we have established, will serve as an illustration of what we have stated above. Convinced that capital and labour are necessary ingredients of wealth and prosperity and that these two factors are absolute essentials for the economic development of our country, and believing that our beloved people will apply themselves to the task of its economic progress, we have acquired loans from friendly countries.

Henceforth, the next step for each Ethiopian, wherever he may be and whatever are his endeavours, is to follow our directions and to devote himself assiduously to the execution of our plan for the betterment of our country. If we fail to use profitably the credits we have acquired for the development of our communications system, port facilities, the establishment of industries and the improvement of agriculture, we shall have brought a heavy liability not only upon ourselves but upon succeeding generations.

Ethiopians, have courage and brace yourselves! Unless you improve your lot by the sweat of your brow, nobody will shoulder your responsibilities. Provided that you pursue your task with unswerving dedication, we, on our part, will do everything possible to assist you in your forward march.

Help made available

Just as we have done in the past, we will make available to you, through various experts, directives which will serve as your guide in your work.

We have instructed the municipalities to prepare and make available to you, at little cost, various types of seedlings. We shall organise teams of experts who will give you advice and counsel in the fields of agriculture and public health. We shall also set up groups of experts who will give you advice and counsel in co-operative farming and trading.

For the purpose of cultivating oleaginous plants and to the end that you may have better marketing possibilities, we shall make experts available to you.

We shall organise for you a team of experts to study your needs and the ways and means of improving the quality of crops and trading systems in relation to present economic and marketing conditions.

As we hold our people in great affection, so do they entertain great feelings of affection toward us. As a father should not only bequeath wealth to his children, but should also provide them with proper education, so that they may have a richer and fuller life, so it is the duty of those for whom much has been done to show gratitude. Therefore, let us unite our efforts to show in deeds what we profess in words.

In conclusion, since the ideals we have conceived and the projects that have been planned for the development of the country can best materialise by the incessant efforts of our people and the application of every one's ability in harmonious co-operation, we call upon our people to be steadfast in this noble and challenging undertaking.

May Almighty God sustain us to realise these high ideals.

The long broadcast message of August 28 was continued and supplemented by a short one on September 18, 1959, which ended as follows:

We have promised you specialists and technicians to assist you in carrying out your projects. But the leadership and initiative must always come from you. Do not expect them to do for you more than you can do for yourself.

Every labourer is a father – his labour is his child. Choose your project carefully, and achieve it worthily, so that neither yourself nor your country may be ashamed on your account. You who have left your home towns and have entered the cities in search of work, now is the time to go back, for there is work waiting for you. We warn you in advance that those who are physically able shall not be allowed to loiter about the cities.

Let us follow the golden rule – 'Do unto others as you would have them do unto you.' Let the officials follow it closely; let them serve their people and their country with humility and diligence.

But diligence and humility and service to one's country are not the tasks of officials – they are not the tasks of anyone alone. The present projects will demand close contact and co-operation between all of us. Officials to whom we have entrusted various degrees of responsibility, be guided by the example of Jesus Christ, who, having declared, 'I came to serve you but not to be served by you,' brought Himself low and washed the feet of His disciples! Render service to the people without charge for these services. As we repeated many times over in our last pronouncement, we want again to emphasise the value of time; we urge you to dedicate yourselves to hard work – and profitably to utilise your time.

There is no energy in the world, including that of the atom, that cannot be controlled. However, there is no scientist on earth who could control, even for a second, the flow of time. For this reason, never idle away your time, however briefly.

Is it not you, her children, that are referred to as Ethiopia? Our lasting hope has ever been, with the help of the Almighty, to promote the interest and well-being of our people – not to become disillusioned by remote hopes and wishful thinking.

May the Almighty God help us in the fulfilment of all our undertakings.

'Emperor Haile Sellassie on His World Tour', *EO*, vol. 4 (1960), no. 2, pp. 34–9; 'Emperor's further broadcast on His World Tour', ibid., pp. 39–40. A further extract from this speech, on land reform, occurs on pp. 148–9, below.

EDUCATION

In all the countries we have visited, we have noted that education is the basis for the greatness, the power, the pride and prosperity of a nation. This impression, together with the satisfaction that we have had from the students of our own educational institutions, whom we consider the principal instruments for the progress and well-being of Ethiopia, renews and strengthens our belief in education. If, therefore, education is the factor of everlasting significance in the greatness of a nation, it becomes the duty of every Ethiopian to strive for education and progress. What we have seen wherever we went has convinced us that education is as vital as life itself.

The foreign technicians and specialists are only employed to provide us with temporary assistance and training. It is the duty of everyone to strive for self-sufficiency by acquiring knowledge and experience. To live always in dependence upon the assistance of others not only prevents a people from attaining its ideal, but also deprives life of its true significance and achievement.

We have seen again during our visit that God has not been partial in His divine creation. The difference of colour is a notion which has no significance and the futility of asserting a difference has now become obvious. The way in which Ethiopian youth has assimilated the knowledge of modern art and science, and the high academic achievements of the young men and women we have sent for higher education abroad, justifies our efforts and expectations. Our whole history testifies to the heroic deeds of our gallant people.

The fact that we have sown on fertile ground strengthens our hope that we shall realise the plans we have prepared in order to achieve our high ideals. After all, Ethiopia is second to none in her agricultural tradition. We are proud to say that our plans and achievements compare favourably with those of others. If we have been able to accomplish what we had in mind to do, it it because the love and prayers of our people have always sustained us.

In conclusion, we would leave with you the thought that Ethiopia belongs equally to each and every Ethiopian, and we rely on you all, young and old alike, to play your proper constructive part in the great common task of fructifying in Ethiopia the results of our visits abroad. Nor will you fail in furthering the success of the programme of modernisation and development that we have outlined for our beloved country.

The thing that harms a nation most and cripples its strength is lack of enthusiasm and zeal to strive through education to raise itself to the level that other nations have attained. There is nothing we desire more than to see the full development of the natural resources of our Empire and the raising of the standard of living of our people. May the Almighty and Everlasting God continue to protect our people and bless our efforts, so that in His good time we may see the fruits of our endeavours.

'The Emperor's speech on his Eastern tour', broadcast Dec. 10, 1956, *EO*, vol. 1 (1957), no. 4, pp. 116–17.

History, serving as the guide for the future, clearly demonstrates that there is no more useful instrument for the attainment of Ethiopia's high objectives than education. To see our unceasing efforts for the promotion of education, upon which depends the future of our country, achieving commendable results is for us a crowning joy. In pursuance of our programme to extend the benefits of education to all of our people, we personally inaugurated, during the last month, the school at Qabredharre in the Ogaden, and we witnessed, on that occasion, the great hunger and deep yearning for education which fill and animate our subjects. We have brought a number of young boys and girls from the Ogaden to pursue their studies in the schools of Addis Ababa. [. . .]

The past year has, consistent with the trend established in previous years, seen large increases in the number of our schools and the students studying there. A considerable number of our students were sent abroad during the past year to continue their higher education, and many of those who went abroad in earlier years have returned after successfully completing their studies. As a result of these developments, education has come to account for an increasing share of our annual budget. However, despite the magnitude of these efforts, we are still unable to meet the ever-increasing desire for education evinced by our people, a desire which is of itself highly pleasing to us, and our educational programme, which is our primary concern, will therefore demand further and greater sacrifices for all.

To Parliament, Coronation Day, Nov. 2, 1958, *EO*, vol. 3 (1959), no. 3, p. 66.

Ethiopia's endeavours have resulted in broadening the bases of national education, and in increasing the number of our own technicians and experts, thereby assuring our intellectual and scientific independence. As we have repeatedly stated, education is the motivating force of our national life and the major safeguard for our future. Our efforts are bearing fruit, and the past year has marked a significant increase in the number of our own scientists, doctors, engineers, lawyers and technicians returning from advanced study abroad to take up their duties throughout the Empire. A growing number of technicians are being sent abroad to acquaint themselves with the latest technical developments. The same is true of our Army, Air and Naval officers.

To Parliament, Nov. 3, 1959, *EO*, vol. 4 (1960), no. 2, p. 60.

Eleven months ago, we participated in the inauguration of one of our most cherished desires, Ethiopia's first university. To be a product of one's national university is to combine modern learning with the heritage and tradition of the nation. The students who pass through this newly-established educational institution will, we hope, be ever mindful of the confidence and faith which not only we but the entire Ethiopian people have placed in them. Education is a precious trust, to be valued above all else by those fortunate enough to enjoy it. We solemnly adjure them to utilise their time wisely in seeking knowledge, that they may later apply the learning which they acquire in its fullest measure to the furtherance of the well-being and prosperity of the Ethiopian people. Only in this manner will they prove themselves worthy of the sacrifices which the nation has made on their behalf and repay the vast debt which they owe to their country and their fellow-men.

To Parliament, Coronation Day, Nov. 2, 1962, *EO*, vol. 6 (1963), no. 4, p. 298.

Our government has given education, public health and related programmes high priority with the conviction that trained manpower and sound health are crucial to the progress of advancing economic growth.

Accordingly, no less than 20 per cent of the national budget was allotted to education. Enrolment in governmental and private elementary and secondary schools has surpassed targets of the Third Five-Year Development Plan. It is also gratifying that enrolment in the University is growing from year to year.

Considerable time and energy have been devoted by experts to the task of making research into the kind of education best suited to Ethiopia's present needs in accordance with a directive we personally issued. The recommendation has reached us through the Council of Ministers and we have given order for its immediate implementation.

To Parliament, Coronation Day, Nov. 2, 1976, *EO*, vol. 16 (1973), no. 3, p. 127.

LAND REFORM

The encouraging progress achieved in these fields has led us, at this time, to initiate a bold and broad programme of land development. In our message of September 18, we proclaimed our programme of land and credit assistance, declaring:

'For those of you who possess land and labour but lack capital, we have made credit available at low interest. For those of you who have the necessary finance but do not possess land to work on, we have, in accordance with our Proclamation which entitled every Ethiopian to ownership of land, established offices in every province through which you may be able to acquire land. Those who have neither land nor money will be granted land and a financial loan at low interest. For those of you who possess land, who have financial resources and manpower – we have made experts available to furnish you with the necessary guidance and advice in your various undertakings.' [This quotation is continued below.]

Long before initiating this new programme, we had authorised our Central Treasury to advance, through the years, loans without interest amounting to $7,500,000, with a view to raising the standard of living of our beloved people. Realising that those who could avail themselves of this fund were few, we have now made it possible for all to acquire not only money but also land to develop. Even at this moment, throughout Ethiopia, experts whom we have sent to the provinces are, together with the Governors-General and Sub-Governors of every province, meeting at our orders, to explain to the inhabitants of our Empire the details of our message, so that they may proceed to benefit by these provisions.

To Parliament, Nov. 3, 1959, *EO*, vol. 4 (1960), no. 2, p. 41.

With the knowledge that unity and co-operation are in themselves strength, take advantage of the possibilities we have opened to you.

You have now to choose in your respective provinces, up to the end of Hidar [third month of the Ethiopian year, which begins in September], twelve people who are known for their integrity, loyalty and sense of responsibility, who will be charged to give out the financial loans and who will collect them as they mature. The procedure to be the basis of your selection of these officers will be sent to you through the governors of your respective provinces. We shall appoint three persons for each province to make preparation for the selection you are to make and to supervise the execution of this programme. The persons to be chosen by you will be provided with Development Bank regulations which they will use as a guide in their work. The interest on your loan will be 2½ per cent and the loan is repayable in five years' time.

Therefore, we exhort you to follow the guidance of your Creator; not to waver from the goal we have designed for your progress and well-being and to labour diligently for the early realisation of that goal.

'The Emperor's further broadcast on His World Tour', Sept. 18, 1959, *EO*, vol. 4 (1960), no. 2, p. 39.

And lastly, we may refer to the Committee on Land Reform. Ethiopia has been, throughout her history, an agricultural nation. The basis of the livelihood for the great majority of the Ethiopian people rests and will always remain in the land. [. . .] Industrialisation is not an alternative to the development of agriculture; rather, the development of agriculture is the essential precondition to the growth of industry.

The fundamental obstacle to the realisation of the full measure of Ethiopia's agricultural potential has been, simply stated, lack of security in the land. The fruits of the farmer's labour must be enjoyed by him whose toil has produced the crop. The essence of land reform is, while fully respecting the principle of private ownership, that landless people must have the opportunity to possess their own land, that the position of tenant farmers must be improved, and that the system of taxation applying to land holdings must be the same for all. It is our aim that every Ethiopian own his own land, in implementation of this principle. We have ourself set the example by ordering that certain lands in Arussi Province heretofore administered by our Ministry of the Imperial Court be distributed to the tenants working on them, against payment by each man only of the nominal fees charged for the transfer and the registration of this property in his own name. This has been the basic objective of virtually every modern programme of land reform; this is the ultimate goal of the study now being undertaken by the Committee on Land Reform.

Programmes of land reform, having as their aim the securing of the ownership of the land to those who fill it, have been implemented in numerous countries adhering to various political and economic systems. By whatever reasoning these programmes have been justified, they have all rested, at bottom, on the belief that it is the responsibility of government to insure the development of the nation's economy, the well-being of its people, and the attainment of social progress and social justice. If initiative elsewhere is lacking, the burden passes to government.

Land reform, which is in large part a social programme, is wholly in keeping with this fundamental principle, a principle which has already found ample expression in Ethiopian life. Today, for example, a large portion of the means of production is owned by the Government. This is not to say that Ethiopia opposes private ownership, or that the Government shall not continue to encourage and facilitate private investment, both domestic and foreign. This does mean, however, that to the extent that private initiative is not forthcoming, the Government has the solemn responsibility itself to act. In embarking upon a sweeping programme of land reform, the Government is only taking those measures essential to the social progress of the Ethiopian nation which it is its duty to undertake . . .

To Parliament, Coronation Day, Nov. 2, 1961, *EO*, vol. 5 (1962), no. 4, pp. 288–9.

Even though the system of land tenure as well as the collection of taxes in Ethiopia may have varying forms, it is quite evident that these have their foundation in the country's past history. However, even though such a system was only suitable to the time when it was being practised, to make it go hand in hand with the age, and thereby serve as a safeguard for the interest and prosperity of the country and be a means for the strengthening of the unity of the people, the old systems of land tenure and certain rights pertaining to the payment of taxes have been kept in operation. Land is also being allocated to those Ethiopians who may not be owning any at present. It has, however, been found necessary that this be improved in the light of present conditions, needs and requirements. Having realised that the money collected from taxes would be used for the development programme of the Empire, and having thought it desirable that tax collection be carried out in accordance with the Proclamation, and that no distinction be made among Ethiopians, and so that all people be given equal rights as regards the payment of taxes, a committee was formed and ordered to study ways of improving on the present system of land tenure. Having reviewed the first part of the committee's report and recommendation, we have passed the following order of amendment:

1. We have ordered that a bill be submitted to Parliament to be deliberated and passed into law to make people possessing land as 'Riste Gult' and 'Siso' pay normal tax on it to the Government Treasury.

2. The proposed proclamation be presented to Parliament for discussion with the final aim of being passed as law to improve on the traditional form of relationship, shown existing in the Civil Code, between land-owners and tenants.

3. Those serving for 'Feresegna', 'Alenga' and Gala land and 'Gult' allowances, to be paid salaries from the Government Treasury.

Those who were formerly living on allowances from 'Gult' and 'Siso' to be given land.

4. Government lands in the Provinces, owned by people on lease, to be given to those who have no land unless the person now possessing it has developed it with his own money and is not simply collecting regular revenue from tenants.

5. Crown lands throughout the Empire, the benefice of which has been allocated to augment the Civil List, will be distributed in three categories: (1) for development projects, such as industrial establishments, the building of townships and settlements; (2) as compensation for those people whose land has been taken over by the government for development purposes; (3) to patriots and exiles and to disabled veterans who have not received land before. The land that may be left over after apportioning in the above manner, is to be given either to tenants living on it or to the landless people nearby, half a gasha each [1 gasha = about 9 acres] each.

6. It is our wish that all Ethiopians who are to be given government land on the basis of the order given above shall, when receiving the land so donated by the government to raise the standard of living of the recipient, pay for registration and transfer of name, Eth. $15 per gasha of fertile land, Eth. $10 per gasha of semi-fertile land and Eth. $5 per gasha of barren land, and so bring the land under their ownership.

As is explicity put down in Article 38 of our constitution, there is no need to point out that the Ethiopian people enjoy equality. Our instruction as regards reform in the land tenure system will reflect the same basic statement in the constitution. It is known to all that every Ethiopian should have land and be given money to cultivate the fallow land and that an organization to carry out this programme, has earlier been set up, is indeed well known by all. Unless the wealth of the people increases and unless they co-operate their unity as a nation will be compromised.

Therefore we have made it in such a way that chiefs and elders, without their service in the past being forgotten, should live by working in co-operation with the people so that their own interest would be safeguarded, not to the disadvantage of others.

While the economic growth of our country and the living standard of our people are being realized to the extent of the effort we are making, . . . it should be the duty of every Ethiopian to co-operate and work hard towards their implementation.

'Ethiopia's Second Five Year Plan and envisaged Land Reform', speech to the

Nation, over Radio Addis Ababa, Oct. 11, 1962, *EO*, vol. 6 (1962), no. 4, pp. 295-6.

EXAMPLES OF PROGRESS

In the field of industrialisation, several large, medium and small scale manufacturing establishments, opening job opportunities for large numbers of people, have come into being during the Third Five-Year Plan period. Upwards of $300,000,000 have been invested for the establishment of new factories.

Industrial production is increasing at the rate of 10 per cent per annum while manufactured products are showing an annual 22 per cent growth.

The realisation by more and more people of the role of modern banking in a country's economy encourages the judicious utilisation of money. With commercial banks expanding their rural network, bank deposits are growing in volume. The banks, by improving their loan and related services, are making a notable contribution to expanding the nation's economy. Expressed in terms of figures, it would be sufficient to note that during the past year bank deposits totalled $380,000,000, while loans advanced to private individuals and organisations reached $470,000,000.

Although international currency has been in a constant stage of fluctuation and the price of world export goods and services keep soaring, the fact that the gold parity of the Ethiopian dollar has remained stable forestalled an unusual increase in the cost of commodities in so far as Ethiopia is concerned. Even so, the erratic fortunes of international currency have created problems that have yet to be solved – and it is our hope that the effort being deployed on the global front in this direction will soon register a lasting effect.

In order to satisfy the nation's evergrowing power needs, the Fincha hydro-electric power plant has already been completed. Moreover detailed preliminary studies have been conducted to establish a new hydro-electric plant at Malka Wakana on the Wabi Shebelli river. In addition, a feasibility study is being made to divert the Amerti river to the Fincha Dam.

To Parliament, Coronation Day, Nov. 2, 1973, *EO*, 16 (1973), no. 3, p. 127.

Likewise, the campaigns launched earlier to eradicate malaria and smallpox from Ethiopia have been gathering more and more momentum. Because the programme drawn up for the eradication of these diseases has been proceeding effectively in all the 14 governorates-general, over 8,000,000 people have already been vaccinated. Studies have revealed that the preventive programme has been effective to the extent that the incidence of the disease has decreased by 75 per cent.

Strenuous efforts are being made to train medical personnel in various training centres and in foreign institutions in order to fully meet the health needs of the country. During the past 12 months alone, many such medical personnel have graduated from these institutions.

Ibid, p. 128.

A step which, we are persuaded, will stand as a landmark in Ethiopia's history is the enactment in recent weeks of urgently required labour legislation. The newly-promulgated Labour Relations Law and Public Employment Administration Order have been carefully prepared for the declared purpose of stimulating a better way of life for the workers of our Empire and of promoting social harmony and content amongst all classes of our people. If we meet the challenge which this legislation represents and, through it, fulfil the needs of an increasingly-enlightened society, these enactments will make an incalculable contribution to Ethiopia's future economic and social expansion.

A nation's goals in any field of endeavour require, for their achievement, the combined efforts of all parts of its society, and, not least, of the entrepreneurial and labouring classes. The employer-employee relationship, in turn, must be based on sound and fair labour conditions. The Labour Relations Law will ensure that these exist. In addition, this law provides the mechanism for the settlement of disputes between employers and employees by peaceful negotiations. Recourse to the technique of collective bargaining will solve before they are created those difficulties which arise when labour and employers come into conflict. Collective bargaining will require from both employers and employees, and from the employers' associations and labour unions which they are authorised and empowered to create to represent them, a high degree of maturity and responsibility, as well as mutual respect and recognition of the other's rights. We expect that these attitudes will be manifested fully in their dealings with one another.

To Parliament, Coronation Day, Nov. 2, 1962, *EO* vol. 6, (1962), no. 4, p. 298.

We have often made mention in the past of the high benefits which can accrue from the expansion of a nation's communications network. The development of the Port of Assab, where we personally laid the foundation stone of the new docks last May, is progressing satisfactorily. Our airline has acquired new and modern equipment, and has been enabled to extend its services to Central Europe. This past year, we directed that 1,256 kilometres of roads be constructed and renovated. Our Imperial Highway Authority is directly in charge of construction and betterment of 954 kilometres of these highways, while the remainder are under private contracts.

To Parliament, Coronation Day, Nov. 2, 1958, *EO*, vol. 3 (1959), no. 3, p. 67.

CONSTITUTIONAL DEVELOPMENT

Throughout our lifetime, we have unceasingly sought an ever increasing degree of participation by our people in the conduct of the nation's affairs.

In 1931, when we granted Ethiopia's first written Constitution, we were motivated by this desire.

In 1955, we paved the way for an even deeper and wider involvement of our people in the direction of the affairs of their country. The Revised Constitution which we promulgated then is both the basis for and an immutable manifestation of the unity of the Ethiopian nation. The presence of you Parliamentarians here today testifies to the wisdom of those steps.

This past year, two additional measures have been taken to accelerate this process and ensure the country's future political stability and growth.

The first, and perhaps the most significant political development of recent years, occurred only eight months ago. We then announced that the principle of collective responsibility embedded in Ethiopia's constitutional framework would be enlarged by the designation by us of our Prime Minister who would, in turn, select his Cabinet for appointment by us.

This innovation, coupled with the principle of Parliamentary responsibility enunciated in the 1955 Constitution, prepares the way for the introduction of a totally new series of modifications into Ethiopia's institutional framework and guarantees the continued dynamic evolution of the nation's political structure.

We are convinced that this step, taken in accordance with the nation's Constitution, will inject new strength into the political framework of the nation, and that the permanence of the advances already accomplished will be secured.

The first consequences of this major reshaping of Ethiopia's political framework may already be seen.

In order to emphasize and give full scope to the priority of co-ordinated economic planning, a separate ministry charged with wide responsibilities in this field has been established, and work has already been commenced on the preparation of a Third Five Year Plan.

Land reform and administration, an area deserving of the highest consideration, has been confided to another new Ministry created at the time of the reorganization of our Government in April.

Responsibility for social affairs has been consolidated under the direction of the Ministry of National Community Development and Social Affairs.

Information and tourism functions have been combined in a single Ministry in order that fuller and more complete publicity may be given to the many varied aspects of Ethiopia's life and activities.

The institutions earlier created to assure that all Public Servants would receive the recognition which their work has earned for them and that they may look to their future security with confidence have now been consolidated in a single agency.

The Ministry of Public Works have been given the special task of ensuring that adequate provision is made for the furnishing of housing, an increasingly important requirement in these days of rapid urbanization.

All of these changes have been carefully considered before their introduction. They will assist in ensuring the efficient and effective conduct of the affairs of our Government and the proper discharge of our duties to the Ethiopian nation and people.

The second of these vital political measures was initiated several years ago when studies were launched into one of the most significant and critical exercises in national political growth yet attempted in Ethiopia. This work matured in the scheme of local administration based at the Awraja level introduced by our Order only a short time ago.

This vast project has slowly taken form through years of painstaking research and profound examination of the needs, the beliefs, the aspirations and the capacities of every segment of the entire population.

As this programme is implemented, major responsibilities in many areas of pressing concern to each individual and community throughout the nation will be entrusted to locally elected Awraja Councils. Council members will be chosen in formal elections. The judgement and discretion of the Ethiopian people will be tested as never before, as a large proportion of the decisions shaping their economic and social life become their responsibility.

Pending before this session of Parliament is the draft Proclamation dealing with Awraja local revenues which will give final substance to the form already devised for this great and crucial experiment in government. You should act upon this proposal as a matter of urgency in order that this immense programme, so vital to every man, woman and child in Ethiopia, may proceed on schedule. Other financial legislation of vital importance to the nation will also be laid before you in the coming year.

The sum of all the developments we have described is consistent, we believe, with the basic policy of our Government, a policy which is aimed at the adoption and implemention of national programmes having the greatest impact upon the largest number. This is our goal and purpose, as it should be the goal and purpose of every Government sincerely and deeply devoted to the well-being of its people.

The system of responsible cabinet government placed in effect last March endeavours to bring to each member of our government a more immediate and lively awareness of his responsibilities for sharing in the total task of governing the nation and, below him, to encourage each Government official and employee to discharge more effectively the greater measure of the authority which has been delegated throughout our Government's structure.

The increased emphasis placed upon development planning is intended to produce ever-increasing economic activity at every level of the economy down to the smallest village and community.

Land reform measures are calculated to affect and improve the living conditions of literally millions of Ethiopians.

The introduction of a widespread system of local administration is directed to the involvement of substantial numbers of our people in the conduct and regulation of their public affairs. [. . .]

It is our task and responsibility, as it is of our Government, to transform these objectives into coherent, acceptable and realistic legislative and financial programmes and to see to their accomplishment. If this is done, the duty owed to the Ethiopian nation and people will be discharged. To succeed will require the single-minded, tenacious and unselfish dedication of each one of us.

To Parliament, Coronation Day, Nov. 2, 1966, *EO*, vol. 10 (1966), no. 3, pp. 166-7.

In 1930, recognising that the programme of development which we envisaged for Ethiopia required a radical departure from the political system of our ancestors, we gave to our people Ethiopia's first Constitution, of our own free will, and against the strenuous objection of many who were close to us and who did not hesitate to shed blood in opposing this step. For the first time, Ethiopia's government acquired a crystallised and defined form. As has been stated by us when we gave the first Constitution, the 'Ethiopian people must share the burden of responsibility which in the past was borne by their monarchs.' By this act we sought to disperse responsibility and authority among our people, that they might exercise it, together with ourself, in securing the advancement and the unity of the Ethiopian nation. In this manner we sought to lay the groundwork for the orderly and natural growth of those political and social institutions which are essential to the development of a dynamic yet stable society.

Our plans were abruptly halted by the invasion of 1935, but, following Ethiopia's liberation, we resumed our work and carried it yet further. In 1943, we caused to be published Order No. 1, which defined the duties and responsibilities of the Minister of our Government and vested them with all powers requiste to discharging them. At this same time, we promulgated a law which provided for the creation of an organised system of courts where our subjects might go to seek redress for wrongs done to them and enforce the rights which the laws and the Constitution guaranteed to them. These steps, again, we took voluntarily – not in response to any demand or pressure, but in full recognition of the principles of life which we enunciated but a moment ago and out of our desire to facilitate and stimulate the further progress of our nation, in fulfilment of the solemn vow which we took to our people when we ascended the throne of our Empire.

As a complement to these measures, we created by special charter a number of autonomous institutions, possessed of full power to act in the domains given over to their jurisdiction: the State Bank of Ethiopia, the Development Bank of Ethiopia, the Ethiopian Electric Light and Power Authority, the Imperial Board of Telecommunications of Ethiopia,

Ethiopian Air Lines, the Imperial Highway Authority – these and many others we charged with the responsibility of securing Ethiopia's advancement in the areas confided to their care.

As our Empire grew and flourished, it became apparent that the Constitution of 1930 no longer responded adequately to the needs of our people. Accordingly, in 1955, again in the face of objections and opposition, we promulgated the Revised Constitution with which you are all familiar. In it, provision was made for our people to enjoy direct representation and participation in the business of government. The division of power among us, our Ministers acting collectively and individually, and our Parliament, was solidified and acquired permanent institutional form. Subsequently, we caused to be prepared a series of legal codes covering all aspects of the lives of our citizens and setting forth, in a precise yet detailed manner, the principles which were to guide them in their relationships with others and with the State. [. . .]

In all that we did, we believed that we were taking those measures essential to Ethiopia's development. As programmes became more numerous and technically more complex, as the nation's budget increased from Eth.$11 million in 1942 to Eth.$279 million in 1960, it became essential that the decision-making functions be increasingly dispersed among the responsible officials of the Government. Who, today, can be an expert in all fields? Who, today, can single-handedly take all the decisions necessary to the administration of a Government's programmes? These questions require no answer.

But we know that man's desires rarely attain full achievement or perfection. And so it was here. What more was required to create a system of truly responsible government? What was yet lacking? The institutional framework existed. A modern Constitution guaranteed to each element in this structure its proper duties and the authority and the right to fulfil its tasks. Our Ministers were vested with attributions no less substantial than those given to Ministers in any nation of the world, irrespective of political colouration or orientation. Our Parliament was given powers to legislate comparable to those granted in any parliamentary system of government. The legal framework governing the dealings of the Ethiopian people with each other and with the State had been fully articulated.

You all realise that it is necessary to have a sufficient number of men who would courageously and honestly accept responsibility and act under it, and, not counting the cost, discharge their duties to the Ethiopian nation. We have always held ourself at the disposal of our people and our Ministers. And so our Ministers came to us with their problems and questions. Always we said: 'But the power has been given to you to do this yourself.' Frequently, our words went unheeded. Responsibility was shirked, decisions were avoided and thrust back upon us. [. . .]

Today, we say to you, no longer shall it be thus. No longer shall you shirk your duties. No longer shall we accept your responsibilities, when we have given the power to you. This power shall not be abused for selfish and for personal ends when it has been given as a sacred trust to be exercised for the benefit of the Ethiopian people and nation.

Henceforth, you shall work in your Ministries and Departments and administer your programmes there. [. . .]

Your programmes and your implementation of them will be subject to free and open comments. 'In the ultimate sense, it is to the people of Ethiopia that you are responsible, and it is to them that you must answer for your stewardship.' That is why you are constitutionally responsible to us and to Parliament. During our lifetime, we have unfailingly done what we have felt, before Almighty God, to be our duty to our people and our nation, no matter what the cost to ourself. You must do likewise.

Throughout the long years of our ceaseless efforts to achieve the advancement and well-being of our nation, we have always anticipated that the stage would be reached at which our ministers and officials, whom we have trained by education and through long years of service in government administration, could, once their duties and tasks are defined, assume by themselves full responsibility and discharge it properly, thus permitting us to devote more of our time to major political decisions and matters of utmost importance to the future of Ethiopia which necessitate our attention.

We are persuaded that this stage has now been reached, and you must realise that the trust given to you entails a sacrifice on your part, that you may be worthy of it. You should be ever mindful that the supreme test of your worthiness of this trust will be manifested not only by the confidence we have reposed in you, but also by your achievements in the implementation of the programmes we have laid down for the welfare of the Ethiopian people.

Your office shall be where you belong. Technical experts and advisors have been provided to aid you in your work. Your Departments and Ministries can function well only if the choice of your staff is dictated, not by ties of friendship and personal relationship, but by evidence of competence and ability. You shall work on your own responsibility, making your own mistakes, achieving your own successes. We shall reserve for each of you a certain period each week when we shall ask you to report on the progress you have made in your programmes and on the difficulties which you have encountered. But time shall not be used to ask or obtain from us decisions which are rightfully yours to make.

Ethiopians are proud of the 3,000 years of their recorded history, as well they may be. We are proud of what has been achieved during our regime, and we thank God for it. We are content to let History judge the wisdom of our actions. But while we cannot escape the consciousness of each day's immediacy and the urgency of the problems which each day presents, we must none-the-less be ever mindful that just as our nation's history stretches far back in time, so does an unlimited future lie before us, especially in this nuclear and space era. We must all act and take our decisions mindful of the far-reaching implications and consequences of each of them. What we have said to you today, we know, carries with it implications for generation upon generation of future Ethiopians. We are persuaded that what we have said will, in the long term, rebound to the everlasting benefit of those who will follow us. Man is mortal; each one of us here will, one day, face his maker and answer for his actions. Those of us to whom the grave responsibilities of government have been given bear a heavy burden before their people and before Almighty God for the proper discharge of their duties. Let us all labour in this sense, that the people of Ethiopia may ever live in happiness and prosperity.

'The Emperor on Ministerial Responsibility', April 14, 1961, *EO*, vol. 5 (1961), no. 2, pp. 98–100.

It is a great responsibility to be elected to legislate upon matters that are the anchor of personal liberty, security, social responsibility – in general of a framework of organised and ordered social order.

One measure of the healthy growth of parliamentary democracy is the insight sense of responsibility and dedication brought into work by deputies in the course of deliberating on issues originating from either the executive branch of government or the Chamber itself.

To Parliament, Coronation Day, Nov. 2, 1973, *EO*, vol. 16, no. 3, p. 127.

It is normal for every individual family or generation to give way to the new by adding something to the heritages bequeathed upon it. [. . .] It is thus our sacred duty and responsibility to be cognizant of the fact that because history is bound to judge us tomorrow by what we are doing today, we must do everything in our power to leave behind us a lasting legacy of work.

Lastly, we would like to remind you members of the Houses of Parliament to deliberate on the bills already submitted, and those which will be submitted to you as a matter of urgency by realising the fact that they are matters of crucial importance for the progress and development of the country.

May God, who proposes and disposes everything, be with you all in the discharge of your duties and responsibilities.

Ibid., p. 130 (same speech, closing sentences).

In this, his last Coronation Day address to Parliament, the Emperor, aware of the impending revolution and anticipating his fall, takes his leave without any sentimentality, with a call to duty to both Houses of Parliament – soon to be dissolved, with most members of the Senate later being executed. The usual closing reference to 'Almighty God' is here shortened to the single word 'God'.

NOTE ON THE SOURCES FOR THE ENGLISH TEXTS OF THE EMPEROR'S SPEECHES

I. (a) Four collections of official publications printed in Ethiopia, by or under the auspices of the Ethiopian government:

— *Selected Speeches of His Imperial Majesty, 1918-1967*, Addis Ababa: Ministry of Information, Publications and Foreign Languages Press Department, 1967 (693 pp., portrait).
— *An Anthology of some of the Public Utterances of His Imperial Majesty Haile Sellassie I*, Addis Ababa: Press & Information Dept., 1949 (78 pp., portrait).
— *Speeches delivered by His Imperial Majesty Emperor Haile Sellassie Ist, Emperor of Ethiopia, on various occasions, May 1957-December 1959*, Addis Ababa: Ministry of Information, 1960 (183 pp., portrait).
—*Important Utterances of His Imperial Majesty Emperor Haile Sellassie I, 1963-1972*, Addis Ababa: Ministry of Information, 1972 (xvi, 624 pp., illustrations, portrait).

(b) Speeches published separately by the Ministry of Information: about 30 pamphlets, most of them with bilingual texts in Amharic and English, some with a frontispiece portrait.

(c) Pamphlets in the form of mimeographed sheets, intended for distribution to actual audiences.

(d) Texts published in newspapers and other periodicals.

II. Publications of other governments: a few ephemeral items, press releases reproducing addresses given by the Emperor on his journeys abroad.

III. Texts reprinted in *Ethiopia Observer*, published in Addis Ababa and printed in England, 1956-74, and its predecessor *New Times and Ethiopia News*, published in England under the editorship of Sylvia Pankhurst, 1936-56.

IV. Texts reprinted in other serials: *c.* 5 speeches are recorded in this way.

Due to lack of interest internationally in the Emperor's speeches, all items belonging to group I above are rarities and are hard to find anywhere: a few widely scattered libraries hold partial collections, mostly of odd single items. For practical purposes, source III (*Ethiopian Observer*) can suffice in most cases, although this too is becoming rare: barely a dozen libraries on the continent of Europe hold a complete set. This publication is an indispensable source for research on the Horn of Africa during the decades of development, and is available on microfilm from World Microfilm Publications Ltd., London.

INDEX

Abba Samuel, 18-19, 52
Abuna, 21, 30
Abyssinian war (1935), 38-41
Addis Ababa: 2, 3, 4, 10, 13, 15, 22, 23, 27, 29, 32, 35, 36, 37, 40, 59, 67, 69, 73, 76, 108, 109, 111; in 1960 coup, 78-84; Italian modernisation of, 100; 'greening' of, 107-8; move to new capital, 75; urbanisation of, 105-11; poverty in, 109, 110
Ahmed ibn Ibrahim al Ghazi, 14
air force, 41, 78, 121
Akalework Habtewold, 71
Aklilu Habtewold, 70-1
Aksum, 5, 13, 67
Alexandria, 34
Amhara people, 92
Amharic language, 17, 35, 36, 44, 111-12
Aquinas, Thomas, 53
Archaeological Institute, 102
army: 23, 25, 27, 28, 100, 117, 121-2, 123, 124, 125, 126, 127; 1960 coup and, 73-4, 76, 77, 78, 79; assumes power (1974), 122-7; modernisation along European lines, 34; revolutionary cells in, 73, 74, 117; Second Division, 121; territorials, 77-8
armaments, 41
Asfa Wossen, Crown Prince, 48, 49, 76, 77, 78, 80, 83, 87, 102, 114
Asmara, 81, 117
Asrate Kassa, Ras, 28, 31, 45, 48, 76
Aswan dam, 105
Augustine of Hippo, 2
Aymero, 36

Bahr Dar, 75

Balcha, Dedjasmatch, 7, 8, 28, 29, 82
Bale, 48
Bank of Abyssinia, 104
Bayene Merid, Dedjasmatch, 48
Beghemder, 6, 7
Berbera, 22
Berhanena Selam, 36
Brazil, 74-5, 81
Brazzaville, 75
Britain, 2, 4, 5, 8, 11, 16, 17, 22, 23, 40, 49, 61, 62, 69, 80
British Council, 35
British Somaliland, 15
Bülow, Chancellor von, 4

Cairo, 104
Caribbean, 40
Central Powers, 10
chika, 105, 106, 107, 108, 109
Chou En-lai, 99
Christianity, 2, 4, 9, 12, 13, 14, 22, 30, 140n; *see also* Ethiopian Orthodox Church
communism, 41
Confederation of Ethiopian Labour Unions (CELU), 119
Congo, 75
constitutional monarchy, 48
corruption, 66, 116
Crown Council, 7, 8, 9, 32, 33, 93, 113

Debre Zeit, 41, 121
Diredawa, 103, 121
Djibouti, 22, 23, 37, 39, 59, 121

East Africa, 22
Economic Commission for Africa (ECA), 59, 97, 99, 102, 117

163

education, 34, 35, 67, 68, 69, 74, 86, 87, 110–11, 113; *see also* Haile Sellassie University
Egypt, 11, 37, 99, 105
Eritrea: 13, 15, 69, 117, 121, 125; insurgency in, 117
Ethiopia, Ethiopian empire: administration of, 13, 20, 89, 97, 100; agriculture, 41, 56–63, 89–98, 102; attempted coup (1960), 73–88 *passim*; Britain and, 5, 15; *see also* Great Britain; civil service, 20, 70, 71; economy, 51, 104–5, 113, 115; emergence of middle class, 34, 104–5, 108–9, 114; execution of members of old regime (1974), 125–6; expansion of, 13; famine in, 56, 57; France and, 5, 11; Germany and, 4, 5, 6, 41–2; 'Greater Ethiopia' concept, 4; hereditary system of, 19–20; imperial treasury, 68, 69; Islam and, 11, 12, 13, 22–4; Italy and, 5, 8, 39; *see also* Italy; legal codes, 3, 13, 14; Ministry of the Interior, 70, 71, 128; modernisation of, 100, 101; new intellectual élite of, 32–3, 73, 114–15, 124, 126; parliament, 114, 123; Rases in, 8, 10, 16, 22, 28–30; relations with colonial powers, 8, 9, 11, 14, 15; religious conflict in, 13, 22–4; social customs, 111–12; taxation, 20, 89; traditionalists, traditional values in, 6, 15, 17, 25, 26, 27, 31, 50, 115
Ethiopian Airlines, 81
Ethiopian Orthodox Church: 2, 4, 6, 7, 12, 13, 14, 17, 22, 30, 34, 45, 92, 103, 115, 53, 59, 75; conservative reaction to Menelik, 6; Islam and, 13–14, 16; Metropolitan of, 78; relationship with Haile Sellassie, 27, 29; as upholder of Ethiopian tradition, 17

FAO, 57, 59, 89, 97
First World War, *see* World Wars
forestry, 57, 59, 61, 62–3
France, 4, 5, 16, 17, 22, 35, 36, 37, 41
French Somaliland, 40; see also Djibouti
Frederick the Great, 2, 3, 18, 19, 42, 126

Galla, 9, 12, 14, 21, 69, 92
de Gaulle, Gen. Charles, 99
Ge'ez, 36, 44
German Cultural Institute (Goethe-Institut), 3, 35
Germany: 4, 5, 11, 20, 22, 41, 42, 61, 118; colonialism, 11; treaty of friendship with Ethiopia, 5; support for Ethiopia against Italy, 42
Girmane Neway, 73, 79, 84, 85
Godjam, 7, 25
Goethe, Johann Wolfgang von, 2, 3
Gondar, 25, 67, 70, 75
Gurage, 68
Gugsa, Ras, 6, 7, 15, 25, 26, 29, 30, 31

Habte Giorgis, Gen., 23, 25, 27, 30, 31, 43
Haile Sellassie I, Emperor: 1, 3, 6, 7, 8, 9, 14, 16, 17, 18, 20, 21, 22, 23–4, 25–55 *passim*; administration, administrative reforms, 33, 68, 91–3, 97, 103–4; and 1960 coup, 73–88 *passim*; and 1974 revolution, 121–7; assumes command of armed forces, 28, 39; becomes Emperor, 30; concept of 'modern' Ethiopian state, 21, 25, 26, 31, 32, 42, 50, 68; as contender for imperial crown, 17, 25, 27–8, 29, 30; as Crown Prince 25, 26–7; cultural policy of, 35; and death of his enemies, 42–3; education, 10, 18, 19, 20, 44; exile of, 39, 71; failure of

his 'mission', 103, 124; family, 45; feudal nobility and, 33, 53, 68, 91, 92, 94, 95; foreign policy, 15, 17, 22, 23, 36, 46, 86, 99–102; as governor of Harar, 7, 8; as guardian of Ethiopia's independence, 24, 27; influence of Western thought on, 2–3, 31, 42, 53, 126–7; introduces reforms in Sidamo, 8; land reforms, 37, 77, 89–98, 106–12, 115; legal reforms, 33–4, 37, 103–4; Menelik's political concepts and, 10, 15, 17, 21, 31–2, 115, 125; and Orthodox Church, 27; overseas travels, 36–7, 99–102, 118, 119; personality, 1, 3, 17, 20, 21, 31, 44–55, 56–8, 64–7, 81, 102; places hope in emergence of urban middle class, 104–5, 108–9, 114; Private Cabinet of, 21, 44, 70, 73, 77; as Regent, 25, 26, 27; relationship with Lidj Yassu, 4, 10, 15, 16, 17, 22, 23; religious influence on, 19, 103; secret service and, 52, 65–6, 70, 71, 77; style of rule, 26, 27, 31, 101; support of European powers for, 25, 26, 40, 43

Haile Sellassie University (till 1960 University College), Addis Ababa, 57, 73, 78, 83, 86, 87, 96, 102, 113, 115; *see also* students, education

Hailu, Ras, 25

Harar: 7, 8, 15, 18, 19, 20, 23, 25, 26, 32, 37; military academy, 70, 73, 102; Haile Sellassie's power base, 27, 45

Harari, 44

health care, hospitals, 35, 41, 111

Heske, Franz, 62

Hussein, King of Jordan, 99

Ilg, Alfred, 58–9

ILO, 57

imperial bodyguard, 70, 73, 76, 77, 82, 86

Imru, Ras, 6, 45, 77, 78, 95

India, 77

Indian Ocean, 4, 111, 117

Islam: 2, 4, 9, 10, 11, 14, 16, 22; Islamic law, 104

Israel, 100

Italy, Italians: 5, 18, 22, 23, 37, 61, 68, 69, 90, 91, 99, 100, 105; defeat at Adua, 8, 18; invasion of Ethiopia, 37, 40, 41, 48; and modernisation of Ethiopia, 100–1

Italian Somaliland, 11, 15

Itchegue, 27

Japan, 32, 42, 124, 125

Jarosseau, Mgr, 36

Kaffa, 4, 15, 16

Kagnew, 117

Kassa, 48

Kebede Gebre, Gen., 77

Kenya, 99

Kesate Berhan, 36

Khartoum, 81

Kulubi, 103

land reform, 37, 77, 90, 91–8, 115, 116

Law of Kings (Fetah Nagast), 5, 6, 10, 21, 31, 66, 103, 104n

League of Nations, 37, 38, 39

London, 80

Lübke, President H., 98

Machiavelli, 2, 19, 126

machine-guns, 23, 29, 41

Magdala, 80

Mahdi, 11, 16

Mahteme Sellassie Wolde Maskal, Balambaras, 93

Maichen, 39

Makonnen Habtewold, 70, 71, 80, 85, 114
Makonnen, Ras: 2, 8, 10, 18, 19, 20, 31, 37; military experience, 8, 11
Mali, 99
Menelik II, Emperor: 3, 4, 5, 7, 8, 10, 11, 12, 13, 14, 19, 20, 21, 22, 30, 31, 32, 42, 43, 58, 61, 82, 100, 107, 124, 125; abdication, 7; curse of, 22, 123, 127; death, 9; foreign policy, 5, 11; German advisers and, 5, 8; plans for modernisation, 6, 33; poisoning of, 6
Menen, Empress, 45, 48, 76, 80
Mengistu Neway, 73, 74, 79, 82, 84, 85, 86, 114
Merid Manguesha, Gen., 77
Mesfin Sileshi, Ras, 81, 126
Mikael Wolde Giorgis, Ras, King of Wollo, 7, 9, 12, 14, 26, 33, 45, 49
missionaries, 8, 19, 35, 36, 53, 69, 111
Mohammed (the Prophet), 14
Mohammed Ibn Abdallah (the 'Mad Mullah'): 11, 12, 16, 22; German support for, 22; war with Britain, 11; war with Ethiopia, 11
monasteries, 27
Morocco, 11, 99
Moscow, 41, 73, 118, 119, 121
Mulugeta Bulli, Gen., 77, 80
Mullugeta, Dedjasmatch, 29
Muslims, 16, 22; *see also* Islam

Namibia, 100
Napoleon, Emperor, 2, 3, 19, 42, 126
National Bank of Egypt, 104
National Library of Ethiopia, 102, 128, 129, 130-1
navy, 121
Ndjamena, 81
Nile River, 5

Nixon, President Richard M., 99, 117, 118
non-aligned nations, Non-Aligned Movement, 74-5, 100

Organisation of African Unity (OAU), 98, 99, 117
Oromo, 125

Pasteur Institute, 102, 111
philosophy, 2, 3
Pinnow, 4
police, 77, 78, 119
population, 61, 69
Portugal, 60
printing, 35-6
Provisional Military Revolutionary Council, 122, 123

qat, 49

rabies, 64
railways, 59
Rastafarianism, 40
Red Cross, 102
Red Sea, 5, 11
Romanaworq, 46
Roman Catholics, 19
Rosen, von, 5

Sahle Sellassie, Prince, 49-50, 80
Sahle Sellassie, King, 4, 10
Samson Bayere, Lidj, 48
Second World War, *see* World War
Segelie, 23
Le Semeur d'Éthiopie, 36
Shah of Iran, 99
shiftas, 52
Shoa, 4, 13, 21, 29, 31, 126
Sidamo, 7, 8, 28
slavery, slave traders: 8, 20, 33, 37, 49, 55; eradication of, 37, 110
Solomonic (Solomonide) dynasty 4, 5, 6, 7, 15, 20, 25, 31, 92, 93
Somaliland, 11

INDEX 167

South Africa, Republic of, 100
Soviet Union, 35, 58, 73, 75, 80, 99, 124
Steinkühler, Dr, 4, 6
students: 66–7, 68, 73, 74, 113, 116, 117, 119; in 1960 coup, 78, 86
Sudan, 11, 16, 81
Sweden, 40, 41, 108

Tafari Makonnen (Lidj–Dedjasmatch–Ras–Negus), *see* Haile Sellassie I, Emperor
Taitu, Empress, 6, 7, 8, 12, 13, 23, 31, 75
Tana, Lake, 75
Technical Assistance, 60, 61, 62, 75, 89–98, 100, 108, 111, 117, 118
Tenagne Work, Princess, 50
Tesamma, Ras, 6, 8, 30, 31
Theodoros II, Emperor, 6, 80
Thomas à Kempis, 2, 126
Tigre, 7, 28, 68, 92, 125
Tito, President J.B., 99, 100
Tripartite Treaty (1906), 5, 14
Tsigue Dibou, 73, 78
Tsushima, 32
tukuls, 105, 106, 107, 109, 110
Turkey, 11, 16

Uccialli, Treaty of, 18
United Nations, 3, 5, 7, 70, 71, 89, 129
United States of America: 5, 58, 76, 79, 99, 117, 124; abandons base in Eritrea, 117; US information Service, 35, 78

Vitalien, Dr, 19
Voltaire, 2, 126

Wilhelm II, German Emperor, 5, 20
Wollo: 21, 49, 87, 88; Asfa Wossen in, 87, 114; famine in, 57
World Health Organisation (WHO), 57, 111
Workineh Gebeyehu, Lieut.-Col., 70, 71–2, 73–84 *passim*, 85, 114, 125
World Wars: First, 1, 2, 3, 10–11, 15, 48, 127; Second, 37, 48

Yassu, (Lidj, later Emperor): 3–4, 5, 6, 7, 10, 11, 12, 14, 15, 16, 17, 20, 21, 22, 23, 25, 27, 30, 43, 45, 49, 124; and Central Powers, 10, 11; Christianity and, 12, 13, 14; declared Emperor, 7, 9; deposed as Emperor, 4, 22, 23; excommunicated, 22; executed, 23; Germany and, 11, 22, Islam and, 4, 10, 13, 14, 16, 24; 'Mad Mullah' and, 11, 12
Yohannes IV, Emperor, 6, 14
Yugoslavia, 96

Zanzibar, 11
Zauditu, Empress: 7, 25, 26, 29, 30, 33, 43; death of, 30, 43; removal by Haile Sellassie, 27–8
Zebit, battle of, 29
Zukunft, Die,